"The topic of supernatural _ scepticism or sensationalism. helpful antidote; based on of y it combines deep pastoral sensitivity, wise reflection and rich spiritual insight."

Revd Canon J.John

"The devil has indeed gone missing in much Western theology and practice. This magnificent book redresses the balance. It is scholarly and balanced. It is fascinating and practical. And it comes not from the lunatic fringe but from a very experienced Anglican clergyman. Buy it – and learn!"

Canon Michael Green, DD

"Theologically sound, practical, wise advice on the ministry of deliverance. John Woolmer writes with clarity and power about the activities of the devil today and how deliverance ministry can set people free. I read this excellent book in one sitting!"

Don Latham

"This is an engaging and compelling personal account of the healing and deliverance ministry combined with rigorous study of Scripture. It provides a breadth of testimony and will be of particular interest to those responding to anyone who believes they are oppressed or possessed by the forces of evil."

June Osborne, Dean of Salisbury

THE DEVIL GOES MISSING?

DELIVERANCE:
THEOLOGY, PRACTICE, HISTORY

John Woolmer

MONARCH
BOOKS

Oxford UK, and Grand Rapids, USA

Published by Monarch Books
an imprint of
Lion Hudson plc
Wilkinson House, Jordan Hill Road,
Oxford OX2 8DR, England
Email: monarch@lionhudson.com
www.lionhudson.com / monarch

ISBN 978 0 85721 791 2
e-ISBN 978 0 85721 792 9

First edition 2017

Acknowledgments
Scripture quotations marked NIV taken
from the Holy Bible, New International
Version Anglicised. Copyright ©
1979, 1984, 2011 Biblica, formerly
International Bible Society. Used by
permission of Hodder & Stoughton
Ltd, an Hachette UK company. All
rights reserved. "NIV" is a registered
trademark of Biblica. UK trademark
number 1448790.
Scripture quotations marked ESV are
from The Holy Bible, English Standard
Version® (ESV®) copyright © 2001
by Crossway, a publishing ministry
of Good News Publishers. All rights
reserved.

Scripture taken from the New King
James Version. Copyright © 1982
by Thomas Nelson, Inc. Used by
permission. All right reserved.
Scripture quotations marked RSV are
from The Revised Standard Version
of the Bible copyright © 1946, 1952
and 1971 by the Division of Christian
Education of the National Council
of Churches in the USA. Used by
permission. All Rights Reserved.

pp. 30 and 32: Extract from *I Believe in
Satan's Downfall* © 1981, Michael Green,
reprinted by permission of Hodder &
Stoughton.

p. 37: Extract from *Prayer in the New
Testament* © 1995, Oscar Cullman,
reprinted by permission of Mohr
Siebeck (Tübingen), SCM Press and
Augsburg Fortress.

p. 197: Extract from *Origen Contra
Celsum* © 1980, tr. Henry Chadwick,
reprinted by permission of Cambridge
University Press.

pp. 197–98: Extract from *Christianising
the Roman Empire AD 100-400* © 1984,
Ramsay MacMullen, reprinted by
permission of Yale University Press.

pp. 224–26: Extract from "Healing and
Deliverance" in *ReSource Magazine*
© November, 2006, John Widdas,
reprinted by permission.

pp. 227–28: Extract from *God Plus One*
© 2016 Andrew Fanstone, reprinted by
permission of New Wine Press.

A catalogue record for this book is
available from the British Library

Printed and bound in Great Britain,
December 2016, LH36.

DEDICATION

For Tony Collins who long ago asked me to write this book and who, subsequently, for many years guided my writing. His friendship and trust have made a great difference to my wider ministry over the last twenty years.

CONTENTS

ACKNOWLEDGMENTS

Thanks to Simon Cox and the team at Monarch for their gentle editing and considerable encouragement; to Michael and Rosemary Green, with whom I first encountered this strange and wonderful ministry, and to Michael for his theological wisdom; to Chris Tookey and Stephen Heygate, Diocesan Advisors in Bath and Wells and Leicester; to Archbishop Bernard Malango and John Simons who first invited me to Zambia; to Alison Morgan, co-author of the healing course "In His Name"; to Bishop Stanley Hotay, whose friendship and encouragement has led to a number of ministry trips to Tanzania; to Priscilla Breekveldt, who works for Latin Link in Argentina, and who translated and prayed with me and put me in contact with her amazing father, Jacques Teeuwen; to Brian Hodgkin, whose invitation to PNG opened my eyes to the wonderful work of the Wycliffe Bible Translators and their spiritual battles; to Jordan Ling who, among many others, has often helped me with this ministry; to my wife, Jane, who, especially in the early years, coped with many troubled visitors and sometimes a troubled husband.

Thanks also to *The Times* letters editor and Ruth Gledhill, their sometime religious correspondent, whose interest and courtesy inspired me to write.

Biblical quotations, unless otherwise stated, are from the NIV. With thanks to Andrew Fanstone for permission to quote from his recent book *God plus One*, and to Alison Morgan for the use of her Zambian diary and extensive notes of one deliverance session. Further thanks to the many people who, over the years, have given me permission to use their stories. In a few cases, names have been changed and very occasionally details have been slightly altered.

INTRODUCTION

Tread all the powers of darkness down,
and win the well-fought day.

("Soldiers of Christ, Arise", Charles Wesley)

In January 2014, there was some theological controversy because a new baptism service, proposed by a senior cleric in the Church of England, omitted any reference to the devil. Now knowing who the author is, I understand that his motives were pastoral rather than theological – an attempt to simplify the service and make it more easily understood. *The Times* ran an article entitled "The Devil Goes Missing". The *Ten o'clock News* programme on Radio 4 had a limp discussion between two sceptical clerics on the subject. Somewhat infuriated and disturbed, late that evening I penned the following letter to *The Times*:

The devil doesn't go missing

Sir,

I write as an Anglican clergyman, with a degree in Mathematics, who has had some forty years' ministry. In this time, it is been my privilege to visit many houses where parishioners, and others, were deeply disturbed by inexplicable frightening phenomena. I have also prayed with a number of people who, usually through dabbling in some sort of occult practice, were troubled by some spiritual presence. I have exercised this ministry in sophisticated Oxford, rural Somerset, working-class Leicester, and many parts of East Africa, Papua New Guinea, Argentina. In every situation, the phenomena have been similar and are most easily explained by taking the opening chapters of Mark's Gospel seriously. Twice, powerful physical forces have left a person or a building, in each case knocking backwards my helper. Once, in rural Zambia, my wife and I were addressed in perfect Oxbridge English by a spirit saying, "Go away, I am not leaving this person!" No English person had visited that village for many years and no one spoke English except the priest. As a mathematician, Bayes' theorem on conditional probability strongly supports the view that this phenomena occurred because it is similar to the Gospel accounts.

I have exercised this ministry in pubs, a factory, offices and many houses. For the most part, the ministry to buildings and people is very quiet and straightforward. One of those that I have been privileged to help is now an ordained minister in the Anglican Church.

Obviously, there is a huge danger of exaggerating the need for this ministry. Over-enthusiastic exorcists can do more harm than the most sceptical liberal cleric. Actual possession, or better, indwelling by evil spirits, is very rare; being troubled by negative spiritual powers, in my experience, is quite common. People are enormously grateful when their troubles are taken seriously and even more grateful when the spiritual forces disappear – which, if the diagnosis is correct, they invariably do when told firmly and politely to leave "in the name of Jesus". Prebendary John Woolmer (retired)

PS It would be very nice to have a letter published on my primary calling rather than on the noble subject of Purple Emperors!

The result was unexpected. The letters deputy editor emailed me to say that the letter was too long to publish but was of such interest that they would like to send their religious correspondent to interview me. Not long afterwards, the very courteous Ruth Gledhill travelled up to Leicester and had lunch with me and my wife, Jane. She then interviewed me for over an hour. Although most of our conversation was probably outside her experience, she remained very interested and asked plenty of searching questions. She then wrote a very positive piece which was published a few weeks later, taking up most of a page on a Saturday edition of *The Times*.[1]

The first purpose of this short book is to argue that the existence of the devil is a necessary part of our theological understanding of God. Furthermore, there are many people in this country and overseas who need help to be released from oppressive spiritual problems.

Secondly, only if the church proclaims a clear and unashamed message will people seek help from her – otherwise people may seek help from alternative sources, which are normally expensive and dangerous. We have a pastoral duty to offer help.

Thirdly, when people do see release for themselves or their homes, they will recognize the true power of the risen Christ. Possibly, readers of these stories may think that the people have received help which is primarily psychological. However, it is difficult to see the dramatic change in the atmosphere in houses, pubs, offices, and factories as psychological – it is safer and simpler, in each case, to attribute any change to the power and the presence of the risen Lord.

It seems highly significant to me that the distinguished American historian, Ramsay MacMullen, writing about the conversion of the Roman Empire,[2] rates exorcism as one of the most significant factors which bring about individual conversions – certainly in the period pre-Constantine's conversion before AD 312. He has little time for recent historians who attribute these conversions to what he calls crowd psychology. He prefers, rightly I think, to give weight to the considerable evidence of the early church fathers.

If this thesis is correct, then this timeless, cross-cultural ministry deserves to be taken very seriously. That is the case which I hope to present. People sometimes object to my teaching about the supernatural (both on angels and demons) by saying something to the effect of, "I've never experienced anything like this so why is it important?"

From my house, I can walk up to Bradgate Park (home of Lady Jane Grey, the unfortunate nine-day queen who was executed in the Tower of London in 1554 aged sixteen) and across the road to Swithland Wood.

In the park, I occasionally see adders. Sometimes they are basking in the sun. In the spring they may be mating on a grassy bank beneath a stone wall in which they have hibernated. In the autumn they may be on the move, looking for a safe place to overwinter. Despite having some idea where to look, I will probably see an adder just once or twice in a year. They are certainly very numerous. Yet many people walk in the park without ever seeing a snake. Many dogs trample through the grass and bracken; very few, if any, are bitten in a given year. The snakes prefer to remain out of the way and out of sight.

Across the road in Swithland Wood, there is a large colony of Purple Hairstreak butterflies. They spend most of their active life high up in the canopy of the oaks. Occasionally they descend to bask on sunlit warm foliage, especially the females. The females also descend to release some of their eggs on low-lying oak saplings. Because I know where to look, I can usually spot the butterflies during their flight season; I can often find their tiny white eggs in the forks of suitable oak twigs. I can sometimes find their caterpillars, which usually haven't strayed far from the empty eggshells. Many people walk in the woods. But few are aware of, or see, the butterfly. Virtually none, I would hazard, see either the eggs or a caterpillar, although they often walk within a foot of where the eggs have been laid and where the caterpillars are sitting, well camouflaged, on the oak buds. Even I, with years of knowledge, have never found a chrysalis.

From these natural observations, I would make the following points. The supernatural world is all around us. But just as I can scarcely sing a note in tune, so many Christians remain blind to anything but the natural world. Angels, I believe, are present. But, like the Purple Hairstreak butterfly, angels are seldom seen. Evil spirits, like adders, prefer to remain hidden. They may be present but are seldom noticed. If their malign effect is observed, usually other explanations will be proffered. As C. S. Lewis writes in one of his most famous books:[3]

> My dear Wormwood,
>
> I wonder you should ask me whether it is essential to keep the patient in ignorance of your own existence. That question, has been answered for us by the High Command. Our policy, for the moment, is to conceal ourselves. Of course this has not always been so. We are faced with a cruel dilemma. When the humans disbelieve in our existence we lose all the pleasing results of direct terrorism and we make no magicians. On the other hand, when they believe in us, we cannot make them materialists and sceptics.

We need to take note of all this and then we will be far better equipped to help our suffering world.

CHAPTER 1

A ZAMBIAN ADVENTURE

The angel of the Lord encamps around those who fear him.

(Psalm 34:7)

On the evening of Monday 11 May 1992, my wife Jane and I, together with a faithful band of helpers, arrived at the small village of Mutwe Wa Nkoko, deep in the bush in the Luapula province in Northern Zambia. It had been a long, dusty and uncomfortable drive. We were given a rapturous, typically Zambian, and utterly unforgettable welcome.

I was leading a SOMA (Sharing of Ministries Abroad) team. We were accompanied by the late Martin Cavender, then director of Springboard, Archbishop Carey's flagship project for evangelism. His son Henry, a student at Kingston University, had come to make a film of our mission. We were accompanied by Archdeacon Tobias Kaoma, Agnes Mupeta who lived in nearby Mansa and was the leader of the important diocesan Mothers' Union, and Martha Zulu who was the administrator and evangelist for Bishop Bernard Malango.

En route, we paid a courtesy call to the local chief. His household was in chaos, with sickness and considerable anxiety concerning a daughter who was about to give birth. We prayed for them all and gave some small gifts of food. About a mile from the village we were met by hundreds of dancing, smiling people. They had garlands of flowers to give us and greeted us, dancing as they sang, "Sangale

sangale" (let's be joyful). In the midst of a life-threatening drought, this was pretty impressive. We left our vehicle and joined in the fun. Clearly foreign visitors were unusual.

The village seemed quite small: a little church, a good deep well, a few houses (shambas) and, in the distance, a school whose roof had been blown off in a storm some eighteen months earlier.

Under the light of the brilliant African sky and the Southern Cross, we washed as discreetly as possible in steaming hot water, protected by a little stockade. Then there was a camp fire, which involved food, singing, drama, and much laughter. The main drama was about a man who tried to steal from his neighbour, but first he had to steal a bone from someone else to silence the neighbour's dog! There was another about stealing a man's wife – which felt distinctly close to the bone.

We went to bed happily and looking forward to two useful days of speaking, praying, and discovering the extent and effect of the drought. This was my second visit to Zambia. The first, two years earlier, had taken me to the old mission centre at Chipili. Mutwe was about four hours' drive from Chipili. I think, because of the circuitous nature of the roads, we could have walked there in about the same time.

Chipili in 1990 had opened my eyes and renewed my faith. Peter Hancock, then the healing advisor for Bath and Wells, and I spent four days addressing a conference of about 2,000 people who were camping in the grounds around the old mission station. We heard a churchwarden give out a notice: "Tomorrow, brother and sisters, you are going to see signs and wonders – not performed by these men, but by Almighty God." And that is what happened. We had four prayer teams. On two successive days we prayed for several hours. Many collapsed to the ground – shrieking as demons left them. Many professed faith or renewed their baptismal vows. There were healings – Peter saw two people with a blind eye healed.

On the Sunday, after a two-hour service and well over 1,000 communicants, we prayed for four hours. I was awaiting a hip replacement, but somehow was able to stand for that length of time with little pain. At the end, Jason Mfula, a local leader who had been Zambian High Commissioner in Australia, said, "You have brought us the water of the Holy Spirit – now the challenge is, do something about the village water supply." I did my best and raised about £2,000 to replace a worn-out pump, which was used to bring water from the river (where thirty years ago the UMCA missionaries had shot the last crocodile) up to the houses and schools situated far above it.

The next morning in Mutwe, a crowd of about 500 gathered. We held a joyful service in the open air. After much singing and dancing, led by the exuberant members of the Mothers' Union (clad in smart white turbans and blue chitengas – the brightly coloured, full-length skirts worn by all the women), I preached about drawing water from "the wells of salvation" (Isaiah 12:3). It seemed appropriate in a village whose deep, cool well was sustaining them in a time of drought.

It was all very quiet and good natured. Blue Charaxes butterflies danced from one great tree to another, providing me with a pleasant distraction. At the end of the morning, we invited people to join us for a time of prayer in the nearby church.

I was used to spiritual drama in Luapula, but nothing had prepared me for the ferocious battle that erupted. Tobias Kaoma, experienced in prayer and exorcism, was surrounded by a group of screaming women. The rest of us found that we only had to utter a word of prayer, or stretch out our hands in prayer towards someone, and they started to flutter their eyelids, shake violently, collapse to the ground, or even start slithering across the floor in a passable imitation of the local snake. Henry, the youngest member of the team, who had come as a late addition to make a video, made an understandably swift exit. He was terrified!

In the midst of this maelstrom, Jane, my wife, called me over and said, "Listen to this." One of the woman, or to be more accurate the spirit that was speaking through her, said, "Go away. I am not leaving this person!" She was speaking in perfect Oxbridge English – Zambians normally speak English with a lilting, soft accent, but this woman's voice was harsh and powerful – a good mimic of mine. We made little progress and retired for a simple lunch, somewhat bruised and chastened. It was one of the few occasions that prayers of deliverance didn't seem to have much effect.

After a quick visit to a maize field, where I was shown the devastating effect of the drought on their crops, I returned to speak to the gathering crowd. Something was stirring within me.

Speaking against the local demons

It was not my normal style, but I felt convinced that we had to stand against the local principalities and powers – especially Masonda, the black snake spirit, and Malenga, the water spirit. Both these names came up frequently when we asked people what was troubling them. The black snake was probably the emblem of local witchcraft. It seemed likely that many of the local mothers sought protection from the medicine men while also bringing their babies to the church for baptism.

Before speaking, I made a public prayer against these two demonic powers – fallen angels in biblical terms. I then challenged the congregation to stop hesitating between two opinions; to choose Christ and to throw away all charms, fetishes, and potions from the local witchdoctors. The response was laughter – not the friendly, good-natured laughter of the morning – but hollow, sinister, mocking laughter.

I asked my great friend Archdeacon Tobias, who was a wonderfully enthusiastic interpreter, what was happening. He said, "They are saying – we have so little and now you are telling us to throw things away." For a split second, I could sense their devastating logic. What right had I, a rich Westerner on only my second visit to Zambia, to challenge their culture and to tell them to throw away some of their most precious possessions?

The anger of God

Suddenly I was overwhelmed. For almost the only time in my life, I felt what I can only describe as the anger of God. The fact that I was an ignorant, visiting Westerner didn't seem important – what mattered was that God was honoured, and that meant that the Demonic Powers had to be opposed. People had to make a choice. No longer could they oscillate between two opinions. Even now, years later, I find it quite awesome to write about that afternoon. I spoke – I have no idea what – firm, even harsh words. I have never spoken like that before or since.

When I had finished, I felt shattered. I felt that I had failed, going way over the top. I don't remember much about the rest of the day.

We had a session planned with Father James Chungolo, the local priest, and his healing team. I was so exhausted that I left Martin Cavender to speak to them, while Jane had a good session with the local Mothers' Union, who are a tower of strength both spiritually and socially in rural Zambia. There are two women's groups in the Zambian church – the Mothers' Union who provide leadership and stability and the Veronicas who provide social assistance, especially to young mothers.

After another hard night on a mattress on the floor, with bats above, mosquitoes all around, spiders on the floor, and the possibility of snakes coming in from outside, I felt distinctly unenthusiastic about the dawning of Wednesday morning. At least our prayer group back in Shepton Mallet would have been praying for us during the previous evening.

The angel around the church

The next morning we began with a communion service in the little church. About 300 people were crammed inside. I tried to ignore a substantial wasp busying itself with building a nest behind the altar, close to where we were sitting. I was aware that I had nothing to say (an unusual occurrence as Jane would agree). I was grateful for the quiet rhythm of the Anglican Liturgy.

Eventually, it was time to preach. I even contemplated a little joke (Mfumu was the Bemba word for God; Mfubu was the word for a hippo!). I could still think of nothing to say. In desperation (or inspiration?), I asked Tobias Kaoma to give his testimony. Tobias was about sixty; his beloved wife, Prisca, had died only a month earlier at the age of forty-nine. Despite his very evident grief, Tobias had left his parish in Chipili to accompany us and to act as our leader, chief exorcist, and my translator.

Tobias' eyes lit up as he testified to his conversion, his calling to the priesthood (when working as a head teacher), and about the day two years earlier when he had been spontaneously, and unexpectedly, deeply touched by the Holy Spirit.

I well remember that afternoon. A good friend of mine was speaking about the Holy Spirit. I, I am embarrassed to say, was falling asleep, only to be awakened by the sight and sound of Tobias leaping around and praising God in many different languages. I am ashamed to admit that my first unworthy thought was, "Here is a drunk Zambian priest." But Tobias was transformed that afternoon. He was drunk – in the sense of Acts 2:15–21. The Holy Spirit filled him (Ephesians 5:18) in a most remarkable way. A quiet, unassuming, retired headmaster became a really powerful minister of the gospel. On another visit, the discerning Peter Hancock described him as the most powerful confronter of demons that he had ever met. Outwardly, he remained quiet, unassuming, and gracious. Inwardly, he was filled with power. His demeanour and character were those of one of the most Christlike people that I have met.

Tobias' testimony was lifting everyone's spirits but, while he was still speaking, a tall, dark lady glided out of the congregation. "Could I say something?" she asked. For a woman not even belonging to the Mothers' Union to interrupt a visiting leader was culturally unheard of, but Tobias graciously and characteristically gave way.

The lady continued to glide slowly forward. Her face shone. Only once have I seen that sort of light on someone's face.[1]

Her story was simple; its effect dramatic. As she spoke, her face continued to shine with what seemed to be a supernatural light. She spoke in Bemba, the local language. Early that morning, she and some friends had walked in the half-light from her village to the church. She and one of her companions had noticed a figure dressed in white following slowly along the path. While she peeled off into the bushes beside the church, the figure went round the other side. She and her companion then walked around the church expecting to see the person dressed in white. There was no one to be seen. The ground around the church is quite open, with a few trees and some shambas (Zambian huts).

The crowded congregation was deeply moved. Zambians do not wear white clothes. The Mothers' Union welcomed the lady, and symbolically placed one of their turbans on her head. Everyone felt that she had seen an angel, who had been sent to cleanse the church from the battles of the previous day. It was, and remains to this day, the most obviously supernatural experience of my life.

The contrast with the futile battles of the previous day was remarkable; the whole atmosphere in the church was quite different. There was a sort of spiritual electricity in the air. It felt a little like the occasion in the Gospels where Luke writes, "The power of the Lord was with Jesus to heal those who were ill" (Luke 5:17). No one can conjure up these times; they are a sovereign gift from God!

I preached a simple evangelistic sermon. I asked those who would like to respond to stand up and come forward. Two young men stood, and then the floodgates opened. We prayed for about forty; then for another sixty, including the local headman. During all this time of prayer, only one demon showed up. The man concerned was taken outside (always wisest to take people away from the limelight – demons are exhibitionists and seem to gain strength when lots of people are around), and evil powers were banished quickly and silently! Then we continued in prayer for the leaders and for many others to be healed, released from any evil oppression, and to be filled with the Holy Spirit.

Lunchtime came. The Blue Charaxes butterflies[2] were courting around the tree nearest to the church, but it was time to leave. We left with much sadness, but also with great joy and a feeling of "mission accomplished".

We paid a return visit to the local chief. This time there was great joy here too. Two hours earlier, his granddaughter had been safely born, the mother was well, and other members of the household were better. We prayed and gave thanks for the little girl and retreated with an honoured gift – a live chicken, which entertained us during the long, dusty car journey by pecking at Martin's trousers.

Soon afterwards, somewhat fired up by these experiences, we had a remarkable day in Mansa, the nearby provincial capital. A young woman brought from the hospital was lying in a side room in the church. She had been in hospital a month and had not walked for over a year. I saw her and mentally hoped that I would not be the one to pray for her. While I was preaching, Martin and Martha Zulu counselled her and prayed for her. They described her as like a "flower unfolding". She walked out of the side room, down the aisle of the crowded church, and went to discharge herself from the local hospital while her astonished father opened his heart to the Lord.

A more sophisticated man, Douglas Mupeta, husband of Agnes, the Mothers' Union leader in the area, asked for prayer for his stiff neck and arthritic knees. Nothing happened. Martin took him aside and counselled him, lawyer to lawyer. Something was released. Two hours later, he was running down the road to catch up with us as we went to lunch.

Later on that visit, we had some memorable ministry in a village near Mansa. An old lady who had walked in with a white stick, apparently almost totally blind, said to Jane after prayer, "What a nice white shirt you are wearing, my dear!"

Mutwe's reputation confirmed

Two years later, part of a team that I was leading revisited Mutwe. They found it tough going, but the lady who had seen the angel was a very visible part of the church, and Father James was providing dynamic leadership. Yet clearly, our visit had only dented the powers of darkness around the village.

In another part of Zambia, I talked to a remarkable priest who, at the age of eighty-two in a mining town on the copper-belt, was still physically building new churches and evangelizing new areas. He was very tall and very dignified. Over lunch, I mentioned Mutwe. He looked very serious and said quietly, "I visited Mutwe about twenty years ago. It is the darkest place that I have ever been to." He added that he'd had some terrible battles with demons there. I found his evidence strangely reassuring.

Clearly Mutwe is a place that has lived up to its name (which literally means "The Village of the Severed Chicken's Head"). Gradually, as the Christian gospel takes a deeper root there, the powers of darkness will be driven back.

Spiritual outcomes – Henry Cavender and James Chungolo

Martin's son Henry had come to Zambia as a late addition to our team. A priest had dropped out at very short notice so Martin suggested that Henry came, mainly to make a film of the trip. Henry, not yet a Christian, was both intrigued and scared by what he was required to film. It wasn't difficult to film his father giving radio and TV interviews, even if it was surprising to see the church taken so seriously by the national media. It wasn't hard to shoot the exuberant Zambian worship, so refreshingly different to what he was used to at home. It was rather harder to watch people being prayed for– and apparently benefiting from the experience. It seemed both intrusive and frightening to film people who seemed troubled by malevolent spirits. These people were mainly young women, often with babies on their backs.

When Henry returned to England, he spent his gap year living in Bath, and frequently found his friends asking him about things he had seen in Africa. When he reported what he had seen and heard the usual reaction was, "You must be joking." For eight years Henry remained on a spiritual knife-edge – believing and yet not quite committed.

Through university life and then on into the corporate world of London, he knew there would come a point when he would have to make a decision. That point came when, at a junction in London, Henry reached again for a Bible and was drawn to the book of Ecclesiastes. The author, Solomon, spoke deeply to Henry's heart and he knew this was it. Rather beautifully, and through an unrelated set of circumstances, Henry's long-term girlfriend, Emma, then living in Bath, also came to faith and made a commitment to follow Jesus. Within months they married and started attending an Assemblies of God church, signing up to get baptized as a symbol of their new beginning.

The baptism was due on a Sunday, but by the Thursday, Henry was having second thoughts: "Is it really necessary to do this? God knows my heart. I've already made a commitment."

That night he dreamed that he and Emma were walking along a sand-blown road on a hot tropical island. They walked through a bustling market and on towards the beach. The day was beautiful and the beach was just ahead, so they ignored the big hotel where they were supposed to check in, and carried on excitedly with all their luggage. When they arrived on the beach, it was brilliant – clean sand, blue sky, and glorious sea, and they lay underneath a palm shelter with some friends. Then the mood changed. Menacing waves reared up and patrolled left and right. They heard thunder, the sky turned black, strong winds blew sand across the beach and, from the dark sky above, bolts of fire began to rain down as people ran screaming for shelter. As they grabbed their bags and raced for the cover of the big hotel, Henry felt a lump of brimstone hit his leg and woke up with a fright. He knew for certain he must check in on Sunday.

His mother arrived for the service. She was a little late, having driven 200 miles. Henry was just about to be immersed and was explaining to the congregation that he had seen it all in Zambia, but had delayed making a real profession of faith until now. In his testimony, he described himself as "Hesitant Henry".

Soon afterwards, Henry became involved in full-time ministry – notably leading a church for surfers in Polzeath in Cornwall. He now works part-time for the Methodist Church as a pioneer minister in the area.

James Chungolo was greatly inspired and twice came to help me minister in other parts of Luapula Province. On one occasion in 1999, he cycled fifty kilometres to Mwenda with a flat tyre to help us. At least three remarkable things happened.

On the Sunday, we were to hold an open air service in a large area surrounded by a fence, where they were starting to build a church. As we were about to begin, a woman came up to me. She said, "I must tell you about my daughter who has just died." I sighed inwardly and wondered how I could comfort her and answer the inevitable question: "Why did God let it happen?" She continued, "Five years ago you came to our village. You prayed for my daughter who was lying paralysed on her bed."

Suddenly I remembered my third visit to Zambia in 1994. We had left Chipili to visit a small village. After a service, I was asked to go and pray for a teenager lying helpless in a shamba. I felt tired after preaching and praying for many people. I asked Albert Owen, a reader from my parish in Shepton Mallet, to accompany me, and left the rest of the team to encourage the local leaders. We were led into a very dark room. We could just see someone lying on a bed; we couldn't really tell how ill she was. We anointed her with oil. To be honest, I didn't have much faith but, to our surprise, the teenager got up off the bed – apparently completely well.

The mother had walked about fifty kilometres to be with us. She said quite simply, "I want to give thanks to God for the five good years that she had. She died of malaria." I wanted to say, "God, if you healed her of the paralysis, why did you let her die of malaria?" The mother, with a much more balanced faith, had just come to give thanks. I was deeply moved. It was one of the most profound testimonies I have ever received.

I thought of the long journey. I remembered the hazardous drive along the Pedicle – the Zambian road which runs through the edge of the Democratic Republic of Congo. And I silently gave thanks to God that he had allowed me to come and see such amazing things.

A few minutes later the service was in full swing. Halfway through, we started to pray for people. After a short time, I heard a commotion in a distant corner of the area. I went over to try and help. Father James was struggling with a young woman. He said she was demonized and speaking in French. We had discovered that the demons were exhibitionists. They seemed to gain strength from crowds of onlookers. We moved her outside the fenced area. She was gently placed in a small pit where clay for making bricks had been extracted. At my instigation, we marched round seven times singing, "In the name of Jesus, demons will have to flee." They did. When we had finished, the young woman was smiling and completely free. No further prayers were necessary.

At the end of the service, we were aware of a young man who couldn't stop grunting. No amount of prayer or command seemed to have any effect. That evening, Martin Cavender, Father James and I listened to his story. He had been brought up in Lusaka. When he was quite young, his parents were murdered. He was moved to stay with some relatives in Chipili. He said they practised witchcraft. He couldn't stop grunting especially during worship. Father James said that the young man had been invaded by a pig spirit. I was very dubious about the diagnosis, but James' prayers seemed effective.

The next day the young man was very happy when his grunting was silenced, with one brief command. He walked back with me to the village in a very relaxed state. It was wonderful to see the transformation. The deliverance ministry, rightly exercised, brings extraordinary freedom and benefit.

When I returned to England, I read the Greek text of Paul in Philippi. The Greek, "πνεῦμα πύθωνα" (Acts 16:16), said that the slave girl who could foretell the future literally had the spirit of a python (translated as spirit of divination or fortune-telling in our Bibles). Evidently I had been wrong to doubt James' diagnosis. If the woman in Philippi could have a python spirit, a young man in Mwenda could certainly have a pig spirit![3]

Concluding thoughts

When in Southwell Minster in about 2005, I was helping to lead a training day for the diocese on the subject of healing and deliverance. After lunch, there was a question and answer session. It was here that an elderly clergyman stood up and said, "Isn't it time we stopped conniving with this medieval mumbo-jumbo?" I whispered to the Christian psychiatrist sitting next to me, "I think more of your profession believe in the reality of evil powers than mine." She nodded. The bishop said, "John, what have you to say to this?"

I related very briefly the story of the lady speaking in Oxbridge English in Mutwe. I said quietly, something to effect of, "I think by far the most likely explanation is that we were witnessing something similar to that recorded in the first chapter of Mark's Gospel. It is the only explanation which makes any sense." There seemed to be a ripple of relieved assent from most of the assembled clergy. Once again, the events of May 1992 in a very rural Zambian village were having a profound spiritual effect.

One final question – why did the village of Mutwe have such spiritual problems? I can only presume that at one level the village must have had exceptionally powerful witchdoctors. Matthew Parris[4] might agree with that! Mentioning them in my afternoon talk provoked the only really hostile reaction that I have been aware of during many years of such ministry in many different countries. That suggests a climate of fear. I find the evidence of the eighty-two-year-old Zambian priest very persuasive. If that godly man thought Mutwe was the darkest place he had visited, then that is strong evidence.

At a deeper level, we might be witnessing the power of territorial spirits. We shall consider that in a later chapter. Praying against the water spirit and the snake spirit certainly provoked a reaction. But I don't want to press the case too far. I am well content to let the glowing face of the woman who had apparently seen the angel, and a well-spoken evil spirit make the case – in Mutwe, the devil had certainly not gone missing!

THEOLOGICAL CONSIDERATIONS

(CHAPTERS 2–4)

CHAPTER 2

THEOLOGICAL ISSUES

I can't help thinking that if the devil doesn't exist and, therefore, man has created him, he has created him in his own image and likeness.
(Fyodor Dostoevsky, *The Brothers Karamazov*, Part 2, Book V, Chapter 4)

"I can't believe that!" said Alice. "Can't you?" said the Queen in a pitying tone. "Try again: draw a long breath, and shut your eyes... Why, sometimes, I've believed as many as six impossible things before breakfast."
(Lewis Carroll, *Through the Looking Glass*)

"I don't believe in the devil," proclaimed a cathedral canon at an open diocesan meeting.

"Believing in the devil doesn't fit my world view," says a future senior cleric over lunch.

"Isn't it time we stopped conniving with this medieval mumbo-jumbo [about the deliverance ministry]?" asks an elderly cleric (see page 28) at a question session at a cathedral training day devoted to the healing ministry.

Such views are widespread particularly, I think, among the clergy. They have been expressed since at least the seventeenth century when the Latitudinarians, a group who were somewhat uninterested in dogma, church organization or liturgy, were very influential. Their dislike of what they called "enthusiasm" paved the way for the Methodist revival, which came partly as a sharp reaction to their views.

During the Second World War, the influential German theologian, Rudolf Bultmann, maintained that it was impossible to believe in the world of angels and devils, and at the same time to make use of aeroplanes and electric light.[1] This paved the way for a very sceptical view of God and Scripture, which was rampant when I was at theological college in the 1960s.

Denial of the supernatural was the order of the day. Angels, especially in nativity plays, were an embarrassment. Evil spirits, especially after well-publicized cases that had ended in murder or other tragedies, were worse. Healing stretched the faith of parish priests. Usually their prayers seemed to be unanswered and they were left trying to explain the apparent absence of God to the bereaved. It was much simpler to construct a theology which avoided all these pitfalls.

There was a general feeling that psychiatry had explained so-called demon possession and that there was no credible evidence for a supernatural world. Some of my fellow students at what was then a very liberal theological college in Cambridge, ended up as social workers. They were honest enough to realize that their views were incompatible with normal parish ministry.

There were at least three other strands of thinking which reinforced this view. Belief in the devil, it was alleged, inevitably led to Dualism. This concept saw the forces of good and evil as "the outcome of separate and equally ultimate first causes".[2] Religions such as Hinduism, which taught of mighty battles between the gods, reinforced this view. Theologians pointed out that the devil gets little mention in the Old Testament, until Judaism comes under the influence of Persian Zoroastrianism during the Babylonian exile. Zoroastrianism teaches a dualistic view of life.

Secondly, the theory of Kenosis (based on the Greek word for "emptying") was drawn from Philippians 2, particularly verses 5–7: "Christ Jesus, who, though he was in the form of God, did not count equality with God a thing to be grasped, but emptied himself, by taking the form of a servant, being born in the likeness of men" (ESV). It was argued that Jesus was limited by the knowledge of his time. Obviously He thought that the world was flat, that creation took six days, that Jonah was literally swallowed by the whale, and that demons existed. A slight variation of this viewpoint postulates that, because Jesus' disciples believed in the existence of evil spirits, Jesus (who knew better) went along with this world view for their sake. This argument is far from being universally accepted. But, even if we do accept it, we shall see below that it shouldn't affect our understanding of evil.

Thirdly, the rise of the charismatic movement caused great concern. Many charismatics (that is people who have received an empowering experience of the Holy Spirit) were keen on exorcism and tended to see the devil as directly behind every misfortune. In some circles it was normal to see all illness as directly implanted by the devil. More particularly, illnesses like cancer were often / usually thought to be caused by evil spirits. At least one influential teacher, using a curious exposition of Luke 17:37 and Matthew 24:28, taught that it was normal for people to be demonized and that new converts would need some sort of deliverance ministry.[3] In extreme cases charismatics, particularly from Africa, would try and beat devils out of their children and perform dangerous and even life threatening exorcisms.

It was argued, not unreasonably, that trying to exorcise people who were obviously suffering from some form of mental illness was offering them a quick fix, which would inevitably make the situation worse and complicate long-term medical treatment. It was felt to be much safer to suspend belief in a negative spiritual world than to encourage people to see evil spirits everywhere, and the devil directly behind every tragic or evil situation.

I met this sort of theology when, just before a parish mission, I survived a direct lightning strike on the Brecon Beacons. "That was Satan trying to destroy the mission," said our leading speaker. Still somewhat shaken, but rejoicing in my escape, I said, "I don't think the devil controls lightning." The idea that the devil would have had the power to organize a lightning strike seems preposterous. A cursory reading of Jesus' comments about the Tower of Siloam falling down and killing people (Luke 13:4–5) should remind us that we live in a fallen world where accidents (and lightning strikes) are part of the warp and woof of our human existence.

Thus, serious-minded clerics and theologians were convinced

that, by writing out the devil from their theology, they were saving people from the double threat of Dualism and the charismatic extremists. They were also expounding the New Testament in a way which took account of twentieth- and twenty-first-century learning. They were following the great Bultmann in demythologizing the Scriptures and making it easier for thinking people to believe. They also were convinced that they were being intellectually honest and using the best tools available to understand the Bible in general, and the life of Jesus in particular. The devil, as my questioner in the cathedral implied, was a figment of medieval mumbo-jumbo, who was best excised from any intelligent modern theology. To be honest, until I unexpectedly had a profound encounter with what appeared to be the forces of darkness, I would have had some sympathy with many of those views. They were, and are, held by people of integrity who are trying to do their best for the church.

One problem would appear to be that such views tend to empty churches (as in seventeenth-century England before the Methodist revival). Another would seem to be that both reason and experience would appear to make them untenable.

Green writes:

> It is interesting to realize that doubt about the existence of a malign evil is to be found, by and large, only in Christian lands. It is only where the victory of Christ is so well known, only where the defeat of evil is so celebrated, that doubts are expressed.
>
> In non-Christian lands it is not so. There you find the most vital awareness of the reality and personality of evil forces, focused in the great adversary himself. Animism, Islam, Hinduism are under no illusions about the great Enemy. There he is known, dreaded and often slavishly worshipped.[4]

The general reaction of intelligent African Christians to accusations of conniving with medieval mumbo-jumbo is, "How can these people be so stupid?" To most Africans, it is obvious that negative spiritual forces exist. Encounters with witchdoctors, for good or ill, leave little room for doubt on these matters. Witchdoctors are powerful and controversial figures. Often they are possessors of really good medicine based on a deep knowledge of local plants. Such knowledge comes at a price and many encounters are frightening, with most being spiritually dangerous.

The well-known atheist, Matthew Parris,[5] some years back wrote an article in *The Times* entitled "Africa needs God" (see Chapter 1, page 28). His main thrust was that the missionaries had done an amazing job in his native Southern Rhodesia (now Zimbabwe) and Malawi. What had impressed him was not their social work, but their spiritual work in giving people dignity and hope – free from the fear of evil spirits and the power of local witchdoctors. He said that, as a convinced atheist, he was surprised to be writing this. He recognized that for the people he grew up with, fear of evil powers was a constant reality. Presumably he believed they were wrong, but he had the understanding to see that, for many Africans, it was a painful reality which needed to be taken seriously.

The Counter Arguments

The counter arguments can take many forms:

(1) It is difficult, if not impossible, to believe in God if there is no spiritual opposition.

(2) It is possible to form a theology which accepts the existence of the devil, but which in no way is dualistic.

(3) We need to listen to the sober evidence of the Gospel writers on the subject. They are contemporary and clear – especially Mark (traditionally based on the preaching of Peter in Rome) and also Luke, who witnessed Paul freeing an apparently demon-possessed woman in Philippi.

(4) While we might not be alarmed that Jesus thought the world was flat, we should be seriously alarmed if He was performing exorcisms which were merely psychological tricks. Although we must not exaggerate the devil's influence, accepting the biblical view provides some explanation of the state of our world – both in regard to illness, accident and malevolent powers. Jesus' teaching in Luke 13 about the collapse of the Tower of Siloam is particularly helpful.

(5) Finally, as we shall see, there is a great deal of contemporary testimony which only makes sense if the resurrection story is true, and the Gospel stories give us an accurate historical and theological picture. Also, pastorally, as we meet people who have had vivid and real experiences, we can offer them hope and a means of reaching freedom.

IS IT POSSIBLE TO HAVE A COHERENT DOCTRINE OF A LOVING GOD WITHOUT SOME UNDERSTANDING OF, AND BELIEF IN, THE EXISTENCE OF SATAN?

Michael Green writes:

I believe the Christian doctrines of God, of man and of salvation are utterly untenable without the existence of Satan. You simply cannot write him out of the human story and then imagine that the story is basically unchanged. At the beginning, at the mid-point of time and at the end, the devil has an indelible place in Christian theology. The fallen nature of man and of everything he does, the self-destructive tendencies of every civilisation history has known, the prevalence of disease, together with nature, red in tooth and claw, unite to point to an outside enemy. I would like to ask theologians who are sceptical about the devil how they can give a satisfactory account of God if Satan is a figment of the imagination. Without the devil's existence, the doctrine of God, a God who could have made such a world and allowed such horrors to take place daily within it, is utterly monstrous. Such a God would be no loving Father. He would be a pitiless tyrant.[6]

This, I think, is a really important statement. The problems of suffering, the horrors of tyranny and the flawed beauty of the natural world all challenge our ability to believe. If we take Satan seriously, we can begin to see the glimmerings of an answer. As Paul puts it in a different context, "now we see through a glass, darkly; but then face to face" (1 Corinthians 13:12 AKJV). Remove Satan from our world view and we are inexorably challenged by the dark thought that God is at best incompetent, and at worst malicious. Human nature alone, however fallen, cannot really explain the horrors of

Auschwitz, Stalin, Mao, Rwanda, Islamic State and all the rest.

It would also mean that the cross has to be seen as a horrible tragedy entirely caused by human sin. Traditional views such as atonement and victory over evil would have to be removed. Then we are left simply to admire amazing suffering, and to wonder how God could be involved in such a tragedy.

To all of this we might add the thought that Satan is well pleased when people deny his existence. As we shall see, evil spirits often lie dormant until people try to make spiritual progress. It suits their general strategy to remain unnoticed.

BUT DOES THIS INEVITABLY LEAD TO DUALISM – AN EQUAL CONFLICT BETWEEN GOOD AND EVIL?

The devil is bound to a line which can be lengthened even to the point where, for a while, Satan can make himself independent and has to be fought against by God. Going slightly beyond the Revelation of St John, this means that the whole fearful character is to be attributed to the evil, which temporarily looses itself from these bonds. If this event is taking place in accordance with the divine plan, then God himself limited his omnipotence for this interim period, without giving it up in the long term.[7]

These words were penned by Oscar Cullmann, a German Lutheran pastor and theologian. Cullmann lived through the horrors of Nazi Germany. On another occasion, he coined the famous analogy that, after D-Day, the war was over but there was still a great deal of fighting to take place. Cullmann, writing just after D-Day, likened this to the cross and second coming. After Calvary, the war against Satan and the forces of evil was won, but there were a great many spiritual battles still to come.

Cullmann's words, to me, make perfect sense. In most situations, there is a spiritual battle where the believer knows that he can be under attack and that things can go badly wrong. In rare situations, the power of evil seems so great that it appears Satan is in total control. The few remaining beleaguered Christians in Syria and IS-controlled Iraq are surely feeling like that.

Cullmann's theory recognizes the reality of the normal spiritual conflict that believers, and others, face. The devil, as the "father of lies", can help fester many negative characteristics. It is a sad fact that Christian leadership is littered with broken people who had problems ranging from adultery and other sexual issues, financial impropriety, alcoholism, pride, jealousy... the list is endless. We have a formidable enemy. The Lord's Prayer with its petition, "Deliver us from evil (or the Evil One)", is a timely reminder of our own vulnerability. Even if the devil doesn't control lightning, he has many powerful weapons in his armoury. Paul writes pertinently: "take up the shield of faith, with which you can extinguish all the flaming arrows of the evil one "(Ephesians 6:16).

More importantly, Cullmann's theory also accounts for those terrible situations where evil has seemed to rule, and still does, with little effective hindrance. Try telling victims of the Rwandan genocide, the holocaust, the Stalinist purges, the Cultural Revolution in China, or the appalling ravages of Islamic State that the devil doesn't exist, and you will get laughed out of court.

WHAT HAVE THE WRITERS OF THE NEW TESTAMENT TO SAY?

Mark has many vivid accounts of Jesus' conflicts with demons. We shall consider the most detailed incident, which involves the Gadarene swine, in a later chapter. What is clear is that Mark recognizes the reality of the spiritual opposition. The accounts are vivid and detailed. Very strong ancient tradition says that Mark based his Gospel on the preaching of Peter in Rome. This would explain why his accounts of events, also recorded in Matthew and Luke, are invariably longer and more detailed. A comparison between Mark 5:1–20, Matthew 8:28–34, and Luke 8:26–39 makes the point very clearly. Mark's vivid account must have come from an eyewitness. It is an extraordinary story with many bizarre points. It beggars belief that anyone could have invented it. It is totally incredible if it is demythologized. Remove the demons, and the poor man becomes a modern psychiatric case. The curious thing is that then he is healed by the power of Jesus' prayer.

One of the main themes of Mark's Gospel is the conflict between the two kingdoms – of God and of Satan. Eliminate Satan and the

Gospel is dramatically altered and made almost meaningless. Add to this the generally accepted view that Mark is the oldest of the Gospels and the effect is even more disastrous.

In Acts 16:10, Luke, who is the author of both the third Gospel and the Acts of the Apostles, joins the missionary group. One of the incidents he reports in Philippi is the exorcism of a slave girl with a "gift" of fortune-telling. This gift earned her owners a great deal of money. They were furious when the deliverance took place. As I mentioned in the previous chapter (see Chapter 1, page 27), in Greek, Luke names her problem as having "the spirit of a python". English translations are less than literal and refer to a spirit of divination or fortune-telling.

In Acts there are at least four places which see major spiritual battles. We may call these, power encounters. These took place in Samaria (8:4–25), Cyprus (13:4–12), Philippi (16:12–40), and Ephesus (19). The last three were led by Paul. Acts 8 records the powerful ministry of the deacon Philip. He performed many miracles and exorcisms. These were confirmed by the later arrival of the apostles Peter and John.

It is worth noting that each of these spiritual battles brought problems for the apostles. Simon Magus, from Samaria, apparently caused great difficulties for many years.[8]

After the conflict in Cyprus, Mark returned home to Jerusalem. This caused a huge row between Paul and his mentor, Barnabas. Without Barnabas' careful discipleship, it is highly unlikely that Mark would have been restored to favour. As a result, he wrote his Gospel and also acted as Peter's scribe for his first epistle.

The exorcism in Philippi led to the beating and arrest of Paul and Silas. Despite being acquitted of all wrongdoing, they were hustled out of the city – leaving the embryonic church presumably in the hands of Luke, Lydia (the converted seller of expensive purple dye), the slave girl, and the jailor who had a midnight conversion after an earthquake. This remarkably disparate group produced a church which earned Paul's admiration.

Similarly in Ephesus after the gospel spread rapidly, the silversmiths rioted because no one was buying the silver statues of the goddess Diana. Once again, Paul was acquitted of wrongdoing; once again he was hustled out of the city.

In the fourth Gospel, there are no exorcism stories, but John writes of the activities of Satan – most notably in the sad and puzzling story of Judas Iscariot. He also writes powerfully about some of the negative attributes of the devil: "You belong to your father, the devil, and you want to carry out your father's desire. He was a murderer from the beginning, not holding to the truth, for there is no truth in him. When he lies, he speaks his native language, for he is a liar and the father of lies" (John 8:44).

Similarly, John's first epistle has many references to Satan. If you remove Satan from your theology, the great epistle of love is severely truncated and its theology seriously undermined.

Paul, in his many letters, is constantly aware of Satan. The most famous passage about his thorn (2 Corinthians 12:1–10) has been subjected to too much speculation. What is clear is that Paul was quite convinced that his thorn, whether it was a physical illness, a spiritual attack, a psychological trauma, or whatever, was sent by Satan, and that the Lord was giving him grace to accept it.

His classic passage on spiritual warfare in Ephesians 6:10–20 becomes completely meaningless if there is no spiritual conflict – whether in heavenly places or in everyday life. If Paul is dangerously wrong on such a basic theological issue, it calls into question all his other great teaching on justification, grace, the fruit of the Spirit and the like.

It is also interesting that Paul in his epistles doesn't give any teaching about the existence of evil spirits nor about how to deal with them. The most likely explanation is that, despite meeting them in Philippi and Ephesus (and very probably elsewhere), they were sufficiently uncommon not to merit any exposition in his doctrinal writings. This sober theology gives no encouragement to counsellors who see demons around every corner. We need to keep a very careful balance. I personally think that well-meaning people who try to expel non-existent demons do even more harm than those who deny that there is any possibility of their existence.

WHAT DOES JESUS HAVE TO SAY?

It is clear from the above that, if we give any credence to the truthfulness of the New Testament writers, then Jesus believed in the existence of Satan and the presence of evil spirits. Even if we accept the Kenosis theory (see page 32) that His knowledge of His world was limited by contemporary thinking, that doesn't mean that His understanding of demonology was similarly coloured.

Not only did Jesus have many successful conflicts with demons, but He also called Satan, "the prince of this world". This view was not found in contemporary theology but, as in so many of His sayings, He strikes an original and definitive line.

Also, the Gospel writers are incredibly careful to distinguish between healings of illness and healings which involve a release from evil spirits. The story recorded in Luke 13:10–17 of the woman "whom Satan bound for eighteen years" (ESV) falls somewhere in between the two. Satan is involved in her illness, but Jesus doesn't explain how this has happened.

To suggest that Jesus was wrong (even if this was due to a knowledge limitation which He had willingly accepted) about such a critical theological matter strikes at the very heart of His integrity and theological judgment. It also flies in the face of the evidence of Luke writing in Acts, many Christian leaders in the next three centuries, and much subsequent witness from the Celtic church, John Wesley and George Whitefield, countless twentieth-century missionaries, and much modern evidence even from places like the United Kingdom.

Jesus' first recorded conflict with demons was recorded by Mark (1:21–28). It took place in the synagogue in Capernaum. There were a number of very striking features. First, the spirit makes a futile attempt to take advantage over Jesus by naming Him: "What do you want with us, Jesus of Nazareth?" The "us" is interesting – it is either a sign of multiple possession (like the seven demons cast out from Mary Magdalene) or of the demon's awareness of other evil entities. Once again, we see that Mark's account is both detailed and graphic. It simply must be based on the words of an eyewitness.

Secondly, the spirit declares who Jesus is: "the Holy One of God". This is the first public declaration of whom Jesus was. If you were trying to convince a sceptical public of the divinity of Jesus, you would scarcely choose an unimportant evil spirit in an out of the way synagogue as your first witness. It is as bizarre as using the formerly demonized Mary as the first witness of the resurrection.

There is a simple explanation. Mark, from Peter's lips, is recording what actually happened!

Thirdly, the spirit is not completely obedient to Jesus. It was ordered to leave silently but was actually ejected convulsing the man and speaking in a loud voice. Again, this detail points to Mark's desire for truth. This is far more important than trying to make a convincing case. The evil spirits, both here and in 5:9, equivocate and bargain with Jesus. Their performance is a reminder of their power, which is not to be underestimated by any involved in this ministry.

Fourthly, the reaction of the crowd is interesting: "What is this? A new teaching – and with authority! He even gives orders to impure spirits and they obey him." This is a new teaching! True, there were Jewish exorcists. Jesus admitted as much in Luke 11:19: "Now if I drive out demons by Beelzebul, by whom do your followers drive them out?" But the entertaining story in Acts 19 of the failed efforts at exorcism of the sons of Sceva may be more typical of what people were used to: "Jesus I know, and Paul I know about, but who are you?"(Acts 19:15). The evil spirits are confident and strong. The sons of Sceva are overpowered and driven out of the house naked and wounded![9] As in the story of the Gadarene man, the spirits have a power that is best understood as supernatural. I once witnessed four policemen trying to control a former marine, who had arrived in our house and interrupted a theological discussion with a psychiatrist on this very subject (see Chapter 4, page 74).

Jesus constantly gave new teaching. His teaching about Satan in particular, and demons in general, was radical. His ministry was powerful and effective. How do moderns dare to question His judgment?

WHAT ABOUT CONTEMPORARY WITNESS?

Much of the rest of the book will be the testimony of contemporary witnesses. We shall also look at the ministry of the early church (AD 100–400) where we shall see that exorcism was regarded as a normal part of a Christian's work. At this stage, the point I want to make is a simple one. If the accounts of exorcism in Mark 1–5 are true, then it is not surprising that such ministry was needed in the early days of Christianity. Nor is it surprising that it occurs on the frontiers of the mission field today. What perhaps is more surprising is that it is needed in sophisticated societies like England.

If the accounts in Mark are true, then by far the simplest explanation of modern phenomena is that we are witnessing something similar to what is recorded in the Gospels. Occam's razor encourages us to accept the simplest explanation. In my days of teaching mathematics, we studied Bayes' theorum on conditional probability (see Endnotes, Chapter 11, note 8). In essence it would, by pure mathematics, strongly confirm the view that the Zambian lady (Chapter 1, page 19) apparently overtaken by another entity and speaking in Oxbridge English (although she lived in a very rural village where no English was spoken), was acting in a way which was to be understood by applying Mark 1 and not by modern theology. This is a view which I think many psychiatrists would accept, even if many of my clerical colleagues would question it.

We shall also see that very few people are actually invaded by evil spirits (hence Paul's lack of teaching on the subject), but many are oppressed and troubled by the forces of darkness. This will be an important consideration when we seek to study how best to pray for people who believe they are directly troubled by Satan.

It may seem strange, but I think a key text is John 14:17. Jesus, speaking to the disciples about the Holy Spirit says, "You know him [the Holy Spirit], for he lives with you and will be in you." This is often seen pastorally. As I write, I am waiting to pray for someone who has been coming to church for a year. He is clearly being influenced by the presence of the Holy Spirit. Hopefully soon, he will have received Him. However, if this is true of the Holy Spirit, it is reasonable to conclude that it is also true of evil spirits. Many people are affected by them but relatively few are actually indwelt by them. By himself, Satan cannot create anything; but he is skilled in the dark art of imitation.

We shall explore too the question of houses, pubs, factories, offices – sites where tragedies have happened, which seem to be deeply troubled. There are no examples of this in the New Testament, but even the most cursory look at the so-called "high places" in the Old Testament will see that they were places of great spiritual disobedience, which cast a huge shadow on the nations of Israel and Judah.

For the rest of the text, we shall assume that *the devil has not gone missing,* and that the church in general, and Christian leaders in particular, would be wise to adopt a biblical theology and to take this ministry seriously.

CHAPTER 3

SCRIPTURE AND SATAN

*For he shall give his angels charge over thee: to keep thee in all
thy ways.*

(Psalm 91:11, BCP)

The Wilderness

Mark's Gospel has a majestic and clear opening: "The beginning of
the gospel of Jesus Christ, the Son of God" (NKJV). Straightaway
we meet John the Baptist appearing in the wilderness, preaching,
baptizing and prophesying: "After me comes the one more powerful
than I." Then Jesus is baptized, the Spirit descends upon him, a voice
speaks from heaven, and:

> *At once the Spirit sent him out into the wilderness, and he was in
> the wilderness for forty days, being tempted by Satan. He was with
> the wild animals, and the angels attended him.*

(Mark 1:12–13)

We need to read these details with care. It is the Spirit (Matthew
and Luke say the same) who drove Jesus into the wilderness. The
wilderness was the place of spiritual encounter for Moses and
Elijah, who will both feature in the Transfiguration narrative. The
wilderness was the place of failure for the children of Israel, who
spent an unprofitable forty years wandering around grumbling,
succumbing to spiritual temptation, and dying. By contrast, the

spiritual encounters of Moses on Mount Horeb when receiving the Ten Commandments, and Elijah when travelling there after the encounter with the prophets of Baal on Mount Carmel, took forty days.

The wilderness was inhabited by wild beasts, and fiery snakes. It was the place that Satan chose for his first assault and where angels would come and minister – perhaps bringing the bread of heaven to nourish Jesus after the great fast. Mark doesn't give us the details of the temptations. For him, Satan's appearance is the prologue to the drama of a lifetime's struggle between the Kingdom of God and the Prince of this World.

We should perhaps digress and consider the details of the three temptations recorded by Matthew and Luke – presumably supplied by Jesus. All three temptations involved the misuse of Scripture. Paul, in 2 Corinthians 11:14, says, "Satan himself masquerades as an angel of light." These misuses of Scripture are typical examples – sadly followed by many false teachers throughout Christian history. While we would certainly have been fatally tempted by the physical need for bread, it is the last two temptations which were more subtle. Jumping off the Temple pinnacle would have been, assuming that He was held up by angels, a dramatic sign to an unbelieving religious leadership. So, bowing down to "the prince of this world" would have guaranteed earthly success, yet would have greatly strengthened Satan's hold on the fallen world.

Conflict in Galilee

As soon as Jesus' ministry begins, there is a confrontation with an evil spirit (Mark 1:21-28). Here the spirit, which presumably would have preferred to lie dormant, is flushed into the open by the powerful presence of Jesus in the synagogue. The spirit, after a futile attempt to dominate Jesus by naming Him, then seeks to inconvenience Him by proclaiming who He is – "the Holy One of God". The onlookers are amazed at the authority and power of Jesus. One cannot help feeling that the normal religious leaders weren't very good at this sort of thing.

Many more evil spirits show up in the queue outside Peter's mother-in-law's house. Mark again mentions that "he would not let the demons speak because they knew who he was". None of this makes any sense if Jesus was merely dealing with extreme psychiatric cases! Again in 1:39, Mark specifically mentions the expulsion of demons as taking place after Jesus' preaching in the synagogues throughout Galilee.

The final incident in the magnificent opening chapter is the healing of a leper. The healing of a leper was something truly noteworthy: "there were many in Israel with leprosy in the time of Elisha the prophet, yet not one of them was cleansed – only Naaman the Syrian" (Luke 4:27). The leper doesn't display much faith. The actual healing is through a touch (which was very unusual, forbidden by law and custom) and, significantly, by a command similar to an exorcism: "Be clean!" My favourite commentator[1] says that the NEB, which adopts the reading that Jesus was moved with indignation (as opposed to the very Jesus word "compassion"), is correct. If it is, this is highly significant. Jesus' indignation is against the ravages of disease, caused occasionally directly by Satan (Luke 13:16), and not against the unfortunate man. Sadly, as so often, the healed man disobeyed Jesus' command to keep silent and greatly hindered His ability to heal others.

The third chapter highlights a new and sinister conflict. Jesus, already battling opposition from the Pharisees (Mark 3:6) and loquacious evil spirits (3:11), faces trouble nearer home. His family try to seize Him and take Him away from the unending demands of His ministry. At the same time, the leaders from Jerusalem, doubtless very alarmed, try a different attack. They cannot deny His power of exorcism so they attribute it to the devil! Jesus routs this argument and warns His opponents against committing the unforgivable sin – essentially calling white black and attributing His gracious ministry to the power of Satan.

Satan makes a brief but significant appearance in the next chapter (4) when, in the guise of the birds of the air, he removes the seed that falls on the path. Paul has a similar thought in 2 Corinthians 4:4 when he says, "The god of this age has blinded the minds of unbelievers, so that they cannot see the light of the gospel that displays the glory of Christ." Satan's most deadly work, which is largely unseen and unnoticed, is to try and prevent people hearing and responding to the gospel.

We shall return, at length, to Mark 5. The story of the healing and subsequent obedient discipleship of the Gadarene man is very significant. It is the only story in which we are given many of the symptoms of demonic possession. Mark, as ever, gives us the most detailed, and highly instructive, account.

In chapter 6, the twelve are sent out on their first mission. They are given authority over unclean spirits. They all, including Judas Iscariot, perform many exorcisms and heal many who are sick. They use oil as an outward sign of the Holy Spirit's healing power. In Luke 10, Jesus sends out the seventy-two. When they return, Jesus says, "I saw Satan fall like lightning from heaven" (Luke 10:18). This seems an appropriate time to ask the basic question: how did Satan come into being?

Green says there are three possible explanations.[2] One is that Satan is an "aetiological tale" – that is an explanation for the inexplicable. His existence is a poetic myth, which is there to explain how God's perfect world got messed up. The second is that he always existed. He is the leader of the opposition in God's parliament. This, Green says, is a view held by many ancient religions. The third possibility is that the devil was one of God's creatures – a spirit of great ability, who became consumed by pride, rebelled, lost his position, and set up in opposition and in implacable hatred against God. This is generally in accord with the biblical evidence.

We look first at the Old Testament.

WHERE DID SATAN COME FROM?

Satan, in the guise of the serpent, slithers onto the stage in the Garden of Eden. It is doubtful if even the author meant us to take this account literally. However we understand it, this is a very important encounter in a very important part of Scripture. The early chapters of Genesis make a number of theological points. God created the world and saw that it was good (1:1–25). God created man, in His own image, as the pinnacle of His creation (1:25–31). Man was given authority over creation (1:26). John Taylor rightly emphasizes this as non-violent dominion.[3]

There is, from the beginning, spiritual opposition (3:1–7). The serpent is a liar. It says, incorrectly, "You will not surely die"(3:4).

The serpent sows doubt, saying, "Did God really say...?" (3:1). It then challenges Eve to disobey (3:5). But even after the disaster of the Fall and the expulsion from the garden, there is the certainty of redemption: "I will put enmity between you [the serpent] and the woman, and between your offspring and hers; he will crush your head and you will strike his heel" (3:15).

Satan is present in many guises. If there is no tempter, the chaotic performance of the children of Israel is even harder to comprehend. We are not told how he arrives on the world stage. The best explanation seems to come in Ezekiel's lament, in chapter 28, over the fall of the Prince of Tyre: "In the pride of your heart you say, 'I am a god' ... you think you are as wise as a god" (verse 6).

If these words seem extreme, what follows is much stronger. In verse 11, Ezekiel switches his attention to the King of Tyre. Here the picture painted is quite extraordinary:

> *You were the seal of perfection, full of wisdom and perfect in beauty (12)... You were in Eden, the garden of God (13)... You were anointed as a guardian cherub for so I ordained you. You were on the holy mount of God (14)... You were blameless in your ways from the day you were created till wickedness was found in you (15)... Your heart was proud on account of your beauty (17)...*

This extraordinary passage seems to step outside history. It seems easiest to interpret it as a reference to Satan's fall from heaven – caused mainly by pride. The language used about the king would seem inappropriate if the writer is speaking of a human being. Could any man be described as an anointed guardian cherub? Could any man be described as blameless from the day he was created?

Isaiah 14:12–14 describes the fall of Babylon in similar terms: "How you have fallen from heaven, morning star, son of the dawn... You said in your heart, 'I will ascend to the heavens... I will make myself like the Most High.'" These are words that would seem inappropriate to even the most arrogant of rulers (and there are plenty of those now and throughout history!). But they are words which would be entirely appropriate to a fallen angel.

As we have mentioned, Jesus in Luke 10:18 sees Satan fall from heaven. The author of Revelation sees Satan and his angels as thrown out of heaven (Revelation 12:9) and 12:4 suggests, to some, that he took a third of the angels with him. Jesus, in Matthew 25:41 at the conclusion of the parable of the sheep and the goats, refers to the "devil and his angels". The idea that Satan is a fallen angel makes better sense than any other theory. However, we would do well to be cautious. For our purpose, *it is his existence rather than his origin that is important.*

Satan's actual appearances in the Old Testament are significant but relatively few. In 1 Chronicles 21:1 we are told, "Satan rose up against Israel and incited David to take a census of Israel." This was a puzzling and disastrous incident with terrible consequences. The author of 2 Samuel (2 Samuel 24:1) attributes the catastrophe more directly to God. David's sin, ironically considering Satan's involvement, was that of pride – relying on Israel's military strength rather than God.

In the opening chapters of Job, Satan appears (having been going to and fro on the earth) among the angels to challenge Job's integrity. Why he is permitted to do this is unclear. Nevertheless, his malevolence is limited by God. On many levels, this book is easier to interpret, and just as profound, if we see it as a discourse about suffering and the sovereignty of God, rather than as a literal history.

In Zechariah 3, Satan stands briefly at the right hand of the angel of the Lord. He is described as the accuser (as in Revelation 12:10). His accusation is rejected. Zechariah is vindicated and given new clothes and assurance of the Lord's support.

If Satan's appearances are brief, much of the Old Testament seems to describe an ongoing battle between those who are faithful to God and those who rebel. The children of God, that is the nations of Israel and Judah, fight a generally losing battle. They are warned not to go after false gods and they constantly disobey. They are warned not to worship idols and they build, among other things, a golden calf. They constantly worship in "high places" and follow the prophets of Baal. They are told not to consult mediums and at least one of their kings goes to consult a witch. They are told to keep their nation pure. In the desert, they consort with women of Moab and, later, one of their greatest kings takes 700 foreign wives. They have some godly rulers but, for the most part, they fail and are in constant spiritual and practical disarray.

Ahab is described as the one who "did more evil in the eyes of the Lord than any of those before him" (1 Kings 16:30). Aided by his horrible wife Jezebel, who makes Lady Macbeth seem like an angel, he corrupted Israel. They introduced the worship of Baal (1 Kings 16:31), they rebuilt Jericho causing the builder to sacrifice two of his sons (1 Kings 16:34), and Jezebel fed 450 prophets of Baal and another 400 of Asherah (1 Kings 18:19). Meanwhile the prophets of the Lord had to be hidden in caves from Jezebel (1 Kings 18:1-4). It all culminated in the famous contest on Mount Carmel. The challenge was to produce supernatural fire to destroy the carcass of a bull. The prophets of Baal cut themselves with swords and lances but this flow of blood produced no fire. Elijah doused his carcass with water and then called down fire from heaven. Despite the dramatic response, and the ending of the drought, Elijah fled from the wrath of Jezebel. His ministry was effectively finished. Depressed and exhausted, he was strengthened by an angel and retired to Mount Horeb for a final encounter with God. Jezebel continued on her wicked way until her eventual destruction some years after Ahab's death.

Israel had a few godly kings – notably Hezekiah and Josiah. Hezekiah is commended for many things. He removed the high places, and broke the pillars, and cut down the Asherah. And he broke into pieces the bronze serpent that Moses had made, for until those days the people of Israel burnt incense to it (2 Kings 18:4-5).

A few generations later, Josiah did much the same. He is also commended (2 Kings 23:24) because he "got rid of the mediums and spiritists". Occult activity was never far from the surface. Deuteronomy 18:9–13 contains a series of prohibitions against child sacrifice, divination, sorcery, consulting the dead and suchlike things, which were seen as an abomination.

The unfortunate King Saul (1 Samuel 28), just before the fatal battle on Mount Gilboa, consulted a medium at Endor. The woman, not knowing who he was, reminded him that Saul had cut off all such people from the land. When the woman raised up the spirit of Samuel, she was terrified. Samuel's message to Saul was a mixture of irritation and impending doom.

This vivid and detailed story ought to act as a warning against all such activity. Augustine of Hippo (see Chapter 7, page 148) and others were puzzled by the account. Did Samuel really appear? Or was the apparition an evil spirit purporting to be Samuel? In the end, it doesn't really matter. We shall often find in these matters that we come up against things we don't fully understand. What we will always find is that, if we act under the authority of Jesus, we will be protected and troubled people will experience freedom.

Accident, illness, false signs, and strategy

After this lengthy digression, we return to the Gospels. The account (Luke 13:1–5) of Pilate's slaughter of some Galileans and then mingling their human blood with their animal sacrifices is particularly unpleasant. The collapse of the tower of Siloam which killed eighteen people was a contemporary tragedy. On neither occasion did Jesus blame Satan. Pilate was responsible for his own conduct; the tower fell because such things happen in a fallen world. The people killed were not worse sinners than any others. Jesus used their deaths to remind his hearers to repent before it was too late.

Nevertheless, in the next healing story (Luke 13:10–17), Jesus attributes the woman's illness directly to Satan (verse 16). She is described as having been crippled by a spirit for eighteen years (verse 11), and Jesus calls her a "daughter of Abraham, whom Satan has kept bound for eighteen long years" (verse 16). However, Jesus does not perform an exorcism; he lays hands on her after declaring that she is free from her infirmity.

The Gospel writers are very careful in these matters. In John 9:1–3, Jesus specifically denies that the man's blindness was caused by sin (or the devil). Our experience today (see Chapter 5, page 84) suggests that, while some illness is caused directly by Satan, most is not. That seems in accord with the teaching of the Gospels.

Satan can perform false signs. Matthew 24:24 warns us that false prophets can perform great signs and wonders which would, if possible, lead even the elect astray. Paul says the same in 2 Thessalonians 2:9. John (see Mark 9:38–39) reported to Jesus that they had forbidden a man who was casting out devils in Jesus' name. Jesus overruled him. The exorcism, in this case, was being carried out in the name of Jesus and was a true and mighty work. Such matters call for considerable discernment. By contrast, at the end of the Sermon on the Mount (Matthew 7:22), Jesus makes it clear that not all exorcisms, even when his name is used, are performed by people who know him.

In John's Gospel, Jesus draws attention to several other aspects of Satan's character. He is the "father of lies" (8:44), which takes us back to the Garden of Eden, and "a murderer from the beginning" (8:44), presumably because he caused Cain to murder Abel. He is also called "the prince of this world" in John 12:31, 14:30, and 16:11. The passage in John 12:31 is particularly important. In the next verse, John tells us that Jesus talked about His impending death. If the prince of this world doesn't exist, the significance of this passage is greatly diminished. John, both here and in his first epistle, sees the defeat of Satan as a highly significant part of Jesus' life, death and resurrection.

The New Testament gives a number of examples of Satan troubling individuals. Luke records a particular warning that Jesus gives to Peter: "Simon, Simon, Satan has asked to sift all of you as wheat. But I have prayed for you, Simon, that your faith may not fail"(Luke 22:31–32).

The well-known outcome was that Peter was severely tested, failed, but was deeply penitent when the Lord turned and looked at him (Luke 22:61). He was then forgiven and restored in the lakeside encounter recorded in John 21. Satan's testing of Peter was severe, almost devastating, but because Peter was loyal and his heart was sound, it ultimately didn't prevail.

Similarly, Satan hindered Paul from visiting the Thessalonians (1 Thessalonians 2:18). We are not told how this was achieved, but we know that Paul was well aware of his activity (2 Corinthians 2:11) and of his ability to deceive by appearing to be an angel of light (2 Corinthians 11:14). He also harassed Paul with the much debated "thorn in his flesh" (2 Corinthians 12:7). Paul and Peter both understood the reality of the spiritual battle. Paul writes powerfully about it in Ephesians 6:10–18, and Peter writes in similar vein in 1 Peter 5:8–9. Satan brings false doctrine into the church (1 Timothy 4:1) and traps apparent believers who become opponents of the gospel (2 Timothy 2:26). He ensnares people with sexual temptation (1 Corinthians 5:1–5), and Paul warns the married, except in specially agreed times of prayer, to keep to normal marital relations (1 Corinthians 7:5).

We also meet a number of people who Satan actually entered, but we are not told how this happened (see Chapter 5 for some modern examples). Mary Magdalene, who was the first witness to the resurrection, had seven demons expelled (Luke 8:2). It is quite extraordinary, and surely something no one would invent, that we only know for certain two things about Mary Magdalene – her freedom from demons and her presence at the tomb on the first Easter morning. Mary Magdalene is a faithful follower of Jesus. Of all people, she had most to lose through Jesus' untimely death. She must have wondered if, without His protection, the demons could return. No wonder, when she realized who she was speaking to on the first Easter morning, that she wanted to hold on to Him.

There are two sadder cases we must mention. Satan filled the heart of two early disciples, Ananias and his wife, Sapphira. He caused them to lie to the Holy Spirit and the apostles about a financial matter. The consequences were devastating for them and the church (Acts 5:1–11).

The case of Judas is even more puzzling. He was chosen. He performed miracles (Mark 6:13). Yet Satan entered him (Luke 22:3 and John 13:27). How could this have happened? John tells us that Judas was a thief (John 12:6). All the Gospels tell us that Judas received a trifling amount of money for the information which led to the quiet arrest of Jesus.

In view of this, we might be surprised at Paul's silence on the subject of deliverance. He has important things to say about spiritual warfare (see especially Ephesians 6:10–20, which I discuss in Chapter 12), but nothing to say about how to set people free, or the marks of people being under the power of Satan. He does, however, refer to the area of false doctrine (1 Timothy 4:1) and extreme misconduct (1 Corinthians 5:1–5 and 1 Timothy 1:20) although, in the latter two cases, Paul hands the miscreants over to Satan rather than suggesting that Satan has entered them. This could be because such examples were very rare although he, himself, had encountered them in Cyprus, Philippi and Ephesus. Or it could be because the issue hadn't been raised by any of the churches he was writing to.

Tertullian[4] reckoned that any Christian could deal with someone who was demon-possessed (a far removal from the careful, but in my view wise, instructions issued to diocesan deliverance teams).

Perhaps Paul agreed with Tertullian and felt that the issue didn't need any ink spilled over it. It should certainly caution us against the folly of seeing demons everywhere – behind all illnesses, difficulties, and sins such as anger.

Paul does see that the "god of this age has blinded the minds of the unbelievers, so that they cannot see the light of the gospel that displays the glory of Christ" (2 Corinthians 4:4). This teaching echoes Paul's account of his conversion mandate "to open their eyes and turn them from darkness to light, and from the power of Satan to God, so that they may receive forgiveness of sins and a place among those who are sanctified by faith in [Jesus]" (Acts 26:18).

Peter (1 Peter 5:8) gives us one famous reference which is regularly heard in the evening service of Compline: "be sober, be watchful. Your adversary the devil prowls around like a roaring lion, seeking someone to devour. Resist him, firm in your faith, knowing that the same experience of suffering is required of your brotherhood throughout the world."

It would seem that Peter was all too well aware of his own fall, the failings of the rest of the twelve, and the disastrous outcome for Judas.

John has few references to Satan in his Gospel and gives us no exorcism stories. By contrast, his first epistle has a number of key references: "I am writing to you, young men, because you have overcome the evil one" (1 John 2:13); "The one who does what is sinful is of the devil; because the devil has been sinning from the beginning. The reason the Son of God appeared was to destroy the devil's work" (1 John 3:8); "We know that anyone born of God does not continue to sin; the One who was born of God keeps them safe, and the evil one cannot harm them" (1 John 5:18).

These three references teach us that Satan can, and should, be overcome by believers. Satan sinned from the beginning, echoing the Old Testament passages in Isaiah and Ezekiel, quoted above. The Son came to destroy Satan's work – most notably in obtaining forgiveness of sins, overcoming death, and bringing spiritual protection. Spiritual protection is emphasized in the third reference – far too many people believe that, even though they are believers, Satan can touch and molest them. John says otherwise!

Satan – tester and tempter

Throughout history, leaders of the church have faced the severest attacks of Satan. Archbishop Cranmer almost gave way under the formidable assault of the leading Catholics in Queen Mary's reign. Recent history is littered with examples of people with great prophetic gifts falling; evangelists being found out with both sexual and financial mismanagement, many Christian leaders disgracefully involved in paedophilia. The list is very long. It is a great relief when we can be confident of the complete integrity of someone like the evangelist Billy Graham.

There are many indirect ways in which Satan tests and tempts people. Green[5] has a long helpful, discussion. His list includes scepticism, especially discrediting the Bible; silence, discouraging people from giving any account of their faith; disunity, very evident in the early church in Corinth; pride, the sin by which we believe that Satan fell; lust, the divorce rate among professing Christians is alarmingly high; false asceticism, 1 Timothy 4:3 warns against those who would forbid marriage and require abstinence from certain foods (it is quite different if a vegetarian feels called to abstain from meat); doubt, "did God really say…?" is a whisper Satan repeats many times; depression, which can follow a spiritual triumph – Elijah's spiritual sulk in 1 Kings 19:4 just after the triumph over the prophets of Baal is an example; lack of self-worth and feeling unclean, which make many Christians feel useless. (This one is particularly true for victims of all forms of abuse, who also struggle with the apparent impossibility of forgiving those who have abused them. A realization that Satan is the accuser of the brethren (Revelation 12:10) and a believing study of Psalm 139 can bring relief.) Still another test is fear, which causes many, like Peter, to deny the faith – none of us know how we would react to the fearsome savagery of Islamic State. There are many other ways too.

Satan attacks the body. The misuse of the body through smoking, excessive alcohol, drugs, overeating, or eating junk food leads to illness and a lack of spiritual wellbeing. Satan attacks the mind. He gets us to read and experience dangerous things. I have met too many Christian men entrapped by pornography on the Internet. Satan induces ambition and causes jealousy among those who are not chosen for promotion. James 3:13–18 tells us with characteristic bluntness that jealousy and selfish ambition are unspiritual and demonic in origin.

All of this would be very depressing if we didn't know that through the protection of the armour of Christ, through the indwelling Holy Spirit, and through the Word of God, we have weapons to resist and even overcome Satan in all these matters.

I remember learning verses of Scripture with the Navigators. One of the first verses to be learnt was "No temptation has overtaken you except what is common to mankind. And God is faithful; he will not let you be tempted beyond what you can bear. But when you are tempted, he will also provide a way out, so that you can endure it" (1 Corinthians 10:13).

We would do well to consider carefully the means of escape. To give one example: if we are tempted to misuse our computer, we could make sure that it is always where other people can see us using it. We can ensure that it is unplugged at night and that when it is on we avoid surfing the net. With a few simple steps, it will be much harder to fall and many sad consequences will be avoided.

We have seen that Paul said of Satan, "we are not ignorant of his designs" (2 Corinthians 2:11, ESV). If we couple that with Revelation 12:10, which describes Satan as "the accuser of the brethren" (NKJV), our defences will be much stronger. We understand that many Christians are crippled by false guilt and bear little fruit because of the power of Satan's temptation. Scripture is one of our most powerful weapons. The devil misused Scripture to tempt Christ in the wilderness; we must learn Scripture and use Scripture to defeat his devices against us and those we seek to help.

Many times, Scripture has seemed to sort out demonic situations. Here are some examples.

Scripture speaks

I well remember some years ago when a young woman came for prayer. She was a very caring person who sought to help and counsel others. But she was weighed down with a depression, which was almost demonic in its intensity. Eventually she startled me and my prayer partner by saying very quietly and in a matter of fact style,

"I was conceived through rape." I could visualize hours of ministry, counselling, prayer involving inner healing, and many other godly approaches. I could imagine a healing process that might take weeks, months, or even years. But the Lord seemed to say, "Get her to read Psalm 139."

Almost in an instant, she grasped that God was present in her darkness, that God knew about her conception, and that God had plans for her life. Healing appeared to be total and instantaneous. The demonic darkness of depression was scattered.

I saw her a while afterwards and all still seemed to be fine. We have lost touch. I can only hope and pray that she is still protected by the armour of Christ and the power of the Scriptures.

Once, at a parish prayer meeting, someone saw a picture of a rose with two black spots. One person promptly interpreted this as saying that our policy on infant baptism was wrong. Knowing this to be one of the speaker's hobby horses, I rejected his interpretation. No one else had any idea what it meant, so the picture was put on one side and the meeting continued. At the end of the meeting, a young girl came up and said, "I am the rose with the two black spots." Apparently a radiant Christian, she had deep troubles from which she needed to be released. A Christian Science upbringing, some exposure to occult things at her birth, lesbianism, and suicide attempts had left her very vulnerable to depressions and migraines.

Rather to our surprise, some days later when we challenged anything within her to show itself, she manifested all the signs of demonization. A long and very difficult deliverance followed. At one moment a spirit started to speak through her and to name itself (this should, I think, be discouraged – Jesus usually commanded silence). We couldn't identify the name. An inner voice directed me to Zechariah 2:7 (RSV). Feeling somewhat foolish, I read out: "Ho! Escape to Zion, you who dwell with the daughter of Babylon."

Michael Green, who was sharing the ministry with me, leapt to his feet. "Of course! The spirit's name is that of a Babylonian mystery religion." Armed with that knowledge and increased in faith, the deliverance was speedily concluded. The biblical text, which needed both spiritual and scholastic insight, was the key to unlocking the girl's difficulties.

The story had a splendid ending. Not many years later, I conducted a very moving wedding. The lady in question was marrying a young ordinand whose own conversion had been influenced by her radiant witness.

On another occasion, we were ministering to someone who had a long and complex history of depression, which seemed to stem from involvement in levitation and the like. Ministry had proved difficult and unsuccessful. I met with one of the leaders of the church for one final session of prayer. The person concerned became quite restless and kicked over a jug of water, which I had blessed. I had by this time discovered that "holy water" can be very efficacious. Evil powers are terrified of the cross of Christ (Colossians 2:15) and consecrated water is a reminder of baptism, which is effectively linked to the cross.

There was now a large, damp patch on the carpeted floor. An inner voice said, "Read Exodus, chapter 3." I was puzzled – until I came to verse 5: "'Do not come any closer,' God said. 'Take off your sandals, for the place where you are standing is holy ground.'"

At first, I couldn't see the point. Then I realized that the damp patch was the holy ground. The woman in question was in a sort of trance. We took off her shoes and tried to place her feet in the damp patch. For a few seconds there was sheer comedy as she walked, still in the trance, managing to step over it. Frantically, I instructed the others to dump her in it. As her feet hit the damp, she slumped to the ground, gently overpowered by the Spirit. This continued for some twenty minutes. The rest of us prayed quietly. When she awoke, all trace of demonic activity seemed to have vanished. She was, in the words of Mark 5:15, "dressed and in her right mind".

One woman, a new member of my church, asked to see me urgently. She explained that something was driving her to commit suicide. As she had had a major attempt once before, I took the matter very seriously. I asked her how she was going to do it. She opened her bag and gave me a very large bottle of paracetamol tablets. I then asked her why she felt driven (her word) to kill herself. She said she felt compelled to repeat a certain word, which seemed to have an evil influence on her. The word she named, Greek sounding, meant nothing to me. We agreed to meet that evening and I prayed for her peace and protection. I was not prepared to minister to her on my own[6]. I had to trust that she would not harm herself now that she had asked for help.

After she left, I searched for the word. My concordance yielded nothing. Then I tried one of my dictionaries. I found that her word, Asmodeus, was the name of a particularly unpleasant evil spirit found in the book of Tobit, directly inciting murder and indirectly suicide. For the first time in my life I read the Book of Tobit, which is to be found in the Apocrypha.

> *Because she (Sarah) had been given to seven husbands,* and the evil demon Asmodeus had slain each of them before he had been with her as his wife. *So the maids said to her, 'Do you not know that you strangle your husbands? You already have had seven and have had no benefit from any of them. Why do you beat us? If they are dead, go with them! May we never see a son or daughter of yours!'*
>
> *When she heard these things she was deeply grieved,* even to the thought of hanging herself. *But she said, 'I am the only child of my father; if I do this, it will be a disgrace to him, and I shall bring his old age down in sorrow to the grave.'*
>
> (Tobit 3:8–10, RSV, emphasis added)

Somewhat shaken, I awaited the evening encounter with considerable anxiety. Nowadays, those who play the computer game *Dungeons and Dragons* will be familiar with the name Asmodeus. However, they will, I assume, have little knowledge of his murderous apocryphal history. Fortunately, Michael Green was able to come and join me. We addressed the spirit by name. It left immediately and with such force that Michael was almost knocked over. I found myself holding up my right hand in authority over the woman and my left hand trying to support Michael. The ministry was brief (as ideally it always should be), authoritative and effective. I am certain that the woman, as a recent convert from a non-Christian background, knew nothing about the names of evil spirits in the Apocrypha.

She became a great friend and an effective member of our ministry team. Then after a while, for a variety of reasons, she fell away from the Christian scene. But a few years ago, before her somewhat early and untimely death, we had long periods of prayer for difficulties related to deep problems and incredible unpleasantness experienced in her teenage years. These were not demonic but in many ways

58

more complex and more painful than anything that Asmodeus could achieve. Eventually, after she left home, she got involved with drugs and onto the edges of a dangerous occult group. I think the earlier terrible abusive experiences left her more open both to these people and to the evil spirits.

After a lot of prayer, but no more deliverance ministry, I think she found a measure of peace. She could never really deny or forget the freedom that Jesus had brought her in her early life. She was able to return to her earlier faith.

I have never ceased to marvel at the power of Scripture in these situations. Scripture, too, can cut out a lot of nonsense. At one stage, Michael and I were being assisted by an American who seemed to have some useful insights. But he had an unpleasant habit – he would tease the demons and tell them (without any authority, I felt) what lay in store for them. This ceased when I discovered that, in the epistle of Jude (verse 9), the Archangel Michael argued in a dignified manner with the devil over the body of Moses.

We agreed that we could learn from that Scripture. I noticed too that when Jesus expelled demons – he didn't send them anywhere in particular. I have always felt it right to command a demon to go to Jesus "for whatever He wills to do". I hope they are destroyed rather than punished. The fate of the pigs, in the Gadarene swine narrative, could be a pointer in that direction. And it is to that most graphic of all biblical stories to which we now turn.

CHAPTER 4

THE MAN WHO LIVED AMONG THE TOMBS

Jesus! the name high over all,
In hell or earth or sky;
Angels and mortals prostrate fall
And devils fear and fly.

(Charles Wesley)

Peter and Mark in Rome

We travel to Rome. It is early in AD 64 and the mad and dangerous Emperor Nero is in power. A terrible fire has swept the city. Christians are blamed.[1] Many have been arrested, tortured and killed. The remaining Christians are apprehensive and frightened. They meet mainly in the catacombs. Their leader, Peter, is still with them but in mortal danger. He preaches, mainly telling stories of the life of Jesus. John Mark, whose mother had owned a house in Jerusalem where the church met, after deserting Paul on a missionary journey has been forgiven and restored to favour. He listens intently to Peter. His new task is to record a life of Jesus for future generations. He has already recorded a letter of Peter's, which has been copied and sent to various other Christian groups. Tonight, Peter is recalling one of Mark's favourite stories.

"Jesus had finished teaching the crowds. He had told them the parable about the sower and the four types of soil. We had got into a boat to cross to the other side of the lake. There was a terrible storm. Even we, experienced fishermen, were very frightened. The wind raged. The waves rose high. The boat was taking water. We tried to bail it out but our efforts were fairly useless. We noticed that Jesus was fast asleep – apparently unaware of the terrible danger. Eventually, one of our group, I'm not sure who, woke Him up. We said, 'Master do you not care if we perish?'

"I shall never forget what happened. He stood up in the stern of the boat. He turned and faced the raging sea. With a loud voice, which even those at the other end of the boat could hear, He shouted, 'Peace! Be still.' Just those three words spoken in Aramaic; and quite suddenly, the storm ceased. The wind calmed. The sea became quiet. We were amazed – almost more frightened by His authority than by the storm. He turned to us and said, 'Why are you afraid? Have you no faith?' We became very quiet. We said to one another, 'Who is this, that even the wind and sea obey Him?'

"I think we knew the answer to our question but we were too tired, too filled with awe and wonder to say anything else. Soon afterwards, we saw land and the boat came ashore. We had landed on a wild, an apparently uninhabited part of the land. All around were steep rocks. Not far away there were tombs inside rocky caves. As we landed, a man, if you could call him a man, rushed towards us.

"He wore few clothes. His eyes were blazing with a dangerous fire. His arms were bleeding. His legs were bruised as though they had been chained. He appeared to have the strength of a lion. He came closer. We were as frightened of him as of the storm. He seemed to see Jesus from a great distance. He was shouting as he drew nearer. Jesus quite calmly said, 'Come out of the man, you unclean spirit.'

"The man appeared not to hear. He came closer and fell at Jesus' feet. As he did so he cried out, 'What have you to do with me, Jesus, Son of the most High God? I adjure you by God, do not torment me.' We had seen this kind of thing before. Several times we had seen Jesus free people from spirits. It was strange that the spirits acknowledged, which we didn't dare, who Jesus was. They even knew His name. The man's voice was very strange. I suppose it was actually the voice of the demon, although we didn't realize it at the time. Another curious fact was that the spirits didn't immediately obey the Master.

"Jesus spoke again. He asked the man, 'What is your name?' Again the voices within the man replied, 'My name is Legion; for we are many.' Then the spirits made a strange request. They asked not to be sent out of the country. Evidently they saw this as their territory where they were entitled to live.

"Then we saw that, up above the rocks, there was a large herd of pigs. We were obviously not near a Jewish settlement. The voices, now in a more whining, submissive tone, said, 'Send us to the swine, let us enter them!' Jesus gave them permission.

"Then something terrible happened. The whole herd took fright; there were some two thousand. The pigs rushed down a very steep bank, hurtled into the sea and were drowned. We saw men above us on the rocks. They must have been looking after the pigs. They ran away.

"The man seemed calm and well. We found him some of our clothes. I noticed that his eyes now looked quite normal. It was amazing. I don't think that I have seen such a change in a person. It was like the storm at sea. One moment there was a raging tempest; moments later the sea was as calm as an inland pond. One moment the man had the strength of a lion and spoke loudly and irrationally; the next he was quiet, subdued, and able to talk normally.

"Jesus spoke to him. While they were talking, people from the village arrived. They were angry and frightened. The herdsmen had told the villagers what they had seen. Everyone could see the man whom they called Legion was quite calm and well.

"They begged Jesus to go away. They were angry about the loss of the pigs. I suppose we ought to have been embarrassed but, to us, pigs were unclean animals, which no one should keep. They had evidently known the man for years. They had tried to subdue him with chains but he had always broken the chains. They were used to him – wild and out of control. Now that he was calm and apparently well in body, mind, and spirit, they were more frightened of him. Again, they begged Jesus to leave. They had had enough trouble to last a lifetime.

"The man asked Jesus if he could come with us. We assumed that Jesus would want him to come with us. But Jesus, quite gently, said to him, 'Go home to your friends and tell them how much the Lord has done for you, and how he has had mercy on you.' And, unlike many of the people whom Jesus had helped, the man obeyed. All who heard his story marvelled. Perhaps they, like us, said, 'Who is this man that even the evil powers obey Him?'"

Here is Mark's graphic text (5:1-20):

They went across the lake to the region of the Gerasenes. When Jesus got out of the boat, a man with an impure spirit came from the tombs to meet him. This man lived in the tombs, and no one could bind him any more, not even with a chain. For he had often been chained hand and foot, but he tore the chains apart and broke the irons on his feet. No one was strong enough to subdue him. Night and day among the tombs and in the hills he would cry out and cut himself with stones. When he saw Jesus from a distance, he ran and fell on his knees in front of him. He shouted at the top of his voice, "What do you want with me, Jesus, Son of the Most High God? In God's name don't torture me!" For Jesus had said to him, "Come out of this man, you evil spirit!" Then Jesus asked him, "What is your name?" "My name is Legion," he replied, "for we are many." And he begged Jesus again and again not to send them out of the area. A large herd of pigs was feeding on the nearby hillside. The demons begged Jesus, "Send us among the pigs; allow us to go into them." He gave them permission, and the impure spirits came out and went into the pigs. The herd, about two thousand in number, rushed down the steep bank into the lake and were drowned. Those tending the pigs ran off and reported this in the town and countryside, and the people went out to see what had happened. When they came to Jesus, they saw the man who had been possessed by the legion of demons, sitting there, dressed and in his right mind; and they were afraid. Those who had seen it told the people what had happened to the demon-possessed man – and told about the pigs as well. Then the people began to plead with Jesus to leave their region. As Jesus was getting into the boat, the man who had been demon-possessed begged to go with him. Jesus did not let him, but said, "Go home to your own people and tell them how much the Lord has done for you, and how he has had mercy on you." So the man went away and began to tell in the Decapolis how much Jesus had done for him. And all the people were amazed.

The marks of the demons

This is a wonderfully vivid account. There is no way that anyone would dare invent or embellish it. It simply has to be true. Mark heard Peter describe it. Then after Peter's untimely death[2] (or possibly some ten years earlier), he wrote it down. Those of us who have the privilege, the anxiety, the surprise, and the joy which can accompany such ministry will cherish this account. The transformations in people's lives and their subsequent effective discipleship is something that is wonderful to behold. I have been fortunate to witness a number of life-changing adult conversions; but I can say, with great certainty, that the biggest changes have occurred after some deliverance ministry was needed.

Others more puzzled may prefer to follow the advice of Sir Desmond Lee, the distinguished headmaster of Winchester College, who, when he heard that I was proposing to be ordained, gave me two pieces of advice – one that I have forgotten, the second, "never preach about the Gadarene swine!"[3]

For our purposes there are four definite signs of the demonic presence, and I shall suggest a fifth that was almost certainly also present. They are:

(1)   The man was simultaneously attracted and repelled by Jesus.

(2)   The man spoke in voices which were not his own.

(3)   The man had superhuman strength.

(4)   The man harmed himself.

(5)   The man had wild and blazing eyes.

I believe that many of these five signs are present in genuine cases of demonization although they do not guarantee the presence of demons. Many psychiatric patients will exhibit similar signs and we must not rush to make diagnoses. Nevertheless, these five signs are important indicators of a possible demonic presence within someone.

ATTRACTION AND REPULSION

The man was drawn to Jesus; the spirits, the legion of them, were frightened and repelled. This happens frequently. People know they need help but are frightened. They make appointments and don't keep them. They turn up to church and retreat screaming. Sometimes, the spirits that prefer to lie dormant and unseen allow them to worship, but then react if there is a strong presence of the Holy Spirit.

A young woman came to church. A visiting bishop[4] was preaching. He invited people to come forward for prayer. She came willingly, but as she approached the altar rail, there was a violent reaction. She was thrown to the ground. The spirits within her took over. A crowd of people tried to pray for her. The spirits, as is their wont when surrounded by people, gained strength and boldness. We all had the impression that she was trying to levitate, which was something that she claimed to be able to do. Prayers, even from a very wise and authoritative bishop, were ineffective. Her time of freedom had to wait another week until a quieter place could be found.

A neighbour surprised me by announcing that God had called her to be a nun. I suggested that it might be wise to become a Christian first! She attended an adult confirmation class. She came to church regularly and happily. Then, one day, she went forward to receive communion. There was a violent reaction. She received the bread but reacted strongly against the chalice. Her face contorted. She wanted to hurl the cup away.

Eventually when everything had calmed down, we tried to find out what had happened. She said there was a mantra she couldn't stop repeating. It was a word given to her in a yoga class. When she renounced this, the word stopped bothering her and she was able to receive the wine without any reaction. She did try to become a nun but twice returned home after one night away. She continued to be a faithful member of her local church.

Once I was preaching in rural Zambia. I was just about to conclude a sermon about Philip's ministry in Samaria, when proceedings were disrupted by a turbaned member of the Mothers' Union falling out of the pew screaming. I stopped speaking and then asked several people to take her outside. I went with them with other members of my team. The local priest carried on with the service.

Outside we tried to find a quiet place. Eventually, the lady calmed down. I asked her to call on the name of Jesus to name the spirit and to renounce it. I have found that, if the person concerned will ask aloud for help and freedom, it comes far more quickly and with much less fuss. Having a shouting match with the demons is exhausting, unedifying, and usually ineffective. Finally, she was able to do this. Almost immediately, she smiled. She knew that she was free. An hour later, she was helping to serve lunch. This reminded us of Peter's mother-in-law (Mark 1:31). It was then that I realized that the woman was the pastor's wife. He had carried on with the service as though nothing untoward had happened.

Voices

People suffering from schizophrenia, or other forms of psychotic illness, often hear voices – sometimes telling them to do terrible things. I may be wrong, but I don't think that they often speak in strange voices. People with demons often speak out – sometimes in languages that they don't know, sometimes in tongues which sound menacing but are unintelligible, and sometimes just trying to take authority over the situation. In the Gospels and Acts, the demons often spoke out – proclaiming truthfully but unhelpfully who Jesus was. In Mark, they are disclosing information that Jesus was not ready to give. In Acts 16:16–18 they are found, within a slave girl, following Paul around and proclaiming truthfully that "These men are servants of the Most High God, who proclaim to you the way of salvation" (ESV). I am amazed that Paul allowed this to continue for many days. Perhaps he understood that his ministry would be far more disrupted by the girl's exorcism than by her proclamation. Similarly in Acts 19:15, an evil spirit rounds on the would-be exorcists, the sons of Sceva, saying, "Jesus I know, and Paul I know about; but who are you?" The encounter concluded dramatically when the spirit, displaying formidable strength, attacked them and caused them to flee from the house "naked and wounded".

Luke carefully records that the spirit recognized both Paul and Jesus. Clearly, the spiritual bush telegraph had told them where the ultimate authority lay. Luke would have been present at the encounter in Philippi[5] but would have heard about this one from Paul or his companions.

Some years ago, towards the end of a well-attended parish holiday, about twelve of us gathered in a small upper room to pray for an infilling of the Holy Spirit. None of us had prayed in this way previously. Before we could start, a woman started to sing choruses. Something seemed wrong. After a short time, lacking the patience of Paul, I told her to stop singing. She left the room. Some days later, others discerned that she needed some deliverance ministry. That evening, the spirit within her was trying to disrupt our important prayer time. There were many positive results. One woman received a measure of healing – in a short time she lost five stones of weight due to water retention – her husband received the gift of tongues, and a third woman felt a powerful blessing. All three soon afterwards felt called to full-time ministry.

On another occasion, Michael and I were asked to pray for the daughter of two prominent members of the church. When we entered the main room, the daughter was lying spreadeagled on a low couch by the far window. As we approached and before we could enter into any pastoral conversation, a voice spoke from within her: "You lot are a load of bumbling amateurs!" Michael smiled and replied, "We may be bumbling amateurs, but in the name of Jesus, you are going to leave – out!" Moments later she was free!

More recently, I was called by a group of clergy to a house where a young woman was showing signs of demonic trouble. After a gentle time of prayer, anointing with oil and some reassuring conversation, all seemed to be well. The only thing that puzzled me was that I could find no reason for her problems. We kept in touch.

About a year later, she visited me accompanied by a clergy friend. She said that, before the previous incident, she had prayed for and received the gift of tongues. Now she was worried as to whether or not it was genuine. Tongues are not an ecstatic gift, and people who have them can use them whenever they will to do so. I told her to pray aloud. The result was dramatic. Her friend and I knew instantly that the tongues were not genuine. My visitor hurled herself to the ground and started writhing around my untidy study floor doing a passable imitation of a snake. After a brief command, this ceased. The tongues stopped, and never returned. She knew that she was completely free – free to pursue useful Christian service and to help others troubled by this kind of thing.

My friend Robin Martin, a member of the Leicester Deliverance Team, remembers that, during a pre-ordination training year at Durham University, Professor Turner addressed the Bernard Gilpin Society (a theological society founded in memory of a distinguished man known as "the Apostle of the North" in the sixteenth century). He was asked a question about "speaking in tongues". He replied that he had recently travelled to a remote region of Africa where the inhabitants spoke in a unique dialect. On his return, he went to worship at a church where speaking in tongues took place – and this was heralded as a sign of the Holy Spirit. Unfortunately, the speaker was using the remote language of the African village – and what was said was a stream of vile language! This is a reminder that we all need to follow Paul's injunction to "test everything" (1 Thessalonians 5:21) and John's instruction to "test the spirits to see whether they are from God" (1 John 4:1). It is all too easy to be dangerously gullible when so-called "spiritual gifts" are used.

All this seems fairly mundane when I remember my first encounter with "voices". Jane and I had been out to dinner with a retired headmaster. We had a serious discussion about an exorcism which had gone wrong in Yorkshire and which had earned the church some negative headlines. I found myself, with no practical knowledge or experience, defending what I believed to be the New Testament position of the reality of evil powers and spirits. We left quite early as, theoretically, Jane was due to go into labour that night. When we arrived home, a dishevelled couple were standing on our doorstep. What followed profoundly changed my thinking on the subject.

"We've come to complain about the social services…"

Wearily and reluctantly, I let them in, made the inevitable cup of coffee, and listened to their story. Jane went upstairs to bed. After a few minutes, the woman, who was doing most of the talking, suddenly said, "My trouble is that I'm in league with the devil." I reacted calmly and suggested that she renounce the devil and all his works. The atmosphere changed. She screamed across the kitchen: "I renounce God!" Even her partner looked a bit apprehensive. Her whole demeanour changed. She started to wander around our very small kitchen, talking in the voice of an old man, walking like an old man, and finally becoming spiritually quite menacing.

First she screamed out, "Your wife will go into labour tonight," to which I replied, "No, she won't. You're lying – in the name of the Lord." Rachel was born safely ten days later. Then, when I tried to contact Michael and Rosemary Green, she mocked me: "They're not coming, they won't come…" It so happened that Michael and Rosemary were out to dinner with the only parishioners who were not on the telephone. I was totally stuck, alone, out of my depth and somewhat alarmed.

Around midnight, about two hours later, Michael and Rosemary turned up. Our visitor had become more and more menacing. She'd started speaking in a strange, guttural voice. It was very unpleasant. The only way I can describe it is that it sounded like Latin backwards being spat out by a machine gun. It was my first experience of "demonic tongues".

Michael commanded me to pray in tongues. I'd received the gift years earlier but had always doubted its reality. This was the first time I'd used it in public. The effect was quite startling! For the first time in the evening, my visitor shut up, and gradually calm was restored. Everybody left. I went to bed. Jane, still awake, asked about the old man in the kitchen. She had heard our visitor's other voice and assumed that it came from a third person.

Ministry to this lady went on over many years. Rosemary, especially, worked with great love and determination to help her. When we began, we learnt from the medical profession that she had a personality disorder, which meant she was unlikely to be cured. We brought in the diocesan exorcist. He anointed with oil. Her response was to leap in the air, complaining vehemently that the oil had burnt her. She threw a cup of coffee over me. I still have the Bible open beside me with coffee stains on the text of Mark 6:13 – where Jesus sent his disciples to cast out devils and where, for the only recorded time, they used oil to anoint people!

Michael has reminded me that, on another occasion, she spoke with the voice of someone called Hilda, showing marks on her arms and throat of having been tied up and burnt at the stake in a previous incarnation.[6]

The next few months produced a wearisome pattern of progress and relapse. Sometimes she would come to a prayer meeting and take part. Then, quite suddenly, she would scream and totally disrupt proceedings. She went to stay with a priest and his wife, and was prepared for adult baptism the following Easter.

The battle continued long after that. Rosemary has remained in touch with her over the past forty years. She leads a more or less normal life with a real measure of faith and freedom.

We were certainly given a baptism of fire. Neither Michael nor I had experienced anything like it before. It remains the most difficult case that we have ever been involved with. The demonic tongues were one of many marks which confirmed the reality of her spiritual trouble.

One of the kindest, gentlest, most Christlike men that I ever met was Fred Smith.[7] He had a remarkable ministry of healing. Although his main ministry was evangelism and healing, he had a number of encounters with evil spirits:

> I was asked to visit a young girl suffering with deep depression. When I entered the room, she started speaking in a very deep voice. "I know you Fred, but you are not strong enough to fight me!" "I know you too, and I am not afraid of you," I replied. "Neither do I intend to fight you in my own strength, but with the power of the name of Jesus, the Son of God." I was immediately kicked in the stomach by this girl who was half-demented. A little time later she was set free from the evil spirit – delivered by the power in the name of Jesus.

Fred, a strong, powerful man, described receiving the kick as like feeling the force of ten men! The voice was clearly demonic. It is strange how different the demonic voices sound to those of the actual person.

The young girl also displayed the next diagnostic symptom.

STRENGTH

The Gadarene man had exceptional strength. Luke (8:29) tells us that he was kept under guard, chained hand and foot. Despite these precautions, many times he had broken his chains and been driven by the demon into solitary places.

Many people I have tried to help, both in Africa and England, have also displayed remarkable strength. Some years ago, Jane and I were entertaining a psychiatrist and her husband to dinner. The psychiatrist was a Christian, her husband an interested agnostic. We were talking about the reality of evil when the doorbell rang. The clergy, when at home, are never off-duty. I sighed and went to the door. A large, tall ex-marine, a man I will call James, came into the house and collapsed, unable to talk. He told me to get on with my dinner party.

After about twenty minutes, he came and joined us and said the problem was that he had just beaten up his wife. He asked me to go and see if she was all right. I knew the family slightly as I had recently baptized their three children. Rather reluctantly, I left the table and cycled round to his house. His wife greeted me. She was quite calm and remarked that "James was a binge drinker and these things happen." She told me to go back to my guests. I can't have been away more than half an hour. When I returned to my house, there was an interesting scene.

The dining room table was on its side, and James was growling and gnawing at one of the legs, with four policemen trying to restrain him. A neighbour was looking uncomfortable, the psychiatrist and her husband had retreated into the relative safety of a nearby alcove, and my wife was looking remarkably calm.

Eventually, James calmed down and the police proposed taking him to the cells for the night, so that he couldn't do any more damage. When he was calm, I asked him if he had ever been involved in any occult activity. His temporary calm disappeared. He snarled at me that he'd "used Ouija when in the Merchant Navy". Then he calmed down again and the police carted him off for a night in the cells.

I was able to see him over the next few days. He agreed to let his doctor treat him for binge drinking. I told his doctor, who was also mine, that there was underlying spiritual problem which would also need sorting out. James started to come to church.

About six months later, he was sitting in my garden talking to me. He said, "I don't really feel comfortable in church – it's as though there is a sort of cloud over me." I told him that, in order to feel at peace, he needed to make a clear renunciation of the past, and a commitment to Jesus.

We went inside to my study. He was sitting on a very solid chair. After a short time, his face changed and he gasped out, "You had better pray quickly!" Before I could do anything, he started to shake violently, an arm of the chair split (it was mended, I am writing sitting on it now!), and he landed on the floor amid a characteristically untidy heap of papers. I remembered that Michael Green, my rector, was away writing *I Believe in Satan's Downfall*,[8] and my other two colleagues were playing cricket for the diocese.Feeling very alone, I prayed – commanding the prostrate, six-foot plus ex-marine to stop shaking in the name of the Lord. To my immense relief, James calmed down. We spent the next hour threading our way through the Oxford rush-hour traffic to remove a Ouija board from his potting shed on his allotment.

A few days later, with the permission of the bishop and the knowledge of his doctor, a small group of us met in the local church to pray for James. I led him through the service of renewal of vows of baptism. I took the vows in the reverse order – beginning with "Do you renounce evil?" For a while, James couldn't speak. Then he started to shake, gripping the pew so hard that I thought it might break. After a short time, he shouted that he renounced evil, and made a full confession of all occult things he had been involved with. He continued with repentance and a public commitment to Jesus. He described it as like a light coming on in his life.

For some years things went well. He became very involved with and valued by the church, and his family started to come to church. Very sadly, some years later (long after I had moved from the area), he left his wife and family. I don't think this was anything to do with the previous problems, but it is a reminder to us all of how fragile faith and commitment can be, even after powerful experiences of God's love and human forgiveness.

There are other curious physical signs that can be present with some kind of demonic interference or indwelling – unexpected deafness, mocking laughter ("you can't help me"), severe shaking, inability to speak (especially the words, "deliver us from evil"), inexplicable fear, retching, uncontrollable coughing. All these can be pointers.

STRENGTH BUT NO DEMONS

In 1994, I led another SOMA team to Zambia. After a period of ministry in the north, we moved to the central diocese. Randy and Dorothy Vickers and I had a strange time in Luanshya. We stayed with an old Etonian white priest who greeted us with the words: "We don't want American fundamentalists in our parish!" I remarked that I was neither an American nor a fundamentalist – it was my only frosty reception in Africa!

The next day, Father Simon reluctantly let us loose on his parish (without the bishop's explicit instructions I am sure he would have banned us). He took Randy and Dorothy off to visit a lad who was chained up by his family. This sort of thing happens to the mentally ill in Zambia. Simon, I think, was expecting an instantaneous failed attempt at exorcism. Randy and Dorothy spent a long time with him, gained his confidence, got him unchained, and brought across to the church. They had discerned that, despite his apparent strength, he was traumatized but not demonized. This "negative" diagnosis is vital. They returned to visit him two days later and there was a marked improvement, which was maintained; Father Simon was impressed.

When Randy later joined me, I had just finished my teaching session. Randy had a session teaching about the Holy Spirit and then went through his procedure of invoking His presence. There was some spiritual reaction, but not the violent screams I had witnessed elsewhere. Then we started to pray for the sick. Randy saw the dramatic healing of a baby who was suffering from chronic constipation. I invited Simon to join me and used plenty of anointing oil. It is useful for flushing out the presence of evil and also reassures high churchmen! A man who was totally deaf in one ear, and who heard badly overall, was completely healed. I heard that he was singing in the choir a few weeks later.

Simon was impressed. But without Randy and Dorothy's careful, loving discernment, we would never have gained his trust. Not unreasonably, though, when we corresponded, he was puzzled as to why God would heal partial deafness and yet so many of his parishioners were still desperate in hunger and poverty.

SELF-HARM

Self-harm is one of the most distressing modern phenomena. Nearly always it is a sign of low self-esteem. Sadly this is often caused by abuse – sexual and physical. I wouldn't mention it in this context but for two things: the Gadarene man practised self-harm (Mark 5:5) and, in many people's experience, a lot of people troubled by demons threaten and attempt suicide (see the story at the end of Chapter 3).

William Lane[9] says that the most likely reason for the Gadarene man's self-harm was that cutting the flesh was a very ancient practice in pagan worship. This is certainly supported by the actions of the prophets of Baal on Mount Carmel (1 Kings 18:28). The demon's address to Jesus as "Son of the Most High God" is a title well attested in Gentile and Jewish syncretistic contexts, which would be appropriate in a wild region not properly under Jewish control – as the presence of the pigs proves.

The ultimate self-harm is suicide. Many demonized people threaten to kill themselves (see Chapter 6); some threaten violence on others. If we try to help people who are suicidal, we have to realize (and it is a very distressing thought) that the people we seek to help may destroy themselves. But it is better for us to try and to fail rather than to wash our hands and say the problem is beyond us.

On one occasion, I was counselling a very sorrowful young woman. She would only agree to see me if I was on my own. In today's politically correct world, I might have had to refuse. We met a number of times. She was beginning to trust me, but I sensed there was a serious block. The Spirit seemed to direct me to read Psalm 16:4:

> *Those who run after other gods will suffer more and more. I will not pour out libations of blood to such gods or take up their names on my lips.*

I read the verse even though I couldn't see its relevance. The woman looked surprised. We turned to pray. Her hands were firmly clenched. Closed hands are a bad sign when you're praying for others. I asked her to open them. She didn't respond. Then I did something that I would never do now. I commanded her to open them and touched her closed fist with my hand. She seemed to close her eyes. Her hand opened and a small knife fell to the ground. She looked embarrassed. Then, with great difficulty, she admitted to her problem and some of the reasons. "Libations of blood" were rather close to the truth. But the really important thing was that she was able to talk honestly and openly about her problem. After that, I think we made considerable progress.

In the context of Mark 5, I would want to emphasize that there was nothing demonic in her actions, but they did display an inner turmoil which needed to be addressed.

WILD EYES

In the Sermon on the Mount, Jesus said, "The eye is the lamp of the body. If your eyes are healthy, your whole body will be full of light. But if your eyes are unhealthy, your whole body will be full of darkness. If then the light within you is darkness, how great is that darkness" (Matthew 6:22–23; see also Luke 11:34). Jesus is saying that the eye is the window of the soul.

It is amazing what you can see when you look into people's eyes. Often they look clouded or flash with a strange light. After prayer, they invariably change. On one occasion, I had spoken at a parish dinner, which was at the beginning of a healing weekend. I prayed with a young woman who had just married a divorcee. They were both Christians, but she was challenged by the talk that I gave, which included reference to the dangers of any occult involvement. She had had readings both from a fortune-teller and from tarot cards. The significant thing was that she had been told she would be involved with one child that was not her own, and would have another which would die. Her husband had a child by his previous marriage, and she had had a miscarriage.

She had a strange spiritual experience as we prayed. I wanted to pray to cut off the effects of these predictions, but she was unable to look into my eyes – complaining that she could see nothing but brightness.

As she explained afterwards, she felt all right with me until I called her husband over to join in the prayer. As I looked into her eyes, all she could see were my eyes – no face, no lips, just an absolute nothingness. She began to feel very frightened. She felt that I was a fake and longed to get away.

I had encountered this sort of thing before and I was anxious to avoid a very public spiritual confrontation. I turned away. Then I asked her to pray aloud and to renounce her involvement in all these occult matters. We then prayed the Lord's Prayer. When we had finished, I turned back, looked into her eyes, and all was well.

My praying partner (and how essential it is to have the support and insight of others) pointed out that we should now begin to feel the grief from her miscarriage. So it proved. Her next thirty-six hours were times of weeping and darkness. But, thanks to my praying partner's sensitivity, we were able to help her and the darkness passed.

When I last saw them, she and her husband looked radiant. In a subsequent letter, she described how she now felt a new awareness of the Lord.

Years later, I met one of the leaders of the church. I enquired about the lady who couldn't look into my eyes: "How is she?" He smiled and replied, "She's overseas on the mission field."

Much more recently, I was praying with a young woman who suffered from severe depression. It became clear that the root of the trouble was her relationship with her father. He had been a very strict disciplinarian. He was also verbally and physically abusive. In addition, I discovered that he was a prominent Freemason. I have mixed views about Freemasonry which I will discuss later. What I do know is that many partners, children, and grandchildren of Freemasons suffer spiritually. When I have prayed with such people, one thing has almost always happened.

The young woman agreed that we should pray and that perhaps, next time, I would contact a generational healing service. As I looked into her eyes, she turned away complaining of their brightness. She agreed that we should continue in prayer. When I sought to cut off the Masonic influence, she felt quite agitated and said that her neck felt as if it was being throttled. I explained to her that the first Masonic ritual involves blindfolding the new Mason, placing a rope around their neck, and a dagger over their heart. I prayed to cut her free. She gasped, smiled, and looked me fully in the eyes. I saw that her eyes had changed. They looked much clearer. The depression had lifted.

The generational healing service was hardly necessary. She seemed very well when I followed her up sometime later.

Concluding thoughts

Certainly, people's eyes can give us a considerable window into their soul. I am virtually certain that the eyes of the Gadarene man would have changed after Jesus had set him free. His case was extreme. We may meet people who are demonized; we shall meet far more who are troubled by some negative spiritual encounter in their past or in their family's past. What I have described in this chapter is at the extreme of a very wide spectrum. In John 14:17 Jesus said to the disciples, "[The Holy Spirit] lives with you and will be in you." As I said earlier, this is also true of evil spirits. They may dwell with people, they may trouble people; possibly they will even enter people. But most of our ministry involves those who are troubled. It is usually simple, straightforward, quick, and highly beneficial.

We cannot leave this story without a brief mention of the pigs. Much ink has been spilled over their fate. I would offer this thought. The man needed assurance that the demons, which had troubled him so grievously and for so long, would never return. When the demons asked to enter the pigs (perhaps hoping to stay in the region which they had infested for some time), Jesus allowed this. The subsequent destruction of the herd proved to the man that the demons were truly gone – *and that they couldn't return.* That is an assurance that all people troubled in this way need. They may well have read Matthew 12:43–45 and be afraid that their last state will be worse than the first. The Gadarene man needed that assurance. So, I believe, does anyone that we are privileged to help.[10]

PRACTICAL MINISTRY IN TODAY'S WORLD

(CHAPTERS 5–9)

CHAPTER 5

HOW CAN IT HAPPEN?

Against all Satan's spells and wiles, against false words of heresy, against all knowledge that defiles, against the heart's idolatry, against the wizard's evil craft, against the death-wound and the burning, the choking wave, the poisoned shaft, protect me Christ, till thy returning.

(St Patrick's Breastplate)

Scripture is strangely silent about why people are taken over, or troubled, by evil powers. We have no idea how the Witch of Endor (1 Samuel 28) acquired her ability to act as a medium. We can only speculate that the slave girl in Philippi acquired her reputation as a fortune-teller, and hence gained her owners a lot of money, from the Temple of Apollo. We have no idea why the Gadarene man was so totally taken over by the demons. What we do know is that any occult activity is decisively forbidden by Scripture. The clearest text is in Deuteronomy 18:9–14.

When you enter the land the Lord your God is giving you, do not learn to imitate the detestable ways of the nations there. Let no one be found among you who sacrifices their son or daughter in the fire, who practises divination or sorcery, interprets omens, engages in witchcraft, or casts spells, or who is a medium or spiritist or who consults the dead. Anyone who does these things is detestable to the Lord; because of these same detestable practices the Lord your

God will drive out those nations before you. You must be blameless before the Lord your God. The nations you will dispossess listen to those who practise sorcery or divination. But as for you, the Lord your God has not permitted you to do so.

The New Testament is equally disapproving. Paul, in Acts 19:11–20, caused a public burning of magic scrolls. This happened after a failed exorcism and a series of miracles wrought "by the hands of Paul". It is reasonable to make the connection that those who indulge in practices forbidden in Deuteronomy 18, and those who practise magic arts and use magic books, are laying themselves open to demons.

This, I believe, is the main reason why people are troubled by evil spirits. We shall also see that some people's problems are due to the activities of ancestors (Exodus 20:4–7 and John 9:1–3); some are due to sexual partners (1 Corinthians 6:16) or extreme character defects (James 3:13–18); some are due to the places or localities in which they live.

An occult injury

Dave Ridge has accompanied me on a number of missions. This experience, with a different team in Nigeria, is a powerful illustration of how healing takes place when Satan's influence is rejected:

In January 2005 I went as part of a team of five to Nigeria to teach at a conference for clergy. There were about two hundred ordained and lay leaders attending the week-long conference. It was a packed programme and we had only one slot in the schedule to pray for physical healing for those who wanted it. As in any country where access to medical care is costly if available at all when we asked those who needed physical healing to come forward, almost every one of those present came forward.

This meant that each member of the team had thirty-plus people to pray for so the approach I took was simply to ask each person what the problem was and pray that Jesus would heal them and then pray for the next person. I guess I gave each person about thirty seconds.

The next day a man, aged about fifty, came up to me saying that his foot had been healed when I had prayed for him. I didn't even remember praying for him let alone that it was his foot! I said something along the lines of how pleased I was for him but he was very excited and wanted to tell me more. So I arranged to see him later with one of the local team to help me as the man's English was not good.

When we met up his story was something like this. As a young boy he had been initiated into a secret society against his will. An occult ceremony was held by his uncle which culminated with some powder being placed into his hand which suddenly and apparently by the powers of darkness burst into flames. He, not surprisingly, tipped the powder out of his hand onto the floor and put out the flames by stamping on it with his feet which were bare. He was told that a curse had been placed upon him so that if he ever renounced the secret society or told anyone about this ceremony he would die, and so had lived in fear ever since. From that time on the foot that had stamped out the flames was apparently somewhat crippled. It was much more than a simple burn which would have healed in time.

So it was decades later, by then an ordained minister, that he came for prayer for his foot – without even mentioning the history – but Jesus healed it and then he knew at last that the curse had been broken and together we were able to pray that he would be free of this bondage to exercise his ministry as God intended. He showed me his foot as proof of the healing – of course I had not seen the "before" picture and I was amazed at how flat his foot was. He had no instep but this is normal for someone who walks everywhere they go! He testified before people who knew him that he had run up the hill by his house the morning after the healing which he had not been able to do before.

A pub with history

A slightly similar case was when I was called to pray in a pub near Shepton Mallet, called the Canard's Grave Inn. The publican, whose family I knew quite well, felt there was a cold atmosphere in the pub. His two children were having terrible nightmares and his young son had terrible eczema, which no one could cure. He associated all this, quite reasonably I thought, with the tradition that the highwayman Canard, who had been hung nearby, was apparently buried in ground under what was now the main bar.

A small team of us prayed through the inn. One member of the team, with longstanding Shepton roots, felt an extreme feeling of cold in one area of the bar. Apart from that, nothing remarkable happened. But the children's nightmares ceased. Two members of our healing team went to pray for the little boy. The eczema disappeared instantly! The publican was suitably impressed and I had the story retold to me ten years later when I was involved in a mission in Kent.

Some people are much more sensitive to negative spiritual atmospheres than others. Children seem particularly in tune with such problems. The experience of children having nightmares in houses that are troubled seems quite common.

A palm reader's prediction

The reality of these powers was underlined by an early experience of my friend Bob Cole. I first met Bob and Helen when taking a communion service in Pullen Court – a sheltered housing area in Shepton Mallet. At first, they were incredibly negative; but gradually became great friends. Both their daughters had received healing from cancer, which they attributed to the prayers of their churches. Eventually, they started to come to church and joined an adult confirmation class. However, when the question of commitment to Jesus surfaced, it was clear that there was a serious block. Eventually Bob told me this story:

Over fifty years ago (around 1930), my mother was visiting an aunt who occasionally took in paying guests. It was late evening, when there was a knock on the door. A Madam Zelda and her husband had been directed to the house by the police, and needed accommodation for three days. She was a professional palmist. Between appointments, she used to rest at the house. During the stay, two friends of my sister called. Madam Zelda agreed to read their palms. In one reading, she suddenly turned pale and almost fainted. We rushed around getting smelling salts and water. Having recovered somewhat, she said to the girl whose palm she had been reading, "Go straight home, my dear, it is important." After the girls left, Madam Zelda said, "That girl's sister has just met with an accident near here. I am afraid it is serious." It transpired that the sister was on the way to our house when she was knocked down by an ambulance and died almost instantly.

On her last day, Madam Zelda read my mother's hand. As she was leaving, she gave my sister an envelope with instructions not to tell my mother its contents, but to read it and act accordingly. The note stated that on a certain day, in the distant future, my mother would meet an accident, connected with a piece of rope, or a dog lead, and that on that day my sister and I should be on our guard. My sister put the note away and, in due course, we forgot about it.

About two years later, I returned from work to find the house in darkness. My mother was lying on her bed where she had been all day. She told me that she had gone to change the bed linen, when she tripped over the earth lead of my radio set, which was attached to a low water pipe. She had hurt her ankle. It had taken her nearly two hours to reach her own room, and she was exhausted. We summoned the doctor, who discovered that she had broken her ankle. Because of a heart condition, the doctor decided that she should go at once to hospital and have the ankle set. The following day, she was given an anaesthetic and the ankle was set. The operation was unsuccessful, and during the second attempt, she died under the anaesthetic.

After the funeral, my sister remembered Madam Zelda's prediction. I asked her where the envelope was. After a considerable search, we found it. The date which Madam Zelda had written down was the day of the accident.

How such predictions work, I have no idea. That they have a negative spiritual effect is certain. During the confirmation classes, Bob struggled towards faith. He obviously wanted to believe but couldn't. I asked him if there were any spiritual blocks in his earlier life. That's when he told me this strange story. After that, we were able to cut off its effect, and to set him free for the remaining years of his life. He was then able to express his faith with great clarity. He and Helen became much valued and much loved members of the church.

A few years later, at one of my village churches, we sang Bob's favourite hymn. They had just moved away and this prompted me to tell his story. It had a dramatic effect on one very calm member of the congregation, who confessed to having had a similar experience for which he needed prayer.

A schoolteacher's marriage

A Christian couple came for marriage counselling. They were having problems – mainly because they felt that they couldn't afford to have children. At that time, the wife was a deputy head and seemed more successful, earning more than her husband. We discussed many issues.

There were no deep problems – just a grey lack of enthusiasm for the marriage overarched by anxieties about careers, children, and money. We had many sessions and I felt that we were making little progress. Almost out of desperation, I asked them if they'd had any psychic, occult, or fortune-telling experience. The man replied that, years ago, he had been to a fortune teller. "Did anything happen?" I asked. I was clutching at straws. "Yes," he said. "She said I would be married twice."

We all drew breath. I wasted no time in breaking the power of this false prediction. The atmosphere changed. Almost immediately, they agreed to start a family. They had, I think, four children. He became a head teacher and then moved on to a good, full-time job with a Christian publishing company. The marriage was transformed. It was incredible, to me, that such a small exposure to a dangerous prediction could have had such a potentially devastating effect.

So-called spiritual healing, using crystals, pendulums and the like, can have similar negative effects. Here is a testimony from a former parishioner:

A Glastonbury experience

Several years ago, I injured my neck following a road traffic accident and a judo injury. Despite seeing various GPs, physiotherapists, and osteopaths, and taking various tablets, I was never free of pain. However, I endeavoured to keep fit and attended a leisure centre for several years. One day when talking to a gentleman, the conversation turned to my neck injury and the ongoing pain. He told me that he and his partner were healers in Glastonbury and offered his help. He gave me his card which read, "Healer and Counsellor", in case I wished to contact him. I said I would think about it.

Eventually, as the pain continued, I phoned and made an appointment. I went to see him weekly for over a year. I wasn't told what type of healing it was despite asking how it worked. Initially, we had a discussion to discover anything I needed to talk about and, on each occasion, I would open up to him. I would then lie on the couch and he would go round my body with his hands just over me. This generally took between one and two hours. I was asked to make a donation of whatever I could afford.

At this time I was involved in a relationship (not with the healer), which ended abruptly, and I found myself very low afterwards. The healer told me that healing would help, so I continued with it. I was given some "sayings" to repeat morning and evening. I can't remember them, but I now realize they encouraged me to isolate myself from others. At one point I asked if this was a religious healing group, but he merely laughed and said, "I thought you would say that."

Gradually, I began to develop an interest in psychic things and was encouraged to go to a spiritualist church. While there, I asked two healers if they thought I could heal. They told me to open my hands, and then said there was something there. I was encouraged by the Glastonbury healer to read widely about healing and started to read any books relating to healing and psychic issues. I was also receiving psychic mail.

I began to have premonitions, which increased my anxiety. One related to the Paddington rail disaster. When I told the healer, he said that I was discovering my psychic powers and that he would teach me to "cover up" and protect myself from this. He also said that being a nurse, I needed to protect myself when I went into the hospital by covering myself (mentally) with a white blanket. This was also important when treating patients. It took me nearly two years to move on and forget this strange idea.

During this time I went to France with my parents and son. I felt strange at times, with a sense of déjà-vu. Once, on a beach, I saw a figure in white which, I believe, was an angel, spirit, or *apparition. Strangely, when I got home I had a compulsion to search and read about Camille Monet (the wife of the Impressionist artist) who had died in her early thirties. When I told the healer, he said it was the work of the infinite spirit world.*

I told my sister that I had psychic/healing powers and that various psychics had confirmed this ability. I tried to heal my sister, but she was angry with me and told me I needed psychiatric help.

About this time I also began to get blinding headaches, and became forgetful and often confused as to my whereabouts when shopping, particularly in the supermarket. My GP prescribed anti-depressants and antipsychotics. I phoned the Glastonbury healer and said I couldn't go any more, and that my family didn't agree with what I was doing. He said this was absolute madness and he told me to phone him anytime, any day, if I wanted to go back.

I was very afraid that these people would use their powers in a telepathic form to encourage me to join them. I also felt that I had been taken over, or possessed by something, and that I was losing control of myself and this "something" was taking over. I began to have severe panic attacks; my mother realized the danger and asked John Woolmer to see me. My doctor also encouraged the church to get involved. John and another senior member of the local church came to see me. They listened to my story, and prayed very gently. Afterwards I felt safe, and no longer afraid. I also felt that the dark presence had left.

My friend is not yet a worshipping Christian, but writes hoping that her words will help others avoid the same sort of mistake. Many books encourage their readers to experience and to pass on to others the sort of psychic healing that the story above warns against.

An even more dramatic example was told to me by my great friend the late Martin Cavender:

The pendulum and the black box

When I was working in Somerset I formed a friendship with a churchwarden from a little rural church, and his wife – I'll call them David and Mary. He had been a soldier with a distinguished

Second World War record as an officer in a fine regiment, and was now retired. They lived in a small cottage in their village.

Our friendship developed, and the two or three of us began to meet for a simple lunch on a reasonably regular basis. We would talk over all sorts of things, shared interests; but we always included a high proportion of faith questions, and often got down to reading passages from the Bible together.

Mary had a wasting disease which medical science seemed unable to explain or touch, and which meant that she was virtually blind and in constant pain. One day David and Mary arrived for lunch as agreed, and Mary came in looking better than I had ever seen her, with her eyes open and bright. They were watching to see if I would notice that something had happened. It was clearly a transformation, and I said so. What had happened? Mary told me she had been healed; prayed for by a member of their congregation. It was all very exciting, and I asked for details over the lunch.

Mary told me this woman had prayed for her "using a pendulum which she swung over a black box". My spirit began trembling. David was watching me carefully. I didn't quite know what to say, so asked if the woman had used the name of God, or of Jesus, or had invited the Holy Spirit in her prayers? No she had not. The atmosphere was getting distinctly apprehensive, but I felt I had to press on. David was clearly getting irritated with me, and Mary was looking increasingly unhappy.

"Do you know of any pendulum or black box in Scripture?" I asked, with a growing sense of unease. "No," said Mary. I said something haltingly about other spirits and counterfeits, about freedom and bondage, and then asked, "Would you want anything to do with this healing if it were not of Jesus?" After a long silence, Mary replied, "No, I would not," looking more and more fearful. We were driving into something from which I couldn't reverse, and by this time David was obviously very angry. Mary was clearly in better health than she had been for years and here I was questioning it and frightening her. It was touch and go whether he would whisk her away. Our friendship was in serious jeopardy.

It occurred to me to open the Bible, picking up the only clear passage I knew on this – James 5:14–16. We read it together. I explained that I only knew of one kind of healing, in the name of

Jesus in the power of the Holy Spirit – and this was what James was talking about.

Casting about frantically for inspiration I suggested that if Mary really didn't want anything to do with this healing then she could pray, with David, and renounce it in the name of Jesus. If it had been a godly happening, there would be no problem. If not? Well, it occurred to me in my naive understanding to warn her that there might be side-effects – if she decided to renounce the "healing" and it was not of God she could well find that her sight would go, and the pain might return. It seemed right to say all this, but I didn't really know what I was talking about. I was quite a young Christian believer, and I was flying by the seat of my pants.

I also said that if all that happened, then they should immediately contact their local parish priest (a young man who had been in post only, I think, for a few weeks), and ask him to pray for Mary's healing. The passage from James might be a useful text. Lunch ended. They left – and I was really not sure if they would ever want to see me again. Chastened but increasingly clear about what had been happening, I went back to my office. I prayed.

Three weeks later, I had a phone call. It was David. "Do you fancy some lunch?" "Yes!" I almost shouted in my relief. We fixed up a date.

The day arrived, and so did David and Mary. She was looking radiant, and they were both grinning at me. "OK, come on, what's happened?" I asked. The story came out.

They had gone home from the previous lunch angry (David) and confused and fearful (Mary). They had thought and talked about what had been said, and then after ten days decided they couldn't put it off any more. They had knelt together beside their bed, and together renounced anything in this "healing" which was not of Jesus Christ. Instantly Mary's sight went, and her pain returned, worse than ever. It was a very frightening moment.

David went straight to the phone and rang the vicar. "I want you to come round and pray with us for my wife to be healed." The vicar explained that he had no experience of the healing ministry. "That's all right," said David, "James 5 will tell us what to do. See you in the church in ten minutes, Vicar."

I thank God for that young parish priest. Despite his lack of *experience he turned up on parade in the church at the prescribed time, knelt on one side of the altar-rail with Mary on the other, read aloud the passage from James, and did what it said in the book. He prayed for Mary to be healed, and anointed her with oil. And Mary was healed, wholly and completely, of her sight problems and all her pain, in the name of Jesus in the power of the Holy Spirit, there and then.*

Mary lived on in her healing for another four years, and then died peacefully in a hospital bed. There was more healing going on than just the physical on that day in Somerset, though.

David and Mary discovered afresh the God of power who loved them. The vicar found a new ministry which was clear and undeniable. I learned so much, in all my awkwardness, and again saw a loving God at work among his people – and I learned that it was vital to speak out, whatever the social or personal risk. My only sadness was that I didn't think more about that woman in the congregation whose offering of healing by the pendulum and the black box had precipitated the whole thing. I can only pray that someone somewhere has helped her see the truth, and helped her recognize that the evil one "masquerades as an angel of light" (2 Corinthians 11:14). I know that my job as a believer is to stand in the name of Christ and ask, "By what spirit?"

A difficult conversation

On one occasion, I was visiting a hospital. I saw a young woman lying in bed, reading *Romeo and Juliet*. I went over to ask her what was wrong. She replied that she had had terrible back pain since the birth of her second child. I said that Jane, my wife, had similar problems before and after the birth of our first. I mentioned how she had been healed through the prayers of my friend Fred Smith.[1] She smiled, icily, and said, "I'm into healing but not your sort." Remembering one quote from *Romeo and Juliet*, I said, "Parting is such sweet sorrow," and thought no more about our brief encounter.

The next day, our office was rung up by a hospital sister. Apparently, the patient had declared herself to be a white witch. The sister, and another nurse, had sensed a great deal of spiritual chaos. They had gone into a quiet room to discuss the problem.

Then they had tried to pray. They said the Lord's Prayer. When they reached, "Deliver us from evil", they had both fallen over. The two experienced members of the hospital staff were considerably alarmed! They rang the church office and asked for prayer cover. I was away but the prayer team was alerted. Within an hour, a doctor had decided that they could do nothing more to help the patient and she was discharged. Almost immediately everything seemed to return to normal.

The sad thing is that the woman in question probably has considerable psychic powers, which may well include healing. She honestly thinks that she is helping people. But from a Christian perspective, the exact opposite is happening.

Negative experiences – Spiritualism and Ouija

I was asked to visit the home of a man who was critically ill – mainly because his family felt that his house had an oppressive, evil atmosphere. I am not sensitive to such things; but I took with me the woman who had been freed from Asmodeus. She confirmed that there was a problem in the house. Before I prayed with the man, who seemed to have a vague, rather uncertain faith, I asked him about any connections he had had with spiritualism.

"Oh yes," he said. "We had a friend who came to pray for my healing. She went into a trance and turned into a German doctor."

We prayed through the house. In one room, my prayer partner felt that further prayers were needed. When we went downstairs to the room where the seance had taken place. I asked to see the chair on which the medium had sat. "It's upstairs," was the reply. It was in the one room where more prayer had seemed necessary – a small confirmation that we were doing something important. We finished praying through the house, prayed for the man, and left.

I saw the man only once more. He and his wife were wonderfully cheerful, and the whole house felt quite different. A few days later, he died. His wife was evidently greatly comforted by the spiritual uplift they had received.

The man attended an evangelical church, which was led by a very wise pastor. I mentioned to him that I knew the man who had died. The pastor, who knew nothing of this ministry, remarked how amazingly changed, and peaceful, the man had seemed in the last few days of his life. It is deeply humbling to have a small part in such ministry.

On another occasion, a prominent citizen in my Somerset parish got in touch because he was troubled about his daughter. He had discovered that she had been involved with Ouija and similar things at her secondary school. She was suffering from nightmares and was generally unable to sleep. I don't know whether her father told her, but one afternoon I went to pray in her bedroom. From then on, she was able to sleep perfectly.

There were two interesting outcomes. Some years later, I was doing some random parish visiting when I met a group of lads. They tried to wind me up: "Seen any good ghosts recently, Vicar?" I realized that they were about the same age as the girl. I asked them if they knew her. Had they been involved in her Ouija? They turned pale. They were honest enough to admit that they had been very scared and felt that something real had occurred. Years later, I heard that the girl in question was doing full-time Christian work.

Often people get drawn into forbidden territory without realizing where they are heading. Christian, in *Pilgrim's Progress*, stepped off the narrow, rather difficult, road into an attractive meadow called By-path. As a result he ended up in Giant Despair's Castle.[2]

A parish worker once brought a woman in her forties to one of our healing services. The woman described how, some fifteen years earlier, she had gone to a professional counsellor. She wanted help because of a great lack of self-confidence and general depression. At first she felt helped, but as the sessions continued, she realized that the counsellor's methods were connected with spiritualism – especially when listening to a tape, which she was given for guidance. She felt a sensation of being attacked by an evil force – physically (hands around her neck, squeezing) and emotionally. She had no peace of mind and great distress. Her mother had gone forward at a Billy Graham campaign a year before; but neither she, nor any other Christians, seemed to be able to help her.

Her parish worker and others thought, not unreasonably, that her reaction showed marks of hysteria and they doubted the reality of the attacks. As usual, we took her through a low-key type of ministry, praying to cut off the effects of the past. As a result of this, she was able to make a real commitment to Jesus, but still felt under some bondage.

A while later she returned, again with her parish worker, to a healing service I was leading, and at which my friend Fred Smith was preaching. She came forward for prayer. This time, she reacted violently. She screamed and fell over. Very quickly, we took authority over the evil spirit, and she was completely freed.

She is now happily married to a Christian, and they often lead services at an old people's home. Her husband preaches and she sings – quite a transformation from the depressed young lady of the past.

A spirit house in New Guinea

Don and Heather McLean have been working in translation and literacy with SIL (Wycliffe Bible translators) in the Western Highlands Province of Papau New Guinea since 2001. They spent several years in other areas of the country when their children were younger. This is their testimony:

In the early 1980s, we lived at Telefomin in the Western Sepik Province of Papua New Guinea. We were working with the Australian Baptist Missionary Society, in an area which was renowned for worshipping a very powerful spirit goddess, Afek. There was a particularly well-known "man house" not far from the mission houses that tourists were very keen to visit. No national women were permitted to go anywhere near the area, but at that time we were terribly naive about the spirit world which is involved in animism and would sometimes allow our two young daughters to take visitors to the area to see the outside of the house. They would have been about ten and eight years old at the time. Although still inexperienced in this spiritual world, I would feel a "creepy" sensation if I ever ventured into the area, even with a group of other people. My husband said that I imagined it, but I knew otherwise.

Several years later, at our home church back in Australia, when our spiritual eyes had been somewhat opened, a visiting pastor asked any of the congregation who had been missionaries to come forward so that he could pray for us in relation to the dark side of the spirit realm with which we had no doubt had some contact. I turned to my older daughter and asked her to accompany her sister, brother and parents to the front, to which she tacitly replied, "There is nothing wrong with me!" The look in her eyes told me something else. Our pastor told us that if she had been in rebellion against us on any of those visits near the spirit house, then there would have been an open door for any of those dark spirits to enter her life.

Our older daughter had returned with us from Papua New Guinea when she was nearly twelve. She seemed to think that she had missed out on a lot of activities and pleasures that her peer group had experienced by that time and set about catching up with them. No amount of counsel or warning could change her downward path. She told us that she would not learn by anything other than her own experience. That is what happened and she was badly burned by those experiences for many years. I had had a very legalistic upbringing which I did not find easy to abandon. They were tumultuous years for the whole family.

After our older daughter left home, we were sometimes able to communicate more effectively. Occasionally I mentioned that her acting as a tour guide to the spirit house back in Telefomin may have had an adverse spiritual effect on her life. She listened, but would never let us pray for her close up and definitely not allow us to touch her while we prayed. She often used to remind us of the times people had told her as a little girl that they believed that God had a very special purpose for her life and would ask plaintively why everything completely opposite seemed to be dominant in her life. She had a broken engagement followed by a broken marriage and she spiralled deeper into depression and a life out of control.

She was a wonderful, caring palliative care nurse by this time, but was no longer able to function in that capacity. We tried everything that we could think of to help her physically and spiritually, but the more we tried, it seemed the worse she became and we were finally advised to just keep on loving her but leave everything else in God's hands. We had asked many people to join us in praying for her desperate situation. Her paternal grandmother was probably one of the most fervent prayers for her beloved granddaughter's deliverance. At times our daughter would seek secular counselling, but always resisted any suggestions that she needed to see a Christian counsellor.

When our other two children had left home and started on their career paths, we began training with Wycliffe Bible Translators. We were finally ready to leave and returned to Papua New Guinea in the year 2000 with the blessing of all the children. Our older daughter's comment was, "I knew that you would go back one day."

During our early years back in the country, we became aware of a nationwide prayer movement called "Operation Joshua". One of the results of this movement was a request from the people of Telefomin for someone to destroy the old spirit house nearby. It was falling into disrepair and the people themselves were becoming frightened of the building and what it had stood for. The leader of Operation Joshua was very happy to oblige and started a fire which destroyed the decaying building for ever. At that time, most of the local people were delighted, but more recent reports indicate that if the man who headed "Operation Joshua" returned to the area, there are some who would willingly take his life.

In Papua New Guinea, from time to time we were able to speak on the phone with our children when we visited a nearby Bible College. At that time we were living in a very primitive village setting with no facilities of our own. Just over two years ago, I was talking on the phone with our older daughter when she told me that she had recently asked a lady from a nearby church whether or not she could have been affected by those times of taking people to visit the area of the spirit house.

This spiritually in tune lady said, "Oh my dear, let me pray for you!" Miracle number one was that she allowed this lady to pray for her and no doubt she touched our daughter while praying. Miracle number two was that for some time our daughter's sleeping pattern improved noticeably. After her marriage broke down, she had not been able to sleep at night and so slept a lot of the following seven years away.

We believe that the burning of that spirit house, way up north in the depths of Papua New Guinea, actually broke the spiritual bondage in our daughter's life and for the first time she was free to ask for spiritual help for her complex problems. This was only the beginning and there were still many hard times ahead for her.

In the year 2004, three of our close family members died within three months of one another. We returned from Papua New Guinea and were able to be with each member in their last stages of illness. Our daughter was present at two out of the three funerals. At the last one, my 96-year-old mother's, our daughter became distraught. She could not understand why, as she had never felt particularly close to my mother. She realized that she had not forgiven her maternal grandmother for the way that she had brought up me, her mother, so legalistically. By this time my relationship with my daughter had become much closer. But, although a committed Christian from the age of nine, until I was in my early forties, I had not discovered the freedom of grace. I had passed many rules and regulations on to my own children, contributing to many of our hard family situations.

Many years ago, my mother had requested that one of my cousins who is a pastor, conduct her funeral service. He gave a beautifully simple gospel message at the funeral chapel. When he saw our daughter's distress, he asked her if she would like to visit some ladies at his church where she could receive some counsel. She agreed but approximately five more months went by before she managed to get herself to the church.

We had returned to Papua New Guinea by this time. She told me on the phone that she was deeply touched by the lovely caring ladies who led her to renounce all kinds of behaviour which she knew had kept her from receiving the release for which she had been longing. She started to read Rick Warren's book, **The Purpose Driven Life**, with a real fervour, looking up every reference in three or four different versions of the Scriptures so that she could glean every ounce of meaning out of them. She felt that the Lord was speaking directly to her and started to mould her life on the wisdom that she was reading.

One day in February 2005, on the same day that a devastating flood had forced us to leave our village house and move to some premises of the nearby Bible College, we received a fax from her saying that she had given up smoking and was going to be baptized by immersion the following Sunday at the church which she had been attending regularly for some months. She hoped that we would understand that she couldn't wait for us to come home in September that year, but felt that she must obey the Lord straight away. Of course we were delighted and arranged for several friends to stand in for us and witness this wonderful step that she was about to take. She was now nearly thirty-three years of age.

From that time, she has gone on from strength to strength, telling others freely about the goodness of God to her. She delights to study the Word of God with a large concordance that we were delighted to give her. Her television viewing and music choices have changed dramatically and she has destroyed many things around her home which she feels are not advantageous to her Christian walk.

She did a course called 'Cleansing Streams' recently and sent a letter to many of her friends, including us, inviting us to tell her frankly any character defects which we might have noticed in her. This is a far cry from that time when she brusquely stated, "There's nothing wrong with me!" She has become fascinated by stories of those who have been prepared to give their lives in martyrdom rather than deny their Lord, and said, "I want to be strong enough to do the same, should my turn come."

What a wonderful change has taken place in her life! We are constantly amazed and continually grateful when we see what she is allowing the Lord to do in her life. If I mention to her that a certain person has been praying for her for many years, she always asks me to thank them for their faithfulness. She has stated to us "You must have been praying for me for so long. I'm so sorry that I couldn't do it for you, but when God told me to change my self-destructive habits, I had to obey!"

Is it any wonder that we are so grateful to our Lord?

Conclusion

The common theme in all these stories is that people had been in touch with, or living in the presence of, the occult. This had brought illness, sleeplessness, false healing, encouragement to use psychic powers, and some form of spiritual malaise. Not everyone who encounters the negative spirit world will be affected. If I have an infectious illness, not everyone I meet will catch it; but anyone who has been in contact would be wise to get a health check!

There are many other reasons why people have deep spiritual problems but, in my experience, the question, "Have you personally had any dealings with the occult world?" is a good place to start. The Deuteronomy text highlights child sacrifice (only alleged in some of the wilder, largely unsubstantiated, claims against black magic and paedophilia), divination and fortune-telling, sorcery (that would include placing curses upon people), and various aspects of attempting to contact the dead: all these are emphatically forbidden.

An equally revealing question is, "Have you had any psychic experiences?" An affirmative answer will usually take us into the remit of the next chapter – generational healing.

One word of pastoral advice: many people who come for help deny any occult involvement. They have either forgotten or don't want to admit to being involved in such things, which most people instinctively know are wrong. When prompted with more specific questions, they often give very different answers. It is my strong impression that more people are turning to these practices. Alternative healing, using crystals, pendulums, or Reiki is very popular. Practitioners of Reiki often fervently deny any occult practice.

One prominent practitioner advertises on the Web as follows:

> As well as Reiki, angel healing and crystal healing, I use my psychic and mediumistic abilities to bring about deep personal growth and emotional, mental and physical health. I also specialise in chakra and aura healing, flower remedies, dowsing and visualisation. I believe we are all the masters of our own lives and as such have the power and the ability to shape our lives in the manner we choose.

The breathtaking arrogance of such claims, and the clear use of occult practices, should be enough to cause any Christian to repent of touching such a means of healing. The fact that it is so popular, and widely acclaimed even by some doctors, shows the extent of the problem we have. If the devil doesn't exist, combatting this sort of stuff rationally is much harder. If the devil has gone missing, such practices will flourish. The fact that these practices achieve some apparently positive results makes them more dangerous. Jesus, and Paul, both warn us that this can happen (Matthew 24:24 and 2 Thessalonians 2:9).

The Christian Medical Fellowship sounds this cautionary note:

> From a Christian perspective, there certainly are spiritual dangers, which cannot be ignored. The concept of Rei as the invisible source

of all being and of Ki as the Universal Life Force are completely at variance with the Christian belief in God as Creator and Heavenly Father. Reiki claims to be independent of any religious belief systems but Buddhist, Hindu and Taoist influences can be clearly identified. Reiki healers often have strong New Age associations, at times using occult techniques, crystals and tarot cards. Divination, necromancy and the receiving of knowledge and power by channelling are forbidden in the Bible. It has been suggested that the Reiki laying on of hands is similar to the healing miracles of Jesus and his disciples. Yet we need to ask, "By what spirit is this being applied?"[3]

The obvious consequence of all this is that those of us involved in the Christian healing ministry will increasingly be asking people who come for help to renounce such dangerous involvement. Usually, a simple renunciation, accompanied by a prayer of repentance, will be sufficient. Sometimes, as in some of the cases outlined above, something deeper will be required.

CHAPTER 6

GENERATIONAL HEALING

"Will there not be peace and security in my lifetime?"
(King Hezekiah, 2 Kings 20:19)

Winchester Cathedral seems a beautifully safe place. Impeccable singing, marvellous architecture, and sensible orthodox Anglican worship, combine with a deep sense of history and beauty, to soothe rather than to challenge.

Jane Austen lies buried on the northern side of the nave. St Swithin, of rain-making fame, lies, finally undisturbed, just outside the walls. Izaak Walton, theologian and fisherman extraordinary, is commemorated in a magnificent stained-glass window. A nineteenth-century diver, who rescued the cathedral from sinking into the mire of the water meadows of the Itchen, has a generous statue. Somewhat less peacefully, the rather gruesome cadaver, or death mask, of the last Catholic bishop – the fearsome Stephen Gardiner of Queen Mary's unhappy reign – is there for all to see. Worshippers and tourists normally flock in.

It was a beautiful June afternoon. The ancient cathedral seemed strangely still. The tourists were quiet and a small congregation was preparing for an unusual event – unusual in the 1970s – a service of healing in an Anglican cathedral.

The speaker was a small, seemingly elderly, man. He was in his sixties, but the ravages of wartime imprisonment by the Japanese made him look older. His high-pitched voice was quite difficult to hear. After the normal pleasantries, he launched into his talk with a personal reminiscence. Before the Second World War, Ken McAll[1] and his wife, Frances, had been missionaries in China. It was a threatening time, with constant danger both from the Red Army, which was trying to wrest control from the Nationalistic government, and from the Japanese who were also invading parts of China. Ken, Eric Liddell, and other mission workers were increasingly aware of God's direction, and protection.

Ken explained that, one day, he was returning to Siaochang along the rough road through the fields and heading towards the village, when he was aware of someone walking behind him. He was told not to go to that village, but to go instead to a different village, where he was needed. Ken took it to be the voice of a local farmer who knew what was going on. It was best not to show any fear by looking round.

When he reached the village, the gate was opened, and he was pulled inside. The villagers asked him what had made him change direction (some of them had watched him from afar). Ken said, "That man out there told me to come." But when he and the locals looked out, there was no one else to be seen. Then Ken realized that his unseen companion had spoken in English – unlikely for a Chinese farmer!

The villagers then told him that if he had continued in the direction he was heading, he would have landed in a Japanese trap, as the village to which he had been walking was occupied by Japanese troops. Moreover, a local skirmish had left several wounded, some of whom had been brought into their village, and several people needed his medical attention. One of the wounded became a Christian, and eventually joined the staff of the teacher training college where Eric Liddell had taught.

Ken knew that his life had been saved by the direct intervention of the Lord. His world view had changed. Writing about the incident, he commented:

My mocking intolerance of the implicit belief of the Chinese in ghosts and the spirit world was gone. I understood, too, that the spirit world holds both good and evil influences, and I realized that my daily prayer for protection had been dramatically answered.

This was the highly unusual beginning to a very challenging talk. Ken continued with an account of his wartime captivity, shared with his wife, during which they had discovered that the power of prayer could replace unavailable medicines. As prisoners, they had been crammed into a freezing cold factory, into which some 1,200 prisoners had been herded by the Japanese.

The talk then moved on to tell of his more recent experiences of healing, including new insights into psychiatry which he had gained during post-war studies. He spoke as though the sort of experiences he was relating should be part of our normal Christian life.

I listened spellbound. I had attended the meeting reluctantly (and how often are the most important meetings and services the ones to which we go with the greatest reluctance?). I should have been umpiring on the nearby school cricket field, or driving my car to help a natural history expedition. Instead, at the bidding of a saintly colleague, who had a seemingly eccentric interest in places and people of healing, I had persuaded Jane, my newly-wed wife, to join me in the cathedral.

Eventually the speaker was done. A time of prayer for healing followed, including the laying-on of hands. My colleague, Philip Willmot, invited me to join him in the sanctuary. It would be nice to record that I witnessed instant answers to our prayers – I am not aware that we did, but I do know that I left the cathedral with a rather different world view. For almost the first time in my life, I had met someone who had experienced the Living Lord not only through conversion, prayer, and worship, but also in power, in His presence, and in miracles!

For me, an inexperienced young priest, listening to Ken McAll was another turning point. That afternoon, in Winchester Cathedral, was the first time I had ever heard someone speak directly about angels and healing. After a period of personal difficulties, during which I had started to question some of the miraculous parts of the Bible, it was a great relief to hear first-hand evidence of the power of God. A living testimony seemed worth a hundred books! I left the cathedral determined to find out more and with much greater expectation of what God was about to do in my life.

The healing of the family tree

As I was to discover, Kenneth's greatest contribution came from his time as a psychiatrist. He became certain that many of his patients were in some way trapped, emotionally and spiritually, by their ancestors. They could, he believed, be released by holding a communion service in which they were cut free from any malign influence caused by suicide, murder, occult activity, and so on. More controversially, he believed that the spirits of the ancestors could also be set free. He wrote of this in his widely read book, *Healing the Family Tree*. I found his case histories persuasive; his theology seemed less convincing.

As a result, when I was chair of the Bath and Wells Diocesan Healing Group, we published a form of service for those who wished to participate in such a ministry. It was largely written by a diocesan exorcist (known to his delightful bishop as the "Diocesan dealer in Spooks") and drew on his experience and quiet wisdom. In essence, it was an Anglican Communion service with a number of special features. Instead of the intercession, there was a lengthy confession based on the person's family tree. At the time of consecration, a carefully prepared family tree was placed on the altar. Specific problems would be highlighted. It is important to say that we were not making spiritual judgments about the ancestors – we were merely stating that some of their actions could still have a negative effect on their descendants. It was an assessment of the person's spiritual DNA. Before we all received communion, we would use a powerful, responsive version of the Lord's Prayer. After sharing communion, there was further prayer with the laying on of hands and, usually, anointing with oil.

The effects were occasionally dramatic. Much more often, the person who had been prayed for received a deep peace, and saw some clear improvements in relationships around the family.

Theologically, the key was the third commandment (Exodus 20:4–7), especially the warnings and blessings attached to it. Psalm 103:17, which is usually read by the graveside of a deceased person, reminds us of generational blessings – which are even more important. I also found John 9:1–3 very helpful. When the disciples asked Jesus, "Who sinned, this man or his parents?" he didn't rebuke them for asking a stupid question but explained that this situation was different. Implicitly he accepted the idea that people could be adversely affected by their ancestors' behaviour.

People often quote Ezekiel 18:1–4, which teaches that each person is responsible for their own spiritual wellbeing. This is obviously true. But it doesn't mean that they cannot be adversely affected by their ancestors. Hezekiah's descendants were doubtless none too pleased by his casual attitude to words of judgment spoken by Isaiah (2 Kings 20:16–19). Here Hezekiah, who was one of Judah's most godly kings, makes one of the most selfish comments to be found in Scripture. Perhaps future generations will judge our casual attitude to global warming in a similar way.

If someone consults a doctor, or me, about migraines, we probably look for one of three main causes: stress (especially noticeable when schoolteachers take a break or reach the end of the term – as they relax, the migraines frequently kick in), diet (red wine, cheese, and chocolate seem to be the main culprits), and hereditary problems (DNA). I will counsel and pray differently in each case. A doctor will possibly prescribe quite differently according to his diagnosis. If the problem seems to be hereditary, I will pray in a non-judgmental way to cut off this influence. Over the years, I have seen many people suffering from this very debilitating problem.

Some case histories

(Some of the facts have been altered very slightly where I have lost contact with those mentioned.)

My very first experience was one of the most dramatic. A young woman came for prayer. She was deeply troubled because she had made a suicide pact with her fiancé. He had died and she had not gone through with it. Guilt, grief, and the seeming impossibility of forgiveness had combined to make a lethal spiritual cocktail.

A friend of hers, and mine, joined me for ministry. None of us knew what to expect. We went quietly through the Anglican Communion service. We prayed for release from guilt and grief. We prayed for forgiveness and for the release of the influence of the fiancé. After communion, we laid hands on the woman and prayed for her peace.

At the end of the service, I asked if anyone had experienced anything. My friend said, "I saw someone with a tattered, patched-up coat walk through your door." The woman we had been praying with said, in a somewhat stunned voice, "That was him – I mended that coat."

Years later, the same friend, now running a house of healing, asked me to pray for someone with a multiple personality disorder. I was somewhat out of my depth. My friend asked me to do a generational healing service as she had discerned that part of the problem stemmed from the past. The person concerned was reluctant to be prayed for – this is almost always a sign that prayer is needed quickly. However, after a straightforward service, she was far more able to go through the healing process that my friend and her team were offering.

THE STRANGLER FIG

Occasionally, people are trapped by powerful experiences, without even realizing what has happened to them. A few years ago, I had the privilege of praying with a woman who it is best not to name (I write with her permission), a refugee from an African country. She often came forward for prayer. Unlike many African ladies, she was seldom smiling and often in tears. Our prayers seemed to have little effect. Her heartbreaking story, in summary, was this:

> My parents had difficulty in conceiving. After fifteen years, they went to a witchdoctor. His spells were efficacious and I was born. Aged fourteen, I was sent to my future mother-in-law's house. She, knowing my parents' difficulties, took me to a witchdoctor so that I would conceive. My husband was a successful businessman. I was so ill after the birth of my first child that I ran home to my parents. They sent me back.
>
> My husband went into politics. He was on the side of the government, and had quite a prominent position. He accompanied me to the hospital when I was pregnant with my second child. He was disgusted by the state of the hospital, and tried to get something done politically. When my third child was born, he found there had been no improvement. He joined the opposition.
>
> On New Year's Day 1997, we were arrested. He was effectively

told to keep out of politics or be killed. He was very determined and wouldn't be silenced. In May 1997, he was murdered in police custody. I and my youngest two children were helped to escape to England. My eldest is still in hiding in the African country.

For five years, this woman had struggled to make a new life in England. She had been helped by good Christian friends. She'd made much progress, but was locked into grief, self-pity, and anger.

One afternoon, I met her with a discerning friend who has provided some testimony about angels. When we began to pray, the main problem appeared to be her inability to forgive. She was overwhelmed by sorrow for her situation – the death of her husband, the loss of contact with her eldest son, and a new life in a strange country. We recognized that she needed to forgive the president, the police, her husband ("if he hadn't been so obstinate this needn't have happened"), her mother-in-law, and her parents. We made no progress. I felt utterly defeated. My discerning friend seemed to have nothing to offer. Then a word came into my mind. I wrote the word, an African-sounding word of about seven letters, on a piece of paper. She looked at it, nodded, and changed the sixth letter from "t" to "b". Her whole demeanour changed. She screamed, "That's it!"

She started to behave like a powerful witchdoctor – screaming, chanting, and displaying blazing eyes. The word had clearly been connected with the influence of a controlling witchdoctor. My friend stared in amazement. I said that all we needed to do was to pray.

After some quiet prayer, about ten minutes later, much to our relief the woman calmed down. Then, very clearly, she said that the spirit had been released. I told her that she'd had a spiritual operation and that she'd be very tired. Although I cannot be certain, I think that the spirit which manifested was connected with the witchdoctor her parents had visited.

When we next met (which was about four weeks later because I had been away on a mission in Tanzania), she said that she had slept for the next week. Now she was ready to pray to forgive all those who had hurt her. We made the important distinction between forgiveness and justice – we could pray for justice, but still pray for forgiveness for those who had murdered her husband and the witchdoctors who had affected her life.

Two years later, her eldest son was brought out of her country – remarkably by one of her husband's political opponents! The woman celebrated this great event with a splendid party attended by many members of her church community.

This story illustrates my point that occult problems cling very deeply to people, and make it hard for them to receive Christ in the first place, and to forgive others. My friend had received Christ, but couldn't make any real spiritual progress because of her grief and understandable anger. While what had happened wasn't in the context of a generational healing service, the principle was the same. She needed releasing from her parents' spiritually disobedient actions.

Her experience reminds me of the strangler figs in Africa. A large bird, often a hornbill, drops the seed of a fig in the crown of a growing tree. The fig takes root and slowly grows downwards. It is not particularly dangerous, just unsightly, until years later it reaches the ground and takes root. At this stage, the host tree is in real danger of destruction. There is a classic example in the Arusha National Park. You can drive a high truck under the celebrated Fig Tree Arch. It looks like a tall tree with the trunk split into two. The split is where the roots of the strangler fig begin; the host tree disappeared centuries ago.

Another experience occured in 1992 (four years earlier), at the end of a long prayer session in Chipili. I was told there was a man in the gallery who needed prayer. I was feeling very tired after several hours of standing on my hip, which was in urgent need of replacement. I asked for him to be brought down into the main body of the church. Soon afterwards, I saw a huge man lumbering up the aisle towards me. When he was about ten yards away, I asked through an interpreter if his father or grandfather had been a witchdoctor. He snarled what I took to be an affirmative reply. I raised my right hand, made the sign of the cross, performed a cutting motion and commanded any ancestral spirit to leave him. He crashed to the ground. When he came round, he was smiling and calm. I was very relieved that the spirits hadn't manifested with strength as I cannot imagine how many people would have been needed to restrain him!

SUPERSTITION AND PSYCHIC EXPERIENCES

A prominent local businessman had a rather unexpected conversion. When he came to see me, he was seeking healing from a persistent stomach disorder. He also mentioned that he was very superstitious – something which affected both his family and business life. Decision-making depended on the omens being right – one magpie on the road spelled bad luck, fingers had to be crossed the right number of times, wood had to be touched, and so on. Failure to apply these rituals in the right way generated great fear of harmful consequences.

After his conversion, the man had accepted Christian teaching on superstition and the occult. He had resigned from the local Masonic Hall – potentially an expensive decision. He renounced the rituals and accepted the protection given to every Christian. Nevertheless, a deep-seated fear invariably surfaced when one of these rituals was broken.

At a distance, it all sounds quite trivial but, as we went for a walk to discuss the problem on a hot July afternoon, that wasn't how it felt. It became clear to me that it was substantially an ancestral problem. The man had been brought up in a notoriously haunted pub, and claimed to have tape-recorded the ghost when he was a teenager. He had traced a history of "white magic" back on his grandmother's side of the family tree.

As we walked, I came to a fork in the path. To the left I saw a man with a net – I thought it was a butterfly net. As we approached it became clear that it was a bee skep. The hives were about twenty metres off the path to the left. The bees were swarming around the bramble blossom. We hastened through. Unfortunately, my friend was stung twice on the ear. I was very embarrassed! When we were safely into the next field, I put my hand on his ear. I prayed with minimal faith. To my intense surprise and relief, the pain instantly disappeared.

Psalm 118:12 – "They swarmed around me like bees, but they were consumed as quickly as burning thorns; in the name of the Lord I cut them down" – seemed an appropriate commentary on our experience. It helped to confirm to me that God did want me to pray to cut off his connection with white magic and other ancestral problems. I made it clear, however, that I was not judging his ancestors.

A few days later, we held a simple, private communion service in the village church near the family pub. I prayed for complete release for him and his family, and future generations, from any such spiritual bondage. There was a great sense of peace.

My friend said that the next day, when he woke up, he felt as if a physical burden had been lifted from his shoulders and a dark cloud from his mind. His stomach disorder was also considerably better. In due course, his discipleship flowered and, as a lay person, he became one of the most valued officers in the diocese.

Years later, I tried to pray in the troubled pub. A succession of publicans had suffered from alcoholism, depression, and suicide. A former vicar was regularly seriously drunk, his son participated in seances in upper rooms, and employees were scared out of their wits. One man from the village came for help because he had become a compulsive liar. He said he had contacted his grandfather, who was a notorious liar, at a seance in the pub, and that his grandfather's spirit had taken him over.

One evening, I preached about the pub's problems. I thought the parishioners would think I had taken leave of my senses. But with one accord, they thanked me.

I went to speak to the present publican. He said he thought it was a load of nonsense. I said that that was the second-best solution – he was unlikely to be troubled. In fact, he did have a difficult time and died when still quite young. We took the church into the pub for Harvest Festival services and regular church dinners. The place seemed to calm down. I often wonder what it is like today.

EASTER IN ARGENTINA 2004 (EXTRACTS FROM MY DIARY)

Friday 9 April:

Arrive at conference centre. This is at Tucuman University Agriculture Centre, high in the misty hills above the city. Prayer and preparation. Beautiful place but permanently in mist or rain (probably as well as JW wasn't tempted to disappear on a hunt for "mariposas"). Everyone arrives in the late afternoon – mainly by special buses organized by the incredible English missionaries Tony and Ros. People from other churches organize children's work and do the catering (unfortunately not quite enough as there are huge queues for meals, which delay meetings. The locals are quite unphased by the delay, which is common for everything in Argentina!). Fantastic music group leads evening worship when eventually the spiritual side starts. There was a very good attendance at all meetings (possibly helped by the rain!).

Saturday 10 April:

Long day. Lots of teaching and answering of questions by JW, three seminars in the afternoon – prayer for healing and prayer ministry by Eileen and Dave; cell groups and evangelism (Tim and Annie); "Healing the Family Tree" (John and Jane) – a woman is delivered from an ancestral spirit after the meeting. In this seminar, we discover that many people have ancestral problems: compulsive gambling, adultery, general immorality and spiritualism were all rife.

In the late evening, there was a short session of teaching followed by much ministry. JW retires at midnight. Eileen and Dave struggle on to 12.30; Tim and Annie stay up half the night, drinking "mate" (the local bitter tea which is a shared drink in Argentina and a necessary social convention) with the young people.

Sunday 11 April:

(Easter Day) teaching and much prayer in the morning (some people do the rounds getting prayer from every available team). There was a lovely communion service in the afternoon. Jane organizes wild white lilies for the communion table and discovers that her father has made an extraordinary recovery (he had lapsed into unconsciousness on Good Friday and had been expected to die – he did die soon after we returned home). Many people had written out elaborate family trees and laid them on the communion table. There were some professions of faith and Family Tree ministry during the silent prayer. One woman collapsed as a spirit leaves. There was a general sense of peace and perhaps spiritual breakthrough.

We returned, exhausted but elated, to our hotel. JW manages to find the best restaurant in town, really pushing the boat out (a three-

course meal plus excellent wine) – we spend £6 each. The waiters play guitars and sing, starting with songs about the resurrection!

Hugo Vergara, the archdeacon and effective leader of the Anglican Church in northern Argentina, estimated that thirty to forty people became Christians during the Easter weekend. We saw at least five clear examples of deliverance, many as a result of Family Tree ministry. There appeared to be many healings, of which the most notable were a woman who twice testified to being blind in one eye and was now able to see normally, and another woman, paralysed down the left side as a result of a stroke, who was able to move her left leg a considerable amount, and her left hand somewhat more (her friends who brought her were amazed).

Monday 12 April and Tuesday 13 April:

Quiet days for shopping, visiting the Independence Museum, and ministry to the PCC on Monday, during which one member has a terrifying vision of the devil during silent prayer – she crashes to the ground and this opens much major and difficult ministry in family areas where she is in denial about problems. (Whoever said PCC meetings were dull?)

We have a service in the church on Tuesday night. The church is a large converted car workshop. About seventy turn up, including a number who have been brought as a result of the weekend.

Wednesday 14 April and Thursday 15 April:

We drive through the Andes, past amazing tall cacti, to a beautiful hotel. Jane and I, with Hugo and the team, celebrate our 30th wedding anniversary before we return to Salta for a final weekend of ministry.

FREEMASONRY

I always get into trouble when I raise the question of the spiritual effects of Freemasonry. Two of my great-grandparents, one a distinguished Victorian cleric and the other a distinguished surgeon in the Indian army, were prominent masons. The cleric even had a lodge named after him.

I have known many regular worshippers, and valued members of churches who were Masons. A retired brigadier, who was also a reader, had started the planned giving campaign on condition that 10 per cent was given to missions. A singularly inward-looking parish concurred. He was a prominent Mason. His widow lent me copies of some of his sermons. I accept that some Masons are good Christians but I always feel that there is a spiritual cloud hanging around them.[2]

Praying for the relatives and descendants of Masons, wives, children, and grandchildren has opened my eyes somewhat. On a number of occasions when I have prayed for such people (always at their request and under no pressure from me), there has been a surprising reaction. In at least half a dozen instances and probably more, it has been identical. As I began to pray, they have exclaimed that they felt as if they were being throttled. They needed a prayer to cut them free from what felt like an invisible noose around their necks. I am reasonably certain that *none of them knew that the first Masonic ritual* involves the candidate being blindfolded, having a rope placed around the neck and a dagger placed over the heart. I have already mentioned such a case at the end of Chapter 4.[3]

One of the more extraordinary cases that I have dealt with was that of a hard-working, committed member of a church. She was particularly gifted at helping with the down and outs. Her husband appeared to be a committed Christian and served on the PCC. The notes below (I have used them in full as I think they give a very realistic picture of how complicated, tiring, and difficult this ministry can be) are from Alison Morgan, who befriended her and did the bulk of the ministry. My own contribution appears to have been somewhat inadequate.

Ruth (name changed) came to see me last week, having asked for an appointment before Christmas, saying she would like to seek some advice. She came, and explained that her father had been ill, she prayed for him, he had not been healed, and she felt hurt by this, and was worried that it was blocking her prayer life. She had prayed about it with a friend, and had been alarmed to find herself retching as the friend prayed for her. What did I think?

Retching during prayer is a common symptom of interference by evil spirits in a person's life. I asked Ruth whether she had experienced this on any other occasion. I hoped this would help me discern whether it was an emotional response or a spiritual one. She said it happens to her sometimes after she has prayed with a group for the homeless and other disadvantaged people in the church. I know that her prayers are real and effective, and I have a great respect for her in this area of ministry. I asked whether she has any occult activity in her past or in her family's past, as this also can cause spiritual interference. She explained that she had, before becoming a Christian, been involved in spiritualism, and her mother had too. She had prayed about this, but only by herself.

I decided that the best thing to do was to make sure that this previous activity (which would have been sufficient to cause disturbances of the kind she was reporting) was properly and formally dealt with in prayer. So I asked Ruth to repeat her baptism vows (I repent of my sins, I renounce evil, I turn to Christ), and then to pray in her own words, telling God that she was sorry for her involvement with spiritualism, that she had not realized the dangers in it, and to ask his forgiveness and cleansing of her. She did this, and then I prayed for her as a minister, asking Jesus to free her from anything that was not of God and proclaiming her to be forgiven. This was uneventful, and she felt peaceful about it.

We repeated the exercise with regard to her mother and any other member of her family. She then said rather hesitantly that the only other possibility was that her husband, Edwin (name changed), was involved in Freemasonry. So I decided that we should pray briefly for him, and for protection for Ruth in any way that she needed it.

As soon as I began to pray, Ruth began to retch. She retched and coughed, and her body became very tense. She was upset by this, but obviously powerless to prevent it. I recognized these symptoms from my previous experience of praying with people in similar situations as being spiritual and not emotional. Ruth was not in control of what was happening to her, and I strongly suspected that we were dealing with the oppression or possibly presence within Ruth of an evil spirit. As I was alone with Ruth, I did not wish to continue to pray; it is standard practice to pray against such spirits only when two or more people are present, in addition to the afflicted person. So I bound anything that was oppressing Ruth in the name of Christ, and anointed her with oil as a sign of God's presence and protection. Ruth said she felt peace, and we arranged that we pray again with another person present.

Last night we met to pray with John W. I asked Ruth to explain in her own words what had happened. John asked her the same questions that I had asked her. We began to pray for her. As soon as John began to pray, Ruth began to retch. This time we continued in prayer, and Ruth retched, coughed, and went rigid. As we continued to pray for her release and healing, the spirit manifested itself within her. Ruth's face completely changed its expression. She began to speak with words that were not hers, to scowl and leer and spit, to defy us. John asked the spirit's name. She said it was called David. When you pray in this situation, you speak to the spirit directly and command it to leave, and you speak to the person by asking them to look into your eyes. This we did; it was like alternate conversations with Ruth and with the spirit. Ruth was traumatized, frightened, and deeply apologetic for behaving like this. She was aware of what the spirit was saying, and aware that it didn't like John or me. From our point of view it is like having a conversation with two people, just you see them both in the same face, alternately. We commanded the spirit to leave Ruth in the name of Jesus. It was very stubborn and for a long time it refused to go. Eventually John blessed some water and splashed it in Ruth's face, praying for her release as he did so. Ruth flopped to the ground, and it seemed that she was free. She then experienced a vision of Jesus and burst into tears that he loved her so much. She seemed very much herself at this point. Again she was deeply embarrassed and apologetic, as well as horrified and frightened at what was happening to her. We reassured her that it wasn't her fault. Ruth felt peaceful and John went home.

Ruth and I stayed in the sitting room for a while; I wanted to make sure that she was calm before sending her home. As we talked, she said that she worried about a particular case in the house which contained items associated with Freemasonry. I reassured her that a case has no power. I said that we would pray about it so that she knew there was nothing to worry about. As I was explaining how to pray against such things, Ruth began to retch again. We appeared to be back at square one. I asked my husband, Roger, to join us. We went through the same procedure. This time it was even more *violent. Ruth was thrown to the ground, her body rigid, convulsing, her arms stretched out wide in the shape of a cross, the spirit spitting defiance and saying it wouldn't go. It said it had a sword. I prayed against this sword in the name of Christ, by the power of the sword of truth which is the Word of God, and told it to drop its sword, which had no power. Ruth's arm contorted, as if she was having something wrenched from her and dropped on the ground.*

I told the spirit to tell me its name. I wanted to be sure that it was the same one and not a different one. It was the same one: David. We prayed in the name of, and by the blood of, Jesus. It writhed and defied us. It contorted and said there were angels in the room, a big white one, and a lot of others. I asked who was the angel. It said Gabriel. It didn't like it. I told it to get out and go to the foot of the cross. It said it would go into the rabbit (our pet rabbit which was in the next room). Roger told it that it would not. It protested that it liked Ruth. It said Ruth was clever. It said her husband was clever. It said it didn't want to go to hell, hell was hot. We continued to insist.

Eventually, Ruth flopped and said she was free. She, too, had seen the angels. She said that the spirit had gone into the sea. She had a picture of waves washing up to the shore at the beginning of the prayer time. This gave her assurance that God was working his purpose out – bit by bit.

We decided that she needed a cup of tea. Then we chatted about what to do next. Roger said that he needed to talk to her husband about this. Ruth was reluctant. Roger, as head of the church, insisted and Ruth agreed. Roger said that he hadn't liked it when the spirit threatened to go into the rabbit. Instantly, Ruth's face turned again to the same leer. It taunted us that there was doubt. Doubt, I thought, was how it had been able to return. Roger prayed for the gift of faith for Ruth. Again we booted it out. Ruth co-operated and this time it was much quicker. It seemed that as soon as Ruth thought about it, the spirit could return.

I asked her to look into my eyes. This time there was no response. Ruth was smiling. We breathed a sigh of relief. Then she tensed up again; but this time she herself spoke to God, and told it quietly to leave. She kicked with her foot, and said it was like a little brown dragon. It had gone. I realized that Ruth was being taught to resist this spirit herself, so that she was not dependent on us.

Roger prayed for the Holy Spirit to fill Ruth and to seal her[4] so that she would be fully protected. Ruth is now free. I feel it is vital to make sure that it has no chance of returning either to Ruth or Edwin, or any member of her family.

Fairly soon afterwards, Edwin read the lesson at a Masonic service and then decided to renounce Freemasonry. Curiously, he was able to do this without any apparent ill effects. Ruth still needed more prayer. These are her thoughts:

I thought it would be helpful for you to know my thoughts why the "job" wasn't finished at the session with Alison. From what I discern from the prayer ministry, the principal demon was dealt with at the time, but I sensed that further demons were kept quiet, for an appointed time, by Jesus' intervention at the time. When we went to Sozo,[5] part of the ministry was for Edwin to renounce the oaths he had made during his time in Freemasonry. It was during this time I sensed the demons were given a time of activity before they were finally dismissed, and all was dealt with and I was free. Freemasonry is very dark and deceptive and the oaths made are against God's Word. My thoughts are that, when a Christian relative becomes aware of the oaths and their meaning, it is then that trouble for the individual begins.

Ruth has also remembered that, during the first prayer time, I discerned that the demon was a prince (which was presumably why the prayer time was so protracted).

She added:

I thought I would mention when the dragon walked away it looked back then disappeared. I strongly believe that, for whatever reason, this all had to do with the regalia that Edwin kept in the bedroom in a long brown leather box. It contained bishop-like clothing with a hat and a sword. Edwin wore these for events at the Knights Templar lodge. I hated it as it had a smell about it.

Not long afterwards, both Ruth and Edwin accompanied me on a mission trip to Argentina. They were both a great help. We did apparently have a dramatic time of prayer when Ruth almost died of altitude sickness in the Andes! Edwin is now training to become a reader.

On another occasion, I was rung up by a Christian friend. The church at which she and her husband served wanted advice. Twin sisters, aged about thirty-five, had both had dramatic conversions. Previously, they had both been seriously involved with the occult. What should the church do? I suggested, as I usually do, that they retake their baptismal vows – beginning with as clear and specific a renunciation of evil as they could manage, followed by repentance and turning to Christ. After this, the laying on of hands and anointing with oil would probably be appropriate.

The results were surprising. One sister flourished, the other sister felt dramatically worse. She felt that she was taken over by something or someone.

After various sessions of unsuccessful ministry, a voice started to speak through her. It claimed to be that of her dead grandfather – who had been the chief Freemason in Queensland. Eventually, the spirit left and she felt fine. Soon afterwards, the sisters returned to Australia. They reported that they had found their cousins and siblings in some spiritual disarray. The negative spirituality of the prominent Freemason ancestor seemed evident.

On another occasion, I was speaking at an Anglo-Catholic Renewal conference. I didn't say much about Freemasonry. But what I said was enough to infuriate one clergy widow. She angrily took issue with me – declaring that her husband, whose faith I had never questioned, had been a Mason and a good Christian.

Five minutes later, the daughter of a Mason came to seek spiritual help. We talked over coffee. She reacted quite wildly and I conducted deliverance prayer in a crowded hall. Fortunately, it was quickly efficacious. It was interesting, but perhaps not surprising, to get two such completely different reactions in the space of such a short time.

At yet another time, some years ago, I was conducting a healing seminar at a renewal conference. A lay leader interrupted me and said that he was feeling very uncomfortable. I suggested that this might have several causes – he might be finding the whole subject troubling, I might have said something untrue or unwise, or he might be in some sort of spiritual trouble. I was at this time talking about the effect of spiritual disobedience of previous generations.

After the session, he remembered that his father had been a Mason. This led us the next morning to a time of general ministry, in which much more serious things were renounced and many people felt a new freedom. That evening, at a communion service, there was a tremendous sense of peace. The confusion experienced by the lay leader led to a deeper realization of the problems that people could face. His temporary discomfort caused many others to feel like Charles Wesley: "my chains fell off and I was free".

TESTIMONY TO MY LIFE AS THE CHILD OF A MASONIC GRANDMASTER[6]

The following is a powerful testimony from someone who has been set free from evil spirits and gradually healed from many childhood hurts:

My father was a clever engineer and toolmaker. He built a large factory and had 150 people working for him. He was a popular and attractive man and what is more he was prosperous.

I grew up, as the only child of two successful people and I was known as "the poor little rich girl". Life for me was lonely and cut off. Not for me was there any laughter or play with my parents. My memories as a little girl were seeing my father's shoes and trousers and looking up to the ceiling to look at his face. He didn't think to bend down to my level, he was too busy. My mother was really gifted. She could knit beautifully, sew the most complicated embroidery. Tailoring and making ball gowns for herself were not difficult and she really enjoyed her skills. My mother was also an accomplished pianist. I can remember as a tiny girl listening to Listen with Mother, *only my mother was busy elsewhere in the house knitting or sewing.*

At my second school I faced persecution from girls and teachers alike. Even the head teacher could not bring herself to present an award to me in front of the school. I was to receive it in her study before school day began. Every aspiration I had was smashed. Every hope of my chosen career dashed even after training for years.

I was frustrated because I knew that I had talent and skills which had not been allowed to develop. Even my piano lessons were stopped just when I was becoming interested in making a good sound and it gave me pleasure.

After leaving home I began to learn to play classical guitar and had a brilliant teacher, but just as I was developing the skills, my situation changed and I could no longer stay in the area.

My parents would take me to Masonic dinners where I would be the only young person there. I began to see that there was something about the atmosphere that I could not understand, but made me feel uncomfortable. My father was always learning words from a small book at home. He would say that he had to learn every word in it. I was not a curious child by that time so I didn't ask too many questions. My mother used to call it his "Boy Scouts".

My parents would have weekend parties at their house where they would play with a Ouija board and I would leave the house.

As a child of eight years I would take myself off to church on a Sunday morning. I later joined the Girl Guides and went to church parade. Then I became a member of the church youth club, where we would all attend Evensong. I don't remember my parents ever coming to church at all. I have since found out that my father raised an enormous amount of money for the Masonic girls' school, but sent me from the age of twelve to fifteen to the worst council school in the area. There always seemed to be a cloud over our house and our almost non-existent relationship with each other as a family. The sense of hopelessness dwelt in our house. It was an emptiness that was filled with darkness.

My mother became depressed and everything that I touched seemed to go wrong. There became a heaviness that was hard to shake off. I had no confidence but somehow, after several career disappointments, I joined an airline and began to learn to fly aeroplanes out of Biggin Hill. And I moved out of my parents' house.

I realized years later that my God in His infinite wisdom and mercy had been watching over me all this time. He had been with me all through the jungle and had hacked a path for me to tread. Flying was my freedom. My instructor seemed to know that the skills he was teaching me were more than just learning to fly. He was giving me something I had never had before. Something that I had been repeatedly told I was not able or not good enough to be trusted with.

So I became a flying instructor and made sure that I was a really good one. My father would never fly with me, which always was a disappointment as I could never prove to him that I could do something. My mother was neurotic by this time, but still gifted. She never realized that the gifts that she had were amazing.

My father then contracted cancer. It took him two years to die. I cannot remember all that happened. I remember the atmosphere being dark and sharp. I can remember fighting to be independent of my parents, and whatever it was that lived with us. My feelings were just numb. It was just like when you burn the ends of your fingers; you can't feel them for a while. I had not felt any emotions for years.

My father died at the age of fifty-six and I knew that my mother had not had much patience with his illness. They had not had a relationship for many years and I was not allowed to have a relationship with him either. At the funeral, the chapel was packed with Masons and the atmosphere was again that heavy weight of oppression.

Life had always been difficult. Nothing was joyful although I had a good sense of humour. Isn't it strange that God gives a sense of humour when everything else is unbearable! Nothing I could do for my mother was the right thing. I married and gave her three grandchildren, but she could not get interested in them very much. I think she did try, but it was just that she could only concentrate on herself in her depression.

She began to try walking into the sea to drown herself; but she was dragged out. She began taking overdoses while phoning to tell me. Her specialist at the hospital where they pumped out her stomach for the umpteenth time said that she was one of the most manipulative women he had ever met. He suggested that I take everything she said with a pinch of salt. It was ten years later that she hung herself with her mac strap from her bedroom door.

However, in the meantime I had met Jesus. How did it happen? I had just had my first child and I was attacked by a malevolent spirit and terrified. I fled to the phone. I rang my local vicar whom I knew vaguely and he came straight away. He gave me prayers to say at night and came back a few days later with another priest who specialized in such things. We had communion and I was given more prayers to say and was prayed over.

This began my long walk back to life, as I realized that over the years I had been half deadened by the evil in my family and house. The minister was faithful and saw me through the worst times.

I always like to think that I came to find the real Jesus not in the church environment, but He came to me in my home. I fought with the devil, who would come and terrorize me at any time. I would try to say the Lord's Prayer and would be stopped again and again. I would be paralysed so that I couldn't move a muscle. It was exhausting especially with a baby to feed in the night. One night at about 3 a.m., I heard children playing in a playground outside the window. It was so real that I got out of bed and went to the window to look and of course there was nothing there. I was pushed and jolted out of sleep at any hour, but I hung on to the psalms and the prayers that I had been given.

One afternoon at about 4 o'clock when I was really tired and sitting on the sofa while the baby was asleep, the evil spirit came to terrorize me yet again. I was ready but too tired to fight again, when gradually I saw with my spiritual eyes Jesus standing in front of me with His arms out as if to shield me. He was looking at the attacker with His back to me and He said, "You shall not have her, she is mine."

I have never looked back from that time to this. I have had plenty of prayer from many different people. I have sat under amazing teaching. I became a teacher in a Christian school. God has used me in healing His children too. I was a counsellor at a Billy Graham rally. I know what it is to be cleansed. I know what it is to walk in the light of Christ.

I still go for ministry as God hasn't finished with me yet. But do you know that Forgiveness is a very big word and it took years for it to have real meaning in my heart? I now walk along the journey of life with Jesus with a much lighter step and joy in my heart. There are songs and laughter because I know that Jesus is Lord and because He died for me, His father is my father, and His God is my God. He is the air I breathe.

Clearly both Freemasonry and Ouija were negative influences. The method of her mother's final, and fatal, suicide attempt has similarities with the first Masonic admission ritual (see this chapter, note 3). Most importantly, these words are a testimony to the power and presence of Jesus who said, "You will know the truth, and the truth will set you free" (John 8:32).

FRED SMITH'S MINISTRY

I often had the privilege of working with Fred (see Chapter 4, page 73). Here is an example of his effective ministry:

> *I once had a long conversation with an evil spirit when I went to see a young woman who had attempted to commit suicide. When I met the woman, I discerned through the power of the Holy Spirit guiding me, that the girl was afflicted by an evil spirit who had caused her to attempt suicide. The spirit started to speak to me, and told me that it was a familiar spirit, that it had been in both the girl's mother and grandmother, and had caused them both to commit suicide. When I commanded this thing to leave her in the name of Jesus she was set free.*[7]

My friend Pat Souter, who features unnamed as my helper in the story of the African lady who couldn't forgive (Chapter 5), and also in two meetings with angels,[8] realized at a very young age that she had an unwanted and disturbing "gift". From the age of eight, she started to see a black frame appearing around the faces of people who were close to her. She soon realized that this meant she wouldn't see them again. Her mother believed she had special powers because she was the seventh child of a seventh child.

At the age of fifteen, Pat became a Christian. The problem with the "black frames" greatly lessened but didn't disappear.

Sometime after her marriage to Nick, she saw the black frame around two of her husband's aunts and two of her own grandparents. This all happened within the space of two months.

> *I realized I needed to pray and I asked Nick to pray with me. I renounced evil and offered the gift to the Lord to do with as He will. Nick took the sword of the Spirit and cut me free from my mother's generational line. Nick told the enemy he had no authority over me and to go to the place that Jesus has prepared for him. We asked*

the Holy Spirit to fill me and to give me one of His gifts in place of the psychic gift; I believe He has given me a gift of knowledge. I mentioned the black frames to my sister when our father was ill with motor neurone disease – she had been telling me of her experiences of astral travel from about the age of eight, and my brother's experience of astral travel[9] from the age of ten. I soon had a call from our mother telling me to ask for the psychic gift back. I said, no, I didn't want it. Mum said I could use it to help people. I said, "No, I don't want it. I didn't ask for it in the first place and I want nothing to do with it." Mum wanted me to tell her when I saw a black frame around my dad, but I said that it didn't happen any more.

I find this story very persuasive and instructive. The psychic ability was clearly travelling down the generations. Pat's mother didn't want her to renounce it but to use it. This seems to be a normal attitude for those with psychic abilities, who seem to want them to continue in future generations. This rather begs the question of how such a "gift" could be useful.

It is important to realize that Pat's psychic ability didn't disappear when she became a Christian. Presumably at the time, she wasn't asked to make any clear renunciation of such matters and so, although less evident, they remained until her husband used his spiritual authority to deal with them. Her prayer to be filled with the Holy Spirit appears to have been abundantly answered and, despite a long struggle with ill health, she has been greatly used to pray with and counsel other people.

It is difficult to offer any explanation except for the obvious one – dangerous psychic abilities can, and usually do, travel down the spiritual DNA from one generation to another. These last two stories are very clear examples of the need for generational healing from unwanted, and unasked for, psychic experiences.

Years ago, I went to a very smart dance where I spent some time with the daughter of a local MP. Much later, she wrote a book, which became the source for a very moving article in *The Times*. She was a GP who knew that she was dying of cancer. Her family, through several generations, had been afflicted by a genetic strain of cancer, manic depression, and suicide. Despite all this, her family were strong Christians exhibiting great courage. The doctor's book[10] was an example of all this. I cannot help but feel that a generational healing service might have reduced their pain and suffering considerably. Perhaps they had one. I am sure that they had much prayer and support. Her family, despite all the handicaps, seem to have achieved far more in their relatively short lives than most of us can come near to attaining.

Another example: I grew up near the family home of the Earls of Craven in Hampstead Marshall, near Newbury. The main house had burnt down in Victorian times and the family was reputed to be under a curse from a villager, who had been made pregnant by an earl many centuries earlier. The curse stated that each eldest son would die before his mother. Be that as it may, successive earls died young. One recently committed suicide and his brother, who succeeded him, was killed in a traffic accident soon afterwards.

When I was slightly involved in a Christian drugs rehabilitation centre, I met the sister of one of the earls, who was professing faith and now seeking to help others be free from addiction. She married the son of a friend. Unfortunately that marriage didn't last. The Cravens would seem to be another family that would benefit from generational healing.

I include these last two examples to underline my plea to take this underused aspect of Christian ministry more seriously. It is invariably beneficial, not just for obvious issues like psychic problems, but also in much more mundane matters. Just as doctors have learnt so much about effective treatment from knowledge of DNA, I believe the church could relieve a great deal of suffering by a better understanding of generational healing – which is based on exploring spiritual DNA.

Generational healing services

(1) We need to establish whether or not such a service will be appropriate. Sometimes when people come for prayer, there seems to be a deeper issue lurking beneath the surface. They talk about family issues, irrational behaviour by themselves or others, deep depression, suicidal tendencies, psychic experiences, and the like.

Something within me reacts. I ask a few questions about their family history and usually strange memories emerge. Sometimes they are adopted, or they have adopted seemingly disturbed children and don't know much about the background.

I am particularly concerned about any occult or psychic "gifting"; past suicides, murders or abortions; hereditary habits such as adultery, gambling, violence, excessive anger, sexual irregularity, alcoholism; hereditary illnesses, especially depression or migraine. Serious medical conditions such as cancer, Huntington's chorea, or motor neurone disease are often, in some cases always, hereditary. At this stage, I often suggest a generational healing service. My normal procedure is to spend an hour, or longer, discussing the issues, explaining the procedure, and getting them to draw up their family tree back, if possible, to their great-grandparents. I also ask them to highlight any obvious problems.

I try to emphasize that we are not making spiritual judgments about their ancestors, but we are concerned with any negative effects that their lives, or lifestyle, may be having on their descendants. I mention too that we can also inherit very positive benefits, as indicated by Psalm 103:17. I explain this with the simple idea: "We are looking at your spiritual DNA."

When making the family tree, it is helpful to mark with a * any negative experiences (for example, Grandfather Henry Fuller * compulsive gambler who committed suicide). Obviously, if a person is adopted (see below) they may have little knowledge of their ancestry.

(2) I then explain that, at a later date, we will hold a simple communion service. They are welcome to bring a friend or a family member. I hope to have someone else present who doesn't know them who can listen for words of knowledge or ask intuitive questions. We also discuss who else in their family might want/need to be present. I emphasize that we will also be praying for their siblings and descendants.

The service will be quite informal.[11] It may last up to an hour and a half. There will be a lengthy time of confession and a sharing of the peace. After the sharing of the bread and wine, there will be prayer, including the laying on of hands and possibly anointing with oil. At some stage, I will formally destroy their family tree as a sign that they have been freed from any generational problems.

I do tell them that they may be very reluctant to go through with the service and that during the service, if they have any strange feelings or insights, they should share them. The service itself I will usually conduct unrobed, in the quietness of my home. There will be plenty of silence and time for them to ask questions, or to share any additional recollections or feelings.

Where the person or one of their parents has been adopted, the service will inevitably involve some "provisional" prayers. One person who had been adopted told me that, as a small child, he had prayed in strange tongues. I prayed that if his natural parents had been involved in some psychic activity, this would be cut off from his family line.

I think we cannot overemphasize the importance of the cross: "And having disarmed the powers and authorities, he made a public spectacle of them, triumphing over them by the cross" (Colossians 2:15). This is the essence of, and the foundation for, all the ministry of deliverance.

(3) I am constantly surprised by both how necessary and how pastorally effective such services seem to be. The low-key nature of the Anglican service is very helpful. The results are seldom dramatic but often surprising. A young mother feels freed from the effects of probable ritual satanic abuse; a new clergyman is completely freed from a plague of boils which has been debilitating and even possibly life-threatening; an ordinand is released from a severe depression and gets engaged soon afterwards; two adopted children start behaving far more normally; a man who has several recent ancestors who have committed suicide sees release from such thoughts in his family after a service...

My fervent hope is that the church will offer this ministry very widely. It has a scriptural base, the sober, dignified liturgy of the Anglican Church, which lessens the spiritual tension and, in my experience, it is always beneficial. Usually, the person who has been prayed for is more than happy for their own parish priest to be contacted. Often he (or she) will have been involved before and during the service.

A fine hymn about healing and renewal contains the verse:

Come, Holy Spirit, to cleanse and renew us:
Purge us from evil and fill us with power:
Thus shall the waters of healing flow through us;
So shall revival be born in this hour.[12]

Generational healing is all about cleansing and renewal; it will purge people, their relatives, and their descendants from evil, and will bring a real measure of renewal into families. The testimonies in this chapter bear witness to this essential truth.

CHAPTER 7

HIGH PLACES AND HAUNTED HOUSES

Wherever God erects a house of prayer, the Devil always builds a chapel there.

(Daniel Defoe, "The True-Born Englishman")

In England, most requests for help in these matters concern problems with buildings not people. Theologically, this raises an issue. Demonization of people is a fairly common feature in the Bible; haunting, or other forms of spiritual disturbance in buildings, do not seem to feature. My first such request came some years after my first encounters with troubled people.

Troubled stables

This account was written for me by the late Anne Goode. She became a great friend, partly as a result of what she recounts:

I had just moved to Somerset. We had bought an overpriced, attractive eighteenth-century building, which was immediately opposite the site of an annual pop festival which was growing in international importance. I was aware of an atmosphere of menace which was affecting my family. My academically brilliant husband began behaving oddly, displaying signs of early dementia; my musically gifted son was being bullied at school; my daughter spent all her time like a ghost child, pale and withdrawn, in the stables; and I was prone to uncontrollable outbursts of rage which upset the whole family.

In spiritual and emotional disarray, I sought the help of John Woolmer whose recently published book, Growing up to Salvation, contained a chapter about the occult which I read with surprise and relief. During prayer, which included the laying on of hands, I experienced liquid light flowing through my whole body. I found that I was totally free of the dark fear which had gripped every area of my life. Problems within the house still needed dealing with, but I was no longer afraid and family life improved. The church began to use the house for staff days, but I sensed that the house needed deeper ministry than the simple blessing that had been given to it.

After the mysterious death in the field of one of my daughter's horses, John decided, during a staff day, to perform a full-scale exorcism of the whole premises, complete with a large jug of holy water (water that had been set aside by prayer for this purpose). My daughter and I were particularly troubled by unpleasant graffiti on the stable walls which seemed to imply somewhat sinister use by previous occupants. I felt that the evil presence had been around the buildings for a long time.

The staff team eventually gathered around the stable which had been previously occupied by the dead horse, and they stood in a semi-circle. John entered the stables, prayed in tongues, and tipped half a jug of water on the straw, commanding any evil presence to leave in the name of Jesus. One of the staff members, not used to this sort of thing, visibly jumped backwards and described how a huge force leaving the stables seemed to hit him at the moment of the prayer.

The results of the prayer were beneficial. Visitors, and there are many of them, invariably comment on the peace and beauty of the place.

I had prayed with some reluctance. I wasn't sure about the theology of praying for buildings. But the staff at the cathedral where, at that time, Anne worshipped were exceedingly reluctant to get involved. This resulted in her joining our church in Shepton Mallet. Soon afterwards, we started holding staff away days in her delightful old house in Pilton. One of her closest neighbours was Michael Eavis, with whom she had a love–hate relationship. She liked him as a person but objected strongly to the Glastonbury festival, which actually took place in Pilton opposite her house. She disliked the intense disruption to the village and also some of the healing offered which, she felt (correctly, I think) bordered on the occult. I think it is fair to say that, in its early days, the festival encouraged a lot of New Age activity.

I remember approaching the prayer time with some scepticism. Blessing and cleansing the house was one thing – but the stables? Did they really need deliverance? "Don't horses always have problems?" was one of my less enthusiastic comments.

To be honest, I prayed with rather less authority and considerably less faith than Anne has indicated in her generous account. The use of "holy" water is quite normal in such circumstances.[1] The power and the clear presence of the expelled spirit amazed us all – not least my wonderful colleague Albert Bushell, no small man, who never forgot the experience.

I never did examine the graffiti on the stable walls. I gathered that it hinted at some pretty unpleasant activities in the stables.

Years later, Albert testified about this experience to a friend who was making a documentary. My friend also interviewed the then leader of the Leicester Diocesan Deliverance Team who said (to my mind, incredibly) that every situation he had been asked to investigate turned out to have a natural, rational explanation. He cited creaking floorboards caused by faulty heating systems and the like. Personally, almost every situation that I have been asked about appears to have had a genuine psychic problem, although I haven't always discovered a reason for the trouble.

About ten years after the stable incident, there was a sequel. Anne's husband had died. She had moved, as people often do, into a different bedroom. She was now suffering from terrifying nightmares. Once again, she asked me to pray.

We went into the room and I placed my Bible on the bed. It fell open at the end of the book of Nehemiah. Now, Nehemiah is one of my favourite books; I love the early chapters – great examples of prayer, courage, and spiritual warfare. But I confess I have always found the end of the book rather dull. On this occasion, I was drawn to chapter 13:4–9, which tells how Nehemiah returned from a visit to Babylon to find that his arch enemy, Tobiah, had set himself up in a room of the courts of the House of the Lord. Nehemiah unceremoniously threw all his furniture out of the room and had it cleansed (a strong Hebrew word, "taher", as we shall see).

Feeling a bit foolish, I asked Anne if she had any furniture belonging to the previous owners, who appeared to have caused the trouble in the stables. To my surprise, she replied that the bedside table and the carpet had belonged to them. I ordered their removal, prayed a prayer of cleansing for the room, and she had no more nightmares!

Years later, I noticed that a few verses earlier, it is recorded that, during the great celebrations of the dedication of the restored wall of Jerusalem, "the Levites purified themselves, and they purified the people and the gates and the wall" (Nehemiah 12:30, ESV).

I think that the purification of the gates is highly significant. When Joshua pronounced a curse on any future rebuilding of Jericho (Joshua 6:26), he said that the rebuilding of the foundations and the gates would each cost the builder a son. This happened in the reign of the notorious King Ahab (1 Kings 16:34). It was well known that the Canaanites used to sacrifice children when laying the foundations of a city gate.[2] Perhaps Nehemiah felt that the pre-Davidic city had been similarly set up. He was ensuring that the restored city would be purified in a much more spiritually acceptable way.

Father Luke Bell, who at one time was the Catholic priest at Shepton Mallet, recalls prayer in Anne's grounds:

> *I remember celebrating the Eucharist with the Catholic exorcist on the hill in Anne Goode's property overlooking the happening Glastonbury Festival, and him getting a stinging in his hands as he prays exorcism over the festival.*

I had a strangely similar experience to Father Luke's nearby.

Someone reported signs of witchcraft activity in a local disused quarry. I investigated this with a respected Catholic exorcist, Father Luke, and the Bath and Wells Diocesan Advisor for the Paranormal.[3] We quickly discovered a stone pentacle set clearly on some ground where there had been fires. The two leaders cleansed the altar and said that anyone who tried to reuse it would get an unpleasant surprise.

We also visited a nearby disused railway tunnel. The Catholic exorcist said that he could sense a great deal of evil. He was sure that the tunnel was used as a place to induct leading satanists. As we prayed, I put my hand above a niche in the wall. I got a terrible shock, similar to one I had received years earlier when I touched the deformed hand of a woman I was praying for. I don't normally feel things but, on this occasion, the sense of an evil power was overwhelming.

It would be nice to report that a spiritual revival in the area followed, but I have to say that things continued much as before. I guess we were only scratching the surface of the problem.

Place memories

Sometimes memories from the very distant past seem to affect buildings. Once, I prayed in a room where a teenage girl claimed she had seen, on several occasions, a fully-clad Roman soldier on her bed – this would seem highly fanciful except for the coincidental fact that she lived in a house built very close to an ancient Roman road, which runs from Lincoln to Exeter via Shepton Mallet and is called the Fosse Way. About ten years earlier, there had been a redevelopment of the land. Skeletons of a large number of Roman citizens of the fourth century were uncovered, taken for forensic analysis, and eventually reburied in the local churchyard.

On another occasion in Papua New Guinea, I was speaking at the biennial conference of the Wycliffe Bible Translators. This was a particular joy as it enabled Jane to revisit Dogura where she served as a VSO, and me to revisit the wonderful PNG Lepidoptera – with the glorious green Birdwings and fabulous Mountain Blue Swallowtails.

The conference took place in Ukarumpa, which is a large missionary village where SIL had had their headquarters for some years. I mentioned some experiences of dealing with evil spirits – which I assumed many of the missionaries would be all too familiar with. It was one of my happiest speaking times and led to a huge amount of personal prayer with the delegates, and some remarkable testimonies about angels for the book I was just completing.[4]

Towards the end of our stay, I was called to the house of a missionary. They were living in a modern house built, with three storeys, into the side of a hill. Their two teenage children had bedrooms on the lowest floor, which would have been below ground level in the past. The missionaries spent most of their time far away in a small village – translating the Scriptures into a local dialect. The house seemed well-ordered and in a quiet location.

Their son and daughter attended the mission school on the mission station. The daughter had had a troubled time. The previous year, her best friend had been expelled and she had been in some considerable trouble. She had been quite questioning about the Christian faith, although her attitude appeared to be softening. She seemed highly intelligent and attractive.

I think she must have attended one of my talks where I had mentioned this type of problem. Unexpectedly, she had admitted to her parents that she had been frightened by strange presences in her bedroom, which had occurred regularly over a period of at least eight years. She agreed that they should ask for help to cleanse the house. Their younger teenage son also, somewhat reluctantly, said that from time to time he, too, had been troubled.

A number of us prayed throughout the house and sensed God's presence and peace. One of her teachers said she was sure that something had left the house. I was glad to have been asked to help and hoped we had done enough to clear the building. The whole process was no different from cleansings and blessings that I have undertaken in England. There are, in my opinion, no cultural differences displayed by the forces of darkness.

Shortly afterwards, the daughter who had been struggling with her faith for a number of years made her first clear profession of commitment to Jesus. She emailed her parents who had returned to their village. She said she had become a Christian. Very soon afterwards, she was baptized in the local river. A few years later, she was married to the son of one of the other missionaries. I don't know, but I wouldn't be surprised if they are now involved in the translation work.

While I cannot be certain, I am inclined to think that the house was built on a place where there had been fierce fighting – probably involving death and cannibalism. SIL were given the land by the

Australian government who couldn't sort out the territorial claims of two rival tribes.

The daughter knew of other pupils who had been involved with Ouija boards (yes, such things can happen even on mission stations!). She said she had never done anything like that and I am sure that the presence in her bedroom was in no way brought about by her behaviour and had no connection with her troubled school life. Her transformation was remarkable. But such things are not uncommon when supernatural problems are released. People who experience the dark side are well able to recognize the reality of the light when it surrounds them. When something is released, they often turn to Christ with great enthusiasm and commitment.

A few days later, our local driver took us to visit his village. As we arrived, he said rather quietly, "By the way, my grandfather knew the taste of human flesh." I thought, as I often think, that the missionaries and the Christian gospel have done rather more good for many people than they are usually credited with.

Over the years, I have visited many other houses where the occupants were troubled by strange phenomena. They always seemed relieved to discover that *they were not alone in having this sort of trouble*. Usually there was some reason of the type that I have indicated in the preceding stories. Invariably, peace to the building and to the residents came after a few visits.

Occasionally, I could find no sort of spiritual explanation, but prayer still brought peace and harmony. Here is an example:

A distraught factory manager

A small factory set on an industrial estate in a city had recently changed hands. The new manager was making medical equipment with a small but dedicated staff. They were being distracted and frightened by a number of phenomena. These included strange smells, particularly of cigarette smoke (smoking was forbidden in the factory), people hearing footsteps, especially on a staircase, inexplicable electrical failures, and a large girder crashing to the ground, which had seemed securely attached.

One night, when the manager was alone in the factory, a door set on a security code was opened. When the manager went to investigate, he found no sign of anyone. Although very sceptical about any supernatural cause, he was sufficiently disturbed to call up the diocesan office and ask for help. There was also said to be a sense of evil and darkness in parts of the factory. Workmen who had come in to do electrical jobs had been terrified. They had refused to carry on working. One employee was particularly sensitive and had been bothered by a whole series of disturbing events.

The previous owner had mentioned that he was having trouble in his new workplace. There was another factory within a quarter of a mile where I discovered that similar things had happened a few years earlier.

We couldn't find any explanation. The factory I had been called to was built where there had previously been fields, and although I felt the previous owner might have contributed to the atmosphere this seemed an insufficient explanation. The troubles seemed to be a mixture of childish misbehaviour and something more sinister. It took three sessions of prayer, culminating with a communion service on the factory floor, to bring calm and peace. The communion service was attended by the managing director and the employee who had been particularly sensitive to all the problems. A year later, all was reported to be peaceful and the business to be doing well.

Sometimes, I cannot find any explanation for troubles. On these occasions, we have to be glad that peace has been restored and not worry about the reasons for the original disturbances.

My friend Robin Martin was vicar of Thurmaston, on the north-eastern edge of Leicester, from 1985 to 2005. He remembers being called into a factory in his parish:

The owner/manager employed about seven female staff. They made ladies' garments. Everyone was complaining that something was "not quite right". I went, accompanied by the current Diocesan Advisor. We said some brief prayers. A few days later, the owner rang to say things had got worse. As no one else was available, I returned armed with some holy water. I came to a small room which was said to be the source of the trouble. I stood outside the door and said a prayer as I sprinkled some water. I can only describe what happened as that, suddenly "something unpleasant" rushed past

the right hand side of my head. I enquired a couple of times after
that to be told that all was now calm.[5]

About the same time, I was asked to pray in some offices near St Margaret's Church in the centre of Leicester. The building was built on part of St Margaret's cemetery. The top floor seemed to have the most problems. The drawers of the filing cabinet used by the managers kept opening on their own. Some people were very frightened, others unconcerned.

The toilets had problems too. Some people could hear voices in them and a couple of Indian ladies were frightened to go to the toilet because they thought they had seen a "white, funny shape", which appeared in front of them. One cleaner, a lady who I knew to be sensitive to these sorts of things, felt something push her when she was in the cleaning cupboard.

Some of the staff played regularly with Ouija boards. This probably contributed to the atmosphere. However, I suspect the main problem was the siting of the office above the graveyard. After prayer things seemed to quieten down.

More troubled houses

Many people seem to suffer spiritual disturbance in their homes. One family living in a small, quiet Somerset hamlet were total unbelievers in the supernatural. But several people had heard footsteps on a now non-existent staircase, as well as doors opening and closing for no reason. As a result they were quite frightened. When I went to visit the house, the owners were being visited by relations who lived in Africa. The relations were not at all surprised by the situation. They said, "Anyone who lives in Africa is likely to believe!" This was very helpful and meant that we entered the prayer time with much more understanding and faith.

It turned out that, over a hundred years ago, a mother who lived in the house had died quite young. Her son, who lived with her, was so distraught that he attempted to extricate her body from the grave, which was in the nearby churchyard. He was carted off to an asylum. Prayers said for him and his mother to be at peace quickly restored sanity to the household.

In another disturbed house, there had been an early and unexpected death and various other strange happenings. Three nearby houses had also suffered premature deaths – all of men in their fifties. We found a well in the garden, which was very close to the other properties, in which the body of a man, probably in his fifties, had been discovered. It would have been difficult to fall down this well by accident. We concluded that the deceased person in the well was probably a victim of murder, as suicide didn't seem likely. As we prayed just above the well, the local vicar heard a hissing sound, and it seems that peace was restored.

In a town house, a pregnant woman was aware of a sinister presence at the top of the stairs. She had only just moved in, but her husband felt no such problems. I did some investigations and found out that about ten years earlier, the female owner had been murdered at the top of the stairs by a schizophrenic lodger.

I took a gifted friend with me to the house – Jordan Ling, who is now an Anglican vicar in Bristol. I said, "Obviously there's a problem or I wouldn't have brought you here. Walk round the house and tell me what you think."

About ten minutes later, she reported sensing three things – first, that the house was very unfriendly to women; secondly, that something had happened on the landing; thirdly, that there was a small room next to the landing which had problems. The first two statements were obviously true, and we concluded that the third room had probably been used, by either the owner or the lodger, for some strange spiritual activities. After prayer, the whole situation calmed down.

Sometime later, I met another family who used to live in the house and had now returned there. They reported that they had had no strange encounters, but that one of their young children had complained of seeing someone on the stairs. This is not surprising. Some people are much more sensitive than others. There is often a problem when one person (usually the wife) has to explain what she is feeling to a sceptical partner who is not sensitive.

My friend Jordan also helped me pray through an old house belonging to someone in my own family. They had experienced a series of inexplicable floods and also a series of practical problems. Their son, aged about two, had seen a man in the downstairs room.

He went to look for him behind the curtain. The next morning, he went to the same curtains and said, "Man gone!"

While we were praying, we were being watched by a pair of Brazilian cleaners, who only came to the house once a fortnight. At the end, they told me their story. They said that they knew about the man. They had been to this house sometime before they started cleaning there. Now they could remember. Apparently, the previous owner had asked for some friends of theirs to get rid of a ghost, and they had been asked to help! It was a strange confirmation that there really was a problem. Since then things have improved – the house has quietened and the practical problems have largely disappeared.

Very recently, I went to a house in a nearby village. There, with the local vicar, I met three troubled ladies. The owner, aged about seventy, was very worried because her husband was in hospital recovering from a serious heart operation. She was being visited by her daughter and granddaughter. A number of strange things had taken place. That morning, they had come down to the living room to find all the cushions scattered around the floor. They had tidied up the mess and gone to have breakfast in the kitchen. The granddaughter finished first. It was suggested that she went into the living room and watched TV. She left the kitchen – and they heard her scream.

When they entered the living room, all the cushions had been scattered for a second time. After some questioning, it emerged that the daughter and granddaughter were both aware of these kinds of happenings. They had had troubles in the house they were living in on the edge of Dartmoor. It also appeared that the deceased mother of the grandfather who was in hospital was a bit psychic. I was of the opinion that she (the deceased great-grandmother) was worried about her son and was drawing attention to herself. We prayed and, as far I know, everything quietened down. I also encouraged the daughter to get in touch with her local vicar and get her own house blessed.

Another time, in one of my former parishes, a distraught man called because he and his partner had seen apparitions and claimed to have taken a video of things moving around his bedroom. He never managed to show me the video, and it became clear that his problem was mainly due to alcohol. If there were psychic disturbances, it was his personality that was the cause. It would have been easy to waste a lot of time listening to someone who had no real desire to change! The house, however, was in a curious place. In the garden, there was an entrance to a cave, which ran deep under the Mendips. I did not wish to speculate on what might have taken place there in times past, or even times present.

By contrast, another family called me to a farmhouse where they were aware of tobacco and experiencing some other strange happenings. No one in the family smoked. It turned out that the previous owner, who was a strong smoker, had committed suicide. After prayers, and a household communion service, everything became quiet. The family were particularly grateful as they needed to move and, prior to the service, no one would even consider buying the house. They made a satisfactory sale soon afterwards. I think I ought to have asked for a commission for the church! Needless to say, unlike many psychic organizations, we make no charge for these services.

One of my more bizarre visits was to a recently bereaved man, aged about sixty. He was experiencing a number of strange occurrences – white feathers, which he showed me, were randomly appearing around the house, a mirror had spontaneously shattered, and a number of electrical appliances were exploding. Not surprisingly, the man was somewhat bewildered and frightened. Then he mentioned that his wife's ashes were kept in a vase on the mantelpiece in the sitting room. Nothing would persuade him to bury them properly.

Despite being alarmed by the psychic experiences, he also felt comforted by them – surely they were a sign of his wife's continuing presence? I, together with a friend who was our parish worker, visited him several times. We tried to explain that the phenomena might be a sign of his wife's displeasure! Nothing would persuade him and eventually we had to give up. Ashes certainly need to be buried reverently.

Around the same time, I had another saga about ashes. The neighbours of a friend were going through an acrimonious split. After leaving the family home, with the prospect of divorce looming, the husband also left his father's ashes buried at the bottom of the garden. This was much against the wishes of his wife and eldest son, who became very fearful about the possibility that "the spirit" of the dead man could still influence their lives. The wife had, several times, experienced a psychic presence in the house, and I think in the local school (see page 146). These were cleared up by the prayers of their neighbours. Her aunt had been a medium, which probably contributed to her spiritual sensitivity.

When he was alive, the father-in-law/grandfather had been angry and dominating. He had frequently displayed an unpleasant nature. The family who remained in the house became very fearful. This was not helped by the very acrimonious departure of the husband/father. There was no way he could have been consulted about his father's ashes. Like his father, he was prone to bursts of rage. He would have become even angrier at any suggestion of removing the ashes.

Bearing in mind the fear and trepidation of the wife and son, a close Christian friend was willing to dig up the ashes for them in the darkness of night. The ashes were then removed and placed in a box. With the help of a sympathetic local minister who was known to the family, they were then placed reverently within a church building. After further prayer in the garden, the family felt both relieved and at peace. Sometime afterwards, they moved away. If the ex-husband ever demanded the ashes, they knew where they were kept and they could be handed over to him.

The result of all this was that the wife, who had been prayed for over many years, became a Christian. Her son also became a committed believer. This illustrates the evangelistic potential which arises when these psychic concerns are taken seriously.

After the end of the First World War, my Aunt Hilda (an incredibly truthful and straightforward lady with no interest in psychic matters) went to play tennis at a house in Yorkshire called Burton Agnes Hall. It poured with rain. The tennis party retreated to the library and started a practice called "table turning". It used to be fashionable and is, I think, similar to Ouija. My aunt was horrified. She was afraid they would try to contact her beloved brother[6] who had been killed a few years earlier at the Battle of the Somme. After a few minutes, the library table took off and crashed into a wall. The table turning ceased. Everyone was suitably chastened. Burton Agnes is a notoriously haunted house, which features a so-called screaming skull that has a long history of causing problems! The psychic energy generated by the table turning was hardly surprising, particularly in such a venue.

We had a number of problem houses in my parish in Somerset. One family complained of icy coldness in one bedroom. Their children refused to sleep in the room. I discovered that the house, a very recent building, had been built on land which had been used in past centuries to bury murderers and suicides. After prayer, things improved, and the family eventually moved away.

I was somewhat chagrined some time later when there was a headline in the local paper about a family who "had been driven out of a haunted house". The next family hadn't sought help – preferring just to get out. I was surprised that the prayers were only efficacious for the first set of occupants.

Our retired local doctor and his wife, who had experienced healing from a very bad back and tinnitus, told me that they had lived for a short time in a house just outside the parish. They said it was definitely haunted and that their dog absolutely refused to enter one of the rooms. This is not uncommon. Dogs seem to be strangely sensitive to unwanted spiritual presences and are quite a good litmus paper test that a building is free from trouble!

Another former parishioner, who arrived in our church in deep disarray on Christmas Eve in 1999, wrote:

I had been through a period of several months of life change ordeals. I had spent six in an acute mental health unit after trying to commit suicide several times during a period of depression, my marriage of more than twenty years was over, I lost my job, the company that I owned and my house. Sometime later, I was still being treated with medication for the depression and I was trying to cope with all the other issues in my life.

I had moved into a flat in an old house, built in 1762, which was overlooked by the high walls of the ancient prison. And I was having problems. These occurred mainly at night. There was a sense of an overwhelming presence in the room. It felt as if someone was in the room always to the right side of my bed and slightly behind me. I did not feel it to be evil or of the Lord, just neutral, and just being there as if it belonged and I didn't.

John visited me. He prayed for me and also for the room. He told the presence to go. I felt nothing at the time but had undisturbed nights, for about a week. There was no longer any feeling of the

142

presence. Then it returned. At first, it seemed weak. Then it got stronger and regular.

John came back with Chris Tookey, who was the official Diocesan Advisor about the paranormal. He prayed in a differing style. His approach was more akin to the healing of the presence than commanding it to depart. Again I felt nothing, but he suddenly turned and placed his hand on me. It was like a dull thud going through my body as he blessed me. I was standing by the door to the bedroom. Just after he blessed me, I felt something pass to my left and out through the door. There was no sense of anger or love from the presence – just a sense of something clammy.

Following that episode, I never experienced any further visitations of any type. However, I did not feel any change within myself.

In sharing my testimony with others, I learnt several things I had been completely unaware of. Chloe Baker, a leading member of the Methodist church, had been a regular visitor to the main house. She was helping someone with literacy problems. Chloe said she always felt something was wrong in the house and felt very uneasy. She continually repeated the Lord's Prayer while entering and leaving the building. I learnt, from another tenant, that drug dealers had been in the next flat. I also discovered that my flat had been lived in by someone who used to have sessions with a Ouija board.

Around the same time, my curate, who was also a prison chaplain, mentioned that both he and the Catholic chaplain felt there was an oppressive spiritual atmosphere in the prison. We knew that, during the war, a number of American soldiers had been executed within the prison walls.

I met up with the Abbot of Downside and the two chaplains. We climbed the church tower. We were now overlooking the ancient prison. We prayed prayers for the freedom and release of evil presences. Then, during the lunch hour, we walked quietly around the prison. We concentrated our prayers beside the wall, where the prisoners were known to have been shot. Both chaplains recorded that they thought there was a considerable improvement in the atmosphere within the prison.

Troubled places

Another strange echo from the past was probably created by the St John's Stone in north Leicester. This stone stood directly two miles north of the ancient ruins of Leicester Abbey. Apparently it was a place where people would gather for various types of illicit and romantic practices on St John's Day, which was also midsummer night. The stone had crumbled away in Victorian times. However, old photographs exist and local maps state where it was situated.

I found that there was a school built close to the site, and various houses had been built exactly where the stone had stood. A number of staff and pupils at the school reported seeing apparitions. Some local young people, including the son of a member of our church, heard trains when they used to play in the grounds. One of the staff also remarked, "When I used to lock up, I used to hear laughter and footsteps running along the top corridor. I could find no one in school."

We used the school as a place of worship for an experimental church. My friend and another lady said they could sometimes see the face of a devil on the white communion cloth.

I also met a woman in the local pub who lived in one of the houses built where the stone had been. She said that she was very psychic, and frightened. She also, as others had done in the past, claimed that my eyes were too bright for her to look at. Sadly, she refused my offer of help. After we had quietly prayed both in the school and the area where the stone had stood, we heard of no further problems.

Another local area that was troubled was where a new estate had been built on the site of an isolation hospital. This place obviously had many tragic memories. A number of residents, including those of the Hindu faith, asked for help. Several Hindus implied that they thought Jesus was more effective than their gods.

Still another account of a troubled place was given to me by David MacGeoch, a former member of my congregation in Shepton Mallet, now Vicar of Glastonbury:

A few years ago three houses were rebuilt over a medieval extended churchyard from St John's Glastonbury. A young woman came to see me saying I was the last resort, as she had tried many other spiritual mediums to rid the family of a presence in the house that was mischievous. Please would I come round and rid them of this because their eight-year-old was struggling in the house. I went round to see them and could feel something in this young boy's bedroom. It felt as though a sprit had become dislodged from the distant past due to new foundations being built of this house. I did what I usually do in these circumstances and took some water, blessed it, and then blessed the family and the home. I then went into this particular bedroom, broke bread, said several times the Lord's Prayer, and then asked the spirit in the name of the Father, Son and Holy Spirit to leave this house. I sensed it leave, and I then reassured the family and said I would contact them in a week's time.

When I did contact the family, they said that all was now settled in the house and they thanked me very much. I didn't give this much more thought after this. Several months later, I got a phone call from a very upset lady saying that pictures kept moving in her house for no particular reason, please could I come and visit. I took down the address and realized that it was the next door house to the one I visited several months before. I went to see them feeling slightly sceptical about all this. When I arrived, I noticed the house I had originally visited was empty and up for sale. I obviously told the family nothing about next door, but they told me that the neighbours never settled in their house. I carried out the same prayers and blessing as I had before and asked the spirit to leave. I spoke to the family after a week, who again said all was now well...

After a few more months I received a call from the last of the three houses, telling me that pictures were moving on a regular basis for no reason at all. I went round within a few hours of speaking with the family. I blessed them and the house with water, broke bread – and then realized what I had done. You guessed it: I was making this spirit move from one house to the next.

This time, I opened all windows and doors and told the spirit that he could now go back to the ground from where he came and that no more building disturbance would take place. There have not been any further developments in these houses or anywhere near.

It seems significant that the spirits were attached to their location, and simply moved from one house to another (strikingly similar to the deliverance in Fortaleza recorded on page 229). Glastonbury is a notoriously psychic place and certainly one which attracts all manner of weird, and dangerous, healing practices (see Chapter 5, page 88).

What are we to make of all of this?

Three main explanations are usually offered for these strange situations in buildings – place memories, unquiet dead, and misuse of the building (or territory) for occult purposes. The Old Testament gives many examples of "high places" where false cults were practised and led the Israelites astray, which had to be cleansed by action of prophets or kings.

There are no examples in Scripture of place memories remotely similar to the story above of the Roman soldier in the bedroom. Nor are there any convincing stories of the unquiet dead. The strange account of Saul visiting the Witch of Endor (see 1 Samuel 28) has puzzled theologians as wise as St Augustine. No one seems sure if the spirit that the witch called up was really the prophet Samuel or an evil entity pretending to be him. One thing is certain, the outcome was disastrous for King Saul and he would have been far wiser not to enquire of a witch!

Augustine wrote:

> it may be, that spirits of the dead do know something of the events on earth. The Spirit of God decides what they need to know, and who needs to know about things past, or present, or even future. The prophets knew some of these matters, but only those which the providence of God chose to reveal to them. Scripture testifies that some of the dead are sent to the living (just as Paul went from the living to Paradise). Samuel, who died, appeared to Saul, and predicted his death. Although some think that it wasn't Samuel "but some evil spirit purporting to be Samuel". In the Gospels, Moses when dead appeared to the living (at the Transfiguration).[7]

It is clear that "the high places" were a constant source of spiritual disobedience in the Old Testament period.

Psalm 78:58 states tersely, "They angered him with their high places; they aroused his jealousy with their idols."

A few more typical references will suffice: "They [Judah] also set up for themselves high places, sacred stones and Asherah poles on every high hill and under every spreading tree" (1 Kings 14:23). In addition, there were male cult prostitutes and behaviour that was described as "all the detestable practices of the nations the Lord had driven out" (1 Kings 14:24). The behaviour of Solomon's son Rehoboam was no better than his opponent, Jeroboam, the son of Nebat, who is constantly described as "causing Israel to sin".

In 2 Kings 17:9 the writer says, "The Israelites secretly did things against the Lord their God that were not right." These included building high places, setting up pillars and Asherah, burning incense and serving idols. Asherah was a Canaanite mother-goddess, pillars were identified with male deities, and incense was often used in the worship of false gods.

Hezekiah (1 Kings 18:1–4) removed high places, smashed sacred stones, cut down poles used in cultic worship and even destroyed the famous bronze serpent which Moses had made (see Numbers 21:9 and John 3:14). The famous serpent had become an idol and an object of false worship.

His son Manasseh who, until his unexpected repentance, was one of the worst of the kings, rebuilt the high places, erected altars for Baal, made an Asherah, built altars in the House of the Lord, burnt his son as an offering, practised soothsaying and augury, and had dealings with mediums and wizards (2 Kings 21:1–9). The Israelites were evidently not immune to the horrid practice of child sacrifice.

The high places were sites of spiritual evil. The many ungodly kings encouraged them; the few godly kings and the prophets railed against them and attempted to remove them. The godly Josiah (2 Kings 23) destroyed, usually by burning or crushing, anything that had been used in false worship. He defiled (presumably a sort of exorcism) false altars and restored a proper celebration of the Passover. Jeremiah (7:31 and 19:5) spoke against the high place at Topheth where child sacrifice was practised. When Ahab rebuilt Jericho, ignoring Joshua's warning (Joshua 6:26), it cost the lives of two sons of the builder – whether this was through child sacrifice or some other cause is not stated.

The Hebrew word "taher" is translated either as cleansed or purified. Ezekiel uses this word in some of his most powerful teaching. Ezekiel 36:25–27, which is often read at Anglican confirmation services, says: "I will sprinkle clean water on you, and you will be clean. I will cleanse you from all your impurities and from all your idols. I will give you a new heart and put a new spirit in you; I will remove from you your heart of stone and give you a heart of flesh. And I will put my spirit in you."

Similarly, in 2 Chronicles 29:18–20, we read how Hezekiah cleansed the House of the Lord – restoring the utensils which the faithless King Ahaz had discarded. Again, Josiah, in 2 Chronicles 34:1–7 is said to have purged (cleansed) Judah and Jerusalem. In the process, he destroyed many images of false gods. The same Hebrew word was used by the prophet Elisha when he instructed Naaman, the Syrian leper, to be cleansed by bathing in the River Jordan. As I mentioned earlier (see Chapter 3, page 47), when Jesus said to the leper, "Be clean!" it was virtually a prayer of exorcism from the hated disease.

The New Testament gives some evidence of a contemporaneous belief in ghosts. When the disciples were straining to cross the Sea of Galilee (Mark 6:45–51), Jesus appeared walking on the lake: "they thought he was a ghost. They cried out, because they all saw him and were terrified" (49–50).

The sea was a great place of fear (see Revelation 21:1); spirits were thought to live there. When Jesus had reassured them and the wind had died down, they were amazed. Holy fear is a frequent occurrence in Mark right up to the final verse (16:8) after the resurrection.

Similarly, in Acts 12:12–16, after Peter's miraculous escape from prison when the church was gathered together for prayer, he knocked at the door. The maid, Rhoda, recognized his voice. But the Christian leaders couldn't believe that their prayers had been answered and, even after she had been very insistent, said, "You're out of your mind… It must be his angel."

Clearly, the disciples believed in the possibility of seeing spirits (or ghosts) and the existence of guardian angels. Scripture doesn't affirm their beliefs but I would imagine that Mark or Luke would have expressed disapproval of their theology if they were dangerously deceived.

I am agnostic about some of the causes of problems in buildings, but I am certain that the problems are real. I am also certain that prayer, said in the name and with the authority of Jesus Christ, through the power of his cross and resurrection, is highly effective. Paul puts it with his customary clarity:

> *Having disarmed the powers and authorities, he made a public spectacle of them, triumphing over them by the cross.*
>
> (Colossians 2:15)

My limited experiences suggest that buildings built on a site which has experienced great tragedies in the past, buildings where tragedies, especially murder and suicide, have occurred recently, places where occult or other unpleasant acts have taken place – all these are liable to experience what are generally called hauntings. Obviously, if the people living there are spiritually sensitive or actively involved in forbidden activities, then happenings are much more likely.

I think we may safely accept that in certain buildings, and with certain forbidden rituals, psychic energy may be released – as for instance in my aunt's presence after the table turning in Burton Agnes Hall. This may also help to explain so-called poltergeist activities. I have heard credible tales of furniture being moved and electrical instruments behaving in strange ways, seen scratches on furniture in one disturbed house, heard tales of videos recording some of the disturbances, and observed the general sense of chaos and fear that has been created.

Of the two troubled pubs which I mentioned in an earlier chapter, the one with a highwayman reputedly buried under the bar was dealt with relatively easily with beneficial results. The other one, with regular seances taking place in an apparently conducive atmosphere, presented a much more serious problem – which, as far as I know, is still to be resolved.

Kenneth McAll[8] has a powerful testimony about prayer offered to release the spiritual influence of thousands of slaves who were thrown overboard in the so-called Bermuda Triangle. He also has an extraordinary story of being asked to a visit a teacher training college. The principal was having trouble with a building which was considered to be haunted. Every midnight, weird noises and screams could be heard. According to legend, this had gone on for the past three hundred years. The principal, herself, had heard strange sounds.

McAll and a team of three others gathered in the building one night. They said the Lord's Prayer and asked for guidance. The upshot was that they formed a clergy team to come and celebrate the Eucharist on the affected site. When they arrived three weeks later, the principal said that all that was needed was a service of praise and thanksgiving:

> We then heard the story that had precipitated our first visit. Some of the more sceptical students decided to stay the night in the building – quite sure that nothing would happen. They had been startled to see a figure dressed as a cavalier emerge through a built-in cupboard door. Then the noise had begun.
>
> They listened incredulously to the loud screams as the cavalier figure appeared to rape and kill a nun, dropping her body down three flights of stairs with a noise like a falling bucket of bricks and then dragging it along a corridor to a point where the noise suddenly ceased. The drama was over. The terrified students knelt by their makeshift beds and prayed!
>
> We retraced the cavalier's route to the point at which the noise had stopped. We noticed that the floor changed from stone to wooden blocks. McAll pulled up a section of the floor covering. Underneath was a rusted trap-door opening onto a flight of steps which led down to a cellar. No one present knew of the existence of the cellar.

McAll wisely adds, "I cannot be certain whether a cavalier actually raped and killed a nun in that place. I do know for certain that binding all the evil that was manifestly there through the Lord's Prayer and the avowed intention to offer a Eucharist for all needing help and release was sufficient to stop the disturbance of the hauntings permanently."

As to ghosts, I am personally disinclined to believe that they are the spirits of actual people. But it is possible, indeed probable, that disturbed people, such as suicides, victims of murder, or other tragic situations, can leave an "unquiet" presence behind where they have died. Alternatively, it may be that an evil spirit taking advantage of a tragic situation purports to be the spirit of the victim of the tragedy. For the most part, I prefer to be agnostic about the explanations and grateful that authoritative prayer invariably restores peace and calm to both buildings and their occupants.

We will consider in Chapter 9 how to approach all these situations prayerfully and how the problems can be resolved.

CHAPTER 8

INAPPROPRIATE DELIVERANCE

No exorciser harm thee! Nor no witchcraft charm thee!
(*Cymbeline* Act 4 Scene 2, William Shakespeare)

The deliverance ministry is high risk. The newspapers love reporting mistakes and seldom report successes. Over the last ten years, *The Times* has recorded a large number of high-profile disasters, somewhat balanced by two positive accounts from Anglican exorcists.[1]

It is easy to make mistakes. Some years ago, I stayed with a relative who was caught up in the midst of a very strange spiritual turmoil. A friend, who had a respected itinerant ministry, had been told "prophetically" by three well-established Christians that his wife was about to die. The man and his wife had taken up residence in the large home of my relative. My initial (wise) reaction was that "God doesn't speak in that way". But when I entered the strange atmosphere of the house, I lost my discernment and was caught up in a tide of spiritual euphoria.

The visiting wife became convinced that she was about to die of stomach cancer. She spent much of the day sitting in a foaming, scented bath, issuing seemingly spiritual messages.

My youth group was about to stay the weekend in the large house. One member of the group was very sensitive to depression. He was convinced that he was possessed by demons. After doing everything I could to explore the possibility, I had tried, with some success, to convince him that demons were not the cause of his problems.

I should have cancelled the visit although this would have been quite difficult in the days before mobile phones and text messaging. The group were quickly caught up in the strange atmosphere. At the time, I didn't realize how the potentially depressive young man was reacting. It turned out that he was badly affected by the generally hyped-up atmosphere. When he went home, he was very ill for some months. He had to go to a mental hospital for a while and then gradually made a recovery over the next few years. I am certain that staying in this strange house triggered his illness. His family were amazingly understanding and forgiving. Their generous attitude helped me to forgive myself for undoing months of good work by allowing him to come into such a highly-charged household.

The weird happenings continued for about a week. Then I said to the husband, "If your wife doesn't die today, this message was not from God." He looked relieved. That evening, at his instigation, she was visited by a local doctor and a psychiatrist. She recovered instantly. But there were aftershocks.

The husband's itinerant ministry ceased and he returned to selling cars. The three established Christians who had prophesied her death all lost their ministry and prophetic gifting. My faith was severely shaken. Paul says, "We are not ignorant of his devices" (2 Corinthians 2:11, NKJV) – I am afraid that we were all terribly deceived. Satan seems far more dangerous as an "angel of light" (2 Corinthians 11:14) than when indwelling a relatively small number of unfortunate people. Certainly wise and mature Christians were disastrously deceived throughout this sobering (for me at least) tale.[2]

Over the years, the cases reported by *The Times* make sad reading. There are a number of reports of children, often from the Congo, subjected to exorcism because their parents think they are a malign influence – often they seem to be unwanted children. There have been several cases, and these must be just the tip of a very large iceberg, where children have been starved, shaken, and shouted at. It all makes very unpleasant reading.

There have been at least two cases where doctors have been reported to the General Medical Council for recommending exorcism instead of medical treatment. There have been several recorded deaths, including that of a nun in Romania, during attempted exorcisms. One pastor in Brazil seems to have claimed that at least six female members of his congregation could receive exorcism successfully after sexual union with him. Much of the reporting beggars belief. A recent court case involved an independent pastor physically "disciplining" female members of his congregations. This included the unbelievable claim that, in some cases, such practices could effect exorcism. One of the worst features of the case was the psychological hold that the pastor had over his victims. Some of them continued attending his "church" after being assaulted.

Many of the practices in these cases seem so obviously evil. It is small wonder that many people prefer to draw a veil over the whole practice and deny the existence of any malign spiritual forces.

As Shakespeare memorably puts it when a group of onlookers speak over a dead body:

> No exorciser harm thee! Nor no witchcraft charm thee!
> Ghost unlaid forbear thee! Nothing ill come near thee!
> Quiet consummation have; and renowned be thy grave![3]

Clearly the bard understood that exorcisers could do harm. We would do well to ponder on his wisdom.

Sexuality

The most disturbing story seems much more typical of the type of ministry practised by some mainstream churches in this country. *The Sunday Times* (8 February 2015) recorded a case which I summarize (with Jayne's permission) as follows:

Jayne Ozanne is an evangelical Christian. She was a highly respected member of the Archbishops' Council (the executive body of the Church of England). Like most evangelicals, she did not believe that faith in God and being actively gay could be reconciled. Torn between her belief and her desires, she had been repressing her homosexuality for more than a decade.

She was in her thirties and desperate when she turned to exorcism to cure her of her homosexual feelings. She would visit "deliverance ministers" in London, who would pray for her to be released from her emotional prison. "They would put their hands on you and pray until you felt the Holy Spirit," she says. "Then they might say something like: 'In the name of Jesus, I command the spirit of lust to come out.'"

Jayne says, "I needed a way to get rid of this terrible set of desires I had. People would suggest that the issues were down to some emotional trauma or genetic spiritual inheritance, some curse that could be cast out. So I tried it. It's a huge world, full of middle-class doctors and lawyers. But no one talks about it — most people would think we were barmy."

She tried a range of strategies to escape her sexuality. She was celibate for many years, lived as a hermit at Lee Abbey in Devon, travelled round the world, and worked herself to the quick as head of marketing for BBC television. Nothing really helped. Eventually, in 2009, she came out to friends and began living with a female partner. Recently, aged forty-six, she announced to the wider world that she was gay and would be taking up a role as director of Accepting Evangelicals, a network of Christians dedicated to promoting the acceptance of same-sex relationships in the church.

Despite much professional success, Jayne was always dogged by her inability to come to terms with her sexuality. Several times she developed close relationships with female friends, but requited love eluded her. "I was completely closed down, but there was this huge need in me, a hole that was really aching and became bigger as time went on," she said.

This led to deep depression and then a full-scale nervous breakdown at the age of twenty-eight. She was rushed into hospital in agony. Psychiatric care followed, during which one doctor at the Priory suggested that she "change her religion". It wasn't likely, and despite moments of doubt, Ozanne's faith in God remains profound. But it might have helped, because more than anything else it was her fear of God that held her back. "It took me so long [to come out] because I just couldn't countenance it. It was like telling me to go and commit murder. It was a sin: it wasn't allowed."

It was when Jayne turned forty that she decided it was time to overcome her fear and find happiness as a lesbian. Few of her evangelical friends accepted it. "It was awful: I lost virtually everybody. They just didn't know what to say." Nonetheless, finding love brought her "transformation and joy" — and the realisation that coming out did not destroy her faith. It was then that she started analysing Scripture and to question the church's stance on homosexuality.

I find this account deeply disturbing. Those well-meaning Christians who sought to help her seem to have assumed that she was invaded by a "spirit of lust" or something similar. A careful reading of Scripture should have suggested considerable caution.

One of my favourite Gospel stories (Luke 7:36–50) tells how a woman, described as a (notorious) sinner, invaded the dinner party given by Simon, a self-righteous Pharisee. She interrupted the supper, which was presumably taking place in an open courtyard or some other easily accessible part of the house. She wet Jesus' feet with her tears, wiped them with her long hair, and then anointed them with expensive ointment. Her whole demeanour was one of penitence and worship as she prostrated herself around Him.

The guests, onlookers at this strange scene, were doubtless amazed. Simon, the host, muttered to himself that, if Jesus was a true prophet, He would know what sort of woman was touching Him. The obvious implication is that she was well-known in the town for offering her sexual favours. Jesus read the situation perfectly. He told His host a short parable about two debtors who owed five hundred and fifty denarii. Neither could pay; both were forgiven by their lender. "Which of them will love him more?" Jesus asked. Grudgingly, Simon replied, "I suppose the one who had the bigger debt forgiven." In passing, it is worth noting the subtle point that the debtor who owed only fifty denarii, presumably Simon, was also unable to pay!

Jesus then commented on various aspects of His host's welcome which, in contrast to the uninvited woman's, had been inadequate – no kiss of welcome, no anointing of His head. Jesus publicly praised and then forgave the woman (making it clear that her sins were many). He concluded with the reassuring words, "Your faith has saved you; go in peace." There was no question of any need for exorcism. *Forgiveness and acceptance, not deliverance,* was what the woman needed. If spirits of lust do actually exist, I would have thought that this unnamed woman was a prime candidate to have harboured one.

The next few verses introduce us to Mary Magdalene, from whom seven demons had gone out. She is one of a group of women who travelled with Jesus and were able, out of their own means, to provide for Jesus and the twelve. Commentators do not look kindly on those who seek to identify Mary Magdalene with the woman in the previous story. It is this inaccurate confluence[4] of the two stories which has led to Mary Magdalene's dubious, and completely undeserved, reputation as a prostitute. We have no idea what kind of demons were cast out from Mary Magdalene. It is clear that the woman who came to the dinner party was sent back to her community – publicly praised, accepted and forgiven by Jesus. By contrast, Mary of Magdala, with several other reasonably wealthy women, was a long-time travelling companion. There is no way that the two women can be thought to be one and the same person.

Only twice does Scripture even hint at the type of demons that Jesus and the apostles encountered. In Philippi (Acts 16:16–18), it seems clear that the slave girl had acquired a demon connected with her ability to tell fortunes. In the story of the Gadarene demoniac (Mark 5:5), one of his symptoms is described as "cutting himself". Some commentators, notably William Lane (see Chapter 4, note 9), suggest that this was a sign that he worshipped demonic deities.

The account in John 8:1–11 of the unfortunate woman caught in the act of adultery tells a similar story. Once again, Jesus demolishes her accusers and refuses to condemn her. He then sends her away with the solemn warning, "Do not sin again". Once more, the emphasis of the story is on forgiveness of sexual misdemeanour and, again, there is no suggestion that any form of exorcism is required.

Similarly, in 1 Corinthians 6:9–11, Paul lists various lifestyles, including some sexual problems, which are contrary to the Kingdom. He writes, "And that is what some of you were." He continues that they were washed (baptized), sanctified, and justified in the name of Jesus. There is no hint that any kind of exorcism was necessary. Now, we have to be cautious here. Paul never mentions exorcism in his epistles, although he frequently mentions spiritual warfare and clearly sees Satan as a very real opponent of both his ministry and his churches. He certainly practised exorcism in Philippi and probably in Ephesus, but it was never deemed sufficiently important to feature in any of his known writings.

It seems to me that Jayne could have travelled down several routes. Perhaps counselling and prayer might have brought relief – it has to some. She appears to have tried this route. She also tried to follow Jesus' hard words in Matthew 19:12: "there are those who choose to live like eunuchs for the sake of the kingdom of heaven". I have known many godly men and women, some, but not all, of a homosexual disposition, who have taken that difficult and self-sacrificing road. Jayne described this route as unbelievably lonely. Some others have followed the Anglican code of conduct for ordained ministers, and lived with someone of the same sex but have refrained from a physical relationship. Others, like Jayne in her final position, have felt that their sexuality was God-given, and then have wrestled with Scripture before entering into a full partnership with someone of the same sex. It is outside the scope of this book to comment on these choices.[5]

A teenager when aged fourteen, whom I know slightly, was participating in a youth mission trip. One evening, she mentioned to the leader of her group that she was attracted to her own sex. The leader, a girl of about twenty-one, took it upon herself to cast out the demon of homosexuality. The result was that the teenager was traumatized and, for some time, was very reticent about joining in groups or even meeting up with Christians. Bravely, about two years later, she is going on another mission trip, but sensibly has asked to be put nowhere near the group leader who attempted the deliverance ministry.

The girl in question seems to be a caring, gifted young Christian, who needs time and care to sort her sexuality and learn how to handle it. Direct prayers for deliverance will usually achieve nothing, except to make the person concerned feel more anxious, introverted and angry.

But the point that I want to make is that any attempt at deliverance is likely to be inappropriate and ineffective – indeed harmful. Sexual spirits do appear in some deliverance situations – but, if present, they invariably manifest and declare themselves. The big mistake seems to be to assume that a particular kind of demon, such as a spirit of lust, will be present. Unless a spirit clearly shows up, usually in some of the ways described in Chapter 4, it is much safer to assume that no exorcism prayer is needed. Scripture gives us no warrant for making dubious assumptions about the expected presence of certain types of spirit.

Sometimes I have felt led to ask troubled people about their sexual relationships. This is because, as Paul puts it, "Do you not know that he who unites himself with a prostitute is one with her in body?" (1 Corinthians 6:16), and he says the same about marriage in Ephesians 5:31.

This, obviously, is a very sensitive area and I always try to explain why this type of questioning may be necessary. I was trying to help one young woman. She readily volunteered that one of her recent sexual partners was deeply involved in the occult. When I asked her to renounce his influence, she drew back and refused all further help. I clearly mishandled the situation, although it is difficult to work out how I could have helped her to be truly free without tackling this issue. Unfortunately it proved impossible to make further contact with her. I would have liked to apologise and to try to put matters right.

In Chapter 3, I recorded our encounter with the woman who identified herself as "the rose with two black spots". A Christian Science upbringing, some exposure to occult things at her birth, lesbianism, and suicide attempts had left her very vulnerable to depressions and migraines.

Rather to our surprise, some days later when we challenged anything within her to show itself, she manifested all the signs of demonization. A long and very difficult deliverance followed. But the key was uncovering the controlling spirit, which was surprisingly connected to a Babylonian mystery religion. No spirit purporting to be of a sexual or suicidal nature showed up. However, the migraines and the depression lifted. She was free from all thoughts of suicide and all desires for lesbian relationships. The effective deliverance ministry brought her many benefits.

Finally, in this context, I think my father's story is relevant. He grew up in a troubled, angry household. My grandmother, an apparently domineering wife and mother, kept pet monkeys, which leapt around the dining room to my grandfather's extreme annoyance. There were frequent family rows. Many people would see this sort of household with a dominant mother as the classic environment for developing a homosexual personality. Both my uncle and father grew up as practising homosexuals. My father served in a regiment where, in places, homosexual practice seems to have taken place. In 1936, he was due to be married to my mother. The marriage was called off at the last moment. I presume that my father had finally told her about his sexual preferences. Two years later, they married very quietly. In the war, he had a near miraculous escape from Dunkirk.[6] Soon afterwards, I was conceived. Then, towards the end of the war, there was a homosexual scandal and he was dismissed from the army.

After his wartime disaster, my mother, a strong Christian, stood by him and gave him a happy home. They slept in separate rooms but they had a very successful marriage. My mother accepted his annual visits to Tangiers and his many gay friends. He accepted her racehorses. They did many things together. In 1968, they celebrated thirty years of marriage. Then the next year, my mother died at the young age of fifty-seven. My father was heartbroken and guilt-ridden. With the help of two of my friends, he made a profession of faith but then, quite suddenly, his morale collapsed and his mind went. He said that he felt hopeless, just as he had done during his wartime crisis. He was convinced that no one, least of all those he called "trick cyclists", could help him. I consulted his doctor who was also a family friend. We both felt nothing could be done, but we hoped that in time he might pull through. . At that time, when I was just beginning theological training, I knew nothing of the ministry of deliverance. With my knowledge today, I think that any attempt to release him by some form of exorcism from spirits of either homosexuality or suicide would have been cruel and worse than useless.

Dangerous dependency

From time to time, people have come to see me, usually questioning some deliverance ministry that they have received from a particular approach. There is a certain sad, repetitive ring to their stories. Often, over the course of several sessions or different visits, they had apparently had multiple spirits removed. After some gruelling sessions, they were then told there were still more demons that needed to be shifted. They felt trapped. They were uncertain about the efficacy of this seemingly never-ending ministry, *but they were now feeling dangerously dependent upon those who had prayed with them.* They wanted to avoid the place of ministry, but felt they could never be free unless they continued with the prescribed prayer ministry until they were pronounced clear of all evil.

At its worst, it reminds me of my lovely mother-in-law receiving through the post a letter giving her the good news that she has won £50,000. But – there's a catch. She needs to buy some unwanted goods to qualify. Then the cycle gets repeated. More useless products have to be bought. The victims are trapped by the illusion of winning the great prize. At best, they gained entry into a grand draw which may have had some real prizes.

This type of situation needs very careful handling. But it bears little resemblance to the speedy deliverances recorded in the Gospels. In some cases, I doubted whether any deliverance ministry had been needed and, in most cases, I was confident that enough had been done. Obviously, I had to be very cautious. I didn't want to leave anyone in even greater confusion.

On one occasion, a woman came to see me. She was a prospective new member of the church. She mentioned she had just visited the place of "ministry" that I was least confident about. I said, "I hope you haven't had a non-existent spirit of anger cast out." This remark was not a great success! She visibly winced and replied, "My husband says that my temper has been so much better since I returned." Needless to say, she didn't join the church. However, there is a serious point. Anger is frequently mentioned by Paul, most notably in Galatians 5:20, in a long list of the "sins of the flesh". It is very unlikely to be caused by an evil spirit and, to suggest that it may be, gives any angry person a simple cop out: "I can't control my anger because it is caused by a spirit." That is not what Paul teaches and I am very happy to follow his directions.

Common sense and discernment needed

Sometimes, enthusiastic Christians seem devoid of common sense. They ignore the fact that "wisdom" is first on Paul's list of spiritual gifts in 1 Corinthians 12. A modicum of wisdom could have prevented the sad saga with which I opened this chapter.

A distinguished house of healing with a good record subsided spectacularly about twenty years ago. Apparently someone had the bright idea that, by anointing every known orifice of the human body, evil spirits could be expelled and/or prevented from (re)entering. The procedure went by the dubious name of "interior ministries".

Allegedly, some even more obviously distasteful methods (which I am unwilling even to describe) were also tried. Not surprisingly, the results were humiliating for those who were being prayed for and disastrous for the healers. Threats of legal action from some of those subjected to this appalling treatment were narrowly avoided. The centre closed. The ministry of several good people was cut short. Just a little ordinary common sense could have prevented this particular disaster. All that was needed was for someone to say, "Can this really be an appropriate way to conduct Christian prayer?"

Another mistake I personally have made is to assume that, because some of the phenomena described in Chapter 4 are taking place, we are dealing with a deliverance situation. I remember once, at the end of a long teaching day, having a prayer session in a village in central Tanzania. It began very quietly. There always seem to be fewer obvious signs of demons in Central Africa than further south in Zambia. I think this may be a long-term effect of the East African revival in the 1950s.

Suddenly there was a commotion. I could see, at the other end of the small church, a woman flailing about on the floor. She was surrounded by shouting, screaming, African would-be exorcists. After a while, I went across. Perhaps an authoritative English voice could sort the situation out. It didn't; in fact it made it worse. Then, an inner sense, which I do often experience in these situations, told me to obey my own rules and calm the situation down. Eventually, everyone stopped shouting. The woman on the floor stopped shaking and screaming. I asked, through an interpreter, if she had a health problem. She replied that she was being treated for a mental illness – I can't remember but I think she may have said schizophrenia. The next few minutes were spent apologizing for a botched deliverance attempt and assuring her that the pastor would support her efforts to get proper hospital and psychiatric treatment. On this occasion, the outcome was satisfactory, but if we had gone on shouting at her non-existent demons, we could have done irreparable damage.

On bright sunny afternoon, I was walking down a steep track in the Udzungwa National park in Tanzania. We had climbed to the top of a fine waterfall, enjoyed the monkeys and the spectacular butterflies – many Charaxes with their double tails extending their long proboscis into any suitable liquid, large Swallowtails flitting by, the glorious Blue Mother of Pearl sunning itself on a warm leaf, Euphaedra with bright purple and gold wings resting on the warm ground in sunlit glades, the rare Euxanthe Tiberius skulking, well camouflaged, perched on a branch in the shade of the forest. As we descended, I could hear loud singing. Clearly, the small Pentecostal church at the foot of the track was holding a service. Then, quite suddenly, the singing changed to an ugly clamour. It was still going on about ten minutes later when we passed by the church. I resisted the temptation to intervene. A noisy, and seemingly ineffective, exorcism was being attempted.

Sometimes in Africa, I try to liven up teaching sessions by picking up my Bible and bashing my translator on the head with shouts of, "Out! Out!" After the laughter ceases, my hosts admit that that is their usual approach. Then I try to explain why this approach is at worst ineffective and sometimes counterproductive. First, the shouting attracts an undesirable crowd of onlookers. Secondly, the spirits seem to gain strength in these situations. One minister, experienced in this type of ministry, has described the demons as exhibitionists. Thirdly, no one person seems in control of the situation and this increases the chaos. Fourthly, and perhaps most importantly, we need the co-operation of the troubled person. This is best achieved by allowing them to calm down and then quietly asking them what spirit they think is troubling them.[7] Often they know; just as they are the first people to realize when the spirits have left. It is good to ask them to call on the name of Jesus. With the person's co-operation, the demon(s) can usually be expelled with little fuss – which is a great improvement on most other methods.

Revival experiences need to be tested

The "Toronto blessing" helped many people. One great friend, who testified in one of my books,[8] was converted from a very sceptical journalist into a wise Christian counsellor. Countless others were greatly blessed. But I well remember, when it was just starting, attending the New Wine Conference in 1994, which was held on the edge of my parish in Shepton Mallet. When the public ministry time started, bedlam broke out. Some people, quite a number, roared like lions – apparently supported by an obscure Scripture in the book of

Amos and encouraged by the leadership team. Other people were performing weird antics and making strange uncontrolled noises. Everywhere enthusiastic members of the ministry team were waving their arms, apparently to assist the flow of the "wind of the Spirit". They were also flitting around the aisles of the large auditorium, encouraging more noise and more chaos. People were laid out on the floor (this can happen in more sober and acceptable times of ministry); people were weeping (this, too, is usually good and a sign of genuine repentance); people were growling (unjustifiable, it seems to me) and even barking like dogs (completely absurd). It was as though a form of spiritual hysteria were sweeping through the large crowd. It was difficult not to be swept along for fear of missing some new encounter.

The wise words of John, "Dear friends, do not believe every spirit, but test the spirits to see whether they are from God" (1 John 4:1), were completely ignored. Anyone apparently unmoved was thought to be missing out on, or closed to, the new spiritual riches. Jane and I looked at each other in amazement. In rural Zambia, where we had ministered two years earlier (see Chapter 2), we would have regarded such behaviour as demonic. Here, in rural Somerset, it was treated as a sign of the Holy Spirit's presence. Such obvious misjudgment threatened to bring the whole movement into disrepute.

I did know some of the leadership team. Undoubtedly, I should have expressed my reservations. But, like others who were bewildered, I sat in bemused silence. However, in the supercharged atmosphere of the Bath and West Showground, I doubt that my comments would have counted for much.

To be fair, the leadership team did realize the error of their ways and, in subsequent years, both worship and ministry were conducted in a manner which was far more sober. Meanwhile, in churches like nearby St John's Glastonbury, evening services, which were open to a more sensible version of the blessing, flourished and many people were genuinely helped.

In 1745, the same sort of thing brought George Whitefield's ministry in Northampton, New England into controversy. His preaching had seen a great revival. It was accompanied by some curious phenomena[9] but all of this was generally, and properly, accepted as a genuine work of the Holy Spirit. Unfortunately, one supporting cleric, James Davenport, went completely over the top. In response to supposed revelations, he commanded his hearers to be cured of their love of "worldly things" and burn wigs, jewels, and numerous other personal possessions. He also made a pyre of books, which even included those written by distinguished Puritans. Soon afterwards, he retired very sick. But the damage was done and the revival was greatly harmed. One critic commented, "The madder the better, the less reason, the more spiritual" – a comment which could certainly have been applied, almost 250 years later, to New Wine 1994!

Both during the late twentieth-century Toronto blessing and the mid-eighteenth-century New England blessing, Satan had managed to undermine things, not by direct assault but by encouraging mature Christians to behave with extraordinary stupidity. Once again the gift of wisdom, well exercised, would have removed a great deal of unnecessary confusion.

Deceiving spirits and wrong diagnosis

These events, and the personal incident with which I began this chapter, underline my assertion that Satan is at his most dangerous when he disguises himself "as an angel of light" (2 Corinthians 11:14). Evil spirits within, or even around, a person are reasonably easy to deal with. But the subtle destruction wrought by "an angel of light" is much more difficult to discern and far harder to counter. One of the people deceived in my opening story was never able to accept that they were victims of deception; likewise, those deceived by some aspects of the Toronto blessing found it almost impossible to recognize the deception.[10]

To revert to my argument in the first chapter, if Satan doesn't exist, these deceptions are even harder to explain. Three intelligent people simultaneously, and independently, believing that a friend's wife is about to die is scarcely credible – unless this is the work of a deceiving spirit.

Paul (1 Timothy 4:1) also warns that deceitful spirits will try to infiltrate the church with false teaching – in this case about marriage and food. Christian history is littered with further examples of this type of attack. It should be clear that this is less obvious and more dangerous than the more direct attacks that have been the main thrust of this book. The significance of the more direct attacks, I think, is that they provide tangible evidence for the existence of malevolent spiritual forces, while also providing a direct link back to the vivid accounts found in the Gospel of Mark.

I would like to have included more examples. One medical journal[11] contains a very worrying testimony which has a silver lining at the conclusion. For various reasons, it has not been possible to comment on this in detail – suffice it to say that a young woman heard a voice "that she knew to be the devil" telling her that she wasn't a Christian. She then underwent several exorcisms and ended up disillusioned with church, giving up music (her one great solace), and seriously clinically depressed. It would seem to me far more likely that she was suffering from some form of psychosis than from demonization. The church concerned had a highly responsible ministry and saw many other people helped. Anyway, at the end of the story her faith has recovered and matured. Now she is helping other people with problems where psychiatric disorder and religious experience seem to be intertwined. Her whole account is deeply moving and, at the end of a long road, very encouraging.

On one occasion, my local doctor, who was sympathetic to Christianity, sent a patient in our direction. She was suffering from acute persecution mania. She was quite convinced that a local Christian family of impeccable reputation, for whom she was working, were trying to poison her. It seemed like a case for some type of deliverance ministry. The temptation, and indeed the trap, was to "confront" her mania. However, we proceeded with due caution.

Friendship began to bring healing. Her demeanour began to change. The hunted, haunted look on her face softened. After counselling and prayer, she was baptized on Ascension Day (about two months after our first contact). Her condition improved and soon she was completely well. She moved away but that year I received a Christmas card from her. She wanted to give us thanks and say that her discipleship was going well.

This woman did not need deliverance ministry! I think this is an important example of making the necessary distinction between an acute mental condition and a demonic one.

There are on-line accounts and stories where people have seemingly been manipulated at a healing centre with unending ministry, and an almost infinite number (legion?) of demons to be removed. All of us involved in this ministry, myself included, are liable to make mistakes. It is a difficult and complicated undertaking. We have to take heart from the many testimonies of those who have been helped.

CHAPTER 9

TEA AND SYMPATHY

I woke, the dungeon flamed with light;
My chains fell off, my heart was free,
I rose, went forth, and followed Thee.

(Charles Wesley, *And Can It Be?*)

Requests for help come in a variety of ways. The most frequent is via
a call from a bemused parish priest. The most expedient procedure
is to visit the worried parishioner as soon as possible. On arrival, I
find it is best to accept the inevitable cup of tea and to prepare to
listen to a tale, which is often somewhat rambling and confused. I
think it is important to state at the outset that you take the problems
seriously and assure them that they are not alone in experiencing
these kinds of difficulty. Most people who seek professional help for
dealing with phenomena they cannot understand need considerable
reassurance. Faces visibly lighten when I tell them that they are far
from alone and they have not taken leave of their senses.

I always like to hear the story from the lips of the householder.
The vicar will have briefed me and we will have spent a little time
together before visiting the house. Disturbances follow a number of
patterns – among the most common are a sense of extreme coldness
in parts of the house, feeling of a presence, being touched by
something, fear, objects moving around, inexplicable smells – such
as tobacco when nobody smokes, or scent which no one wears –
footsteps, doors opening and closing, electrical problems (appliances

switching on or off inexplicably). Rather less frequently, a "person" has been seen or strange voices have been heard. Children and dogs seem particularly sensitive.

It is best to listen with minimal interruption. I always ask permission to take notes. This aids my memory and also means that I can note down key questions to ask when the account has finished. Then there are a number of straightforward diagnostic questions. How many people have experienced any of the happenings? How long have the problems been around? How long have you lived here? Have you, or anyone else who lives here, had similar problems in previous houses? This is an important question. An affirmative answer will tend to suggest that one (or more) of the occupants is carrying the problem with them. Do you know anything about the history of the house? Do you know anything about the land on which the house is built? This too can be important.

As I have indicated in the previous chapters, the past history of the house and the grounds on which it stands is often the reason for the present troubles. I heard recently of a troubled converted barn, which was built very close to the scene of a Civil War battlefield. One person told me of a clear psychic experience they had had at the site of the Battle of the Imjin River in Korea.

Changing direction, I will then want to ask about the spiritual history of those who have been affected. Has anyone used Ouija? Has anyone been involved with spiritualism or any form of psychic healing – such as Reiki? Have any close ancestors had any known psychic powers or experiences? Are there any Freemasons in the family or among the ancestors? Does the family have a history of depression or suicide? Is there any other information which might help us understand what is happening? Do they have any pornographic books or videos? Do they have any books about the occult?

Looking at the cases mentioned in Chapter 7, which are the more memorable in my ministry but still fairly typical, Anne Goode's problems in her stables were caused by curious goings on there – I do not care to speculate as to whether they were spiritual, sexual, or a combination of both. Nor do I know whether they took place relatively recently or a very long time ago.

The young woman who saw a Roman soldier on her bed was fairly highly strung. If the incident was genuine then it was caused by a place memory from the past, which was created by the disturbance of the Roman graves beside the Fosse Way. Those skeletons that were unearthed were given a dignified reburial in the parish churchyard. The service was conducted in both English and Latin! Unfortunately, I left the area soon after the prayer with the young woman. I should have followed her up to see if all was well. As I heard nothing, I am inclined to believe that the trouble has passed.

The young woman in PNG was clearly helped by the prayers. Although I cannot be certain, I think it is highly likely that the house had been built on a site where not only killing in battle, but subsequent cannibalism, had taken place.

The factory in Leicester was somewhat more serious. The level of disturbance was considerable. Contracted electricians don't down tools, reliable workmen aren't scared out of their wits, and a sceptical factory manager doesn't get the shock of his life without good cause. My problem is that I have no real idea what the cause was. I am just glad that the prayers were eventually efficacious.

The next three cases seem to involve place memories and extreme tragedy. The story of the young boy being locked up after trying to dig up the coffin of his dead mother is deeply tragic. Likewise, the corpse in the well by the roadside, who was probably murdered, would have left a distinctly negative memory. Whether the disturbance was caused by the person's spirit or a place memory is irrelevant; what matters is that peace was restored and untimely deaths in the neighbouring houses ceased. The case of the house where the owner was murdered at the top of the stairs is unpleasant but straightforward. Again, exactly what was released through our prayers is unclear, but the result was beneficial.

Why the two-year-old was troubled in the family house is unclear. But the fact that the previous owner of the house, not a practising Christian as far as I know, had asked her cleaners to exorcise it suggests that the problem was long standing.

The house where the cushions were being thrown about was less serious – nevertheless troubling for the owner, especially when her husband was recovering from a major operation. It would seem that there is a psychic line running in the family. Until that is cleared up, I am afraid they will experience troubles of one sort or another.

The next case was also clearly caused by the owner. He had taken a video of strange happenings and seemed to relish them.

The farmhouse, which the new owners couldn't sell, obviously needed to be cleansed from the shadow of the sad suicide of the previous owner. When we pray for cleansing, we are not making any judgment about the deceased person. People who commit suicide do not take this drastic action without reason, or unless their mind has been seriously disturbed. But the memory has to be erased, so that future occupants can move forward.

Burton Agnes Hall seems to enjoy its reputation for haunting and, until some owner takes the matter in hand, the screaming skull is likely to dominate those who live there.

The council house built over ground where, in the Middle Ages, there had been unconsecrated graves, had landed on an unfortunate site. I am sorry that my prayers for the first occupants were not sufficient to help the next family.

It seems clear that both the St John's Stone, site of dubious midsummer activities, and the isolation hospital had caused problems for future residents. These incidents would seem fairly typical and may help understand the need for sensitive questioning when we are asked to help people.

How should we proceed?

After spending time in the troubled building, whether house, factory, office, or pub, I have to form a judgment as to how to proceed. Sometimes, either because the problem seems straightforward or particularly urgent, I will pray immediately. Normally, I will give a simple prayer of blessing and make a date for a return visit. Ideally, I will bring a gifted person with me who, without being briefed, may be able to give an insight into the problems. I will, occasionally, conclude that there is nothing particularly spiritually wrong. Then, I will make a prayer of blessing and ask the local vicar to keep an eye on the family. I usually give the family my contact details, and ask them to be in touch with me or the local vicar if they are experiencing problems.

The second visit will usually be the time for serious prayer. The local family and the vicar will decide who should be present. Usually,

I would not want young children to be present, but there may be a reason why a particular time of prayer should include the children. I do not robe for such visits – the last thing the troubled family wants is for the neighbours to see a robed clergyman turning up with bell, book, and candle!

We usually get straight down to business. Tea and any refreshments are best left to the end. We may begin with a time of confession. I will bless a bowl of water. I am careful to explain the theology. Colossians 2:12–15 is a good reading. The evil spirits, or whatever is troubling the house, do not like consecrated water. It reminds them of baptism. Baptism, to be effective, depends on understanding the cross and resurrection of Jesus. What we are doing makes no sense (indeed it is medieval mumbo-jumbo!) unless Jesus is Lord and risen from the dead. Those who are present need to understand that they, too, need to turn to Jesus – both for future protection and their own wellbeing. But that is work for the local vicar and any lay people he can enlist to help them. The water is not magical; but it is efficacious. It is also helpful for the beleaguered household to see that something is happening.

Before we start, I also tell the household that they may experience or see something (a little girl recently felt something gripping her). I encourage them to speak up. They may feel cold or frightened; they may remember something. All the help that they can give is to be welcomed.

I then read some Scripture. Psalm 121 is usually appreciated. Some people, and dogs, seem to act strangely at times of a full moon (verse 6). We then pray through the house – room by room. In each room, I sprinkle some water in the name of Father, Son, and Holy Spirit. We remember any difficult experiences (last time it was a duvet being lifted off a little girl's bed to the ceiling – this was witnessed by her mother and older brother), and pray for their effects to be removed and any evil presence to depart. The prayer is a command not an "if it be thy will" type of prayer.

Eventually, we have finished. We sit down, drink a cup of tea, and share any thoughts or experiences. Quite often, as we are praying, other memories come to mind. Sometimes we need to pray more. Always, I try and point them to Jesus. These occasions are great evangelistic opportunities. The warning in Matthew 12:43 (about seven worse spirits returning to a cleansed house) is always at the back of my mind. Sometimes I mention it.

If there is a need for a third visit, it will usually take the form of a home communion. The service will be informal. I invite the residents to take part, even if they are not communicants. It seems wisest to fully involve them. The Eucharist is strangely powerful and reassuring. The Eucharist I led on the floor of the disturbed factory in north-west Leicester was very moving. I don't think that any of the management and workforce who were present will ever forget it. After that, the disturbances in the factory ceased. I don't think I have ever had to return to a house for further ministry after celebrating communion there.

Praying in people's homes is a great privilege. People are so grateful to find that someone takes their problems seriously. They are even more grateful when the problems disappear. I am happy with the theology that I outlined in the last chapter. I am content to be agnostic about some the causes. I never cease to wonder at the power of the risen Lord. Usually, there are no particular phenomena, but when someone like Albert Bushell has an experience as the cleansing takes place (see Anne Goode's story, Chapter 7, page 131) it is even more marvellous. The publican in the Canard's Grave Inn (see Chapter 5, page 85) never quite became a Christian, but he did witness to all and sundry to the power of the ministry and the healing of his son.

Ministry to people

Some people, particularly those with serious mental issues, think they are demonized. Indeed, they can even hope that they are demonized as it provides an explanation, and a potential cure, for their problem. Sadly, this is seldom the case.

Sometimes people are told that they have a "spirit of anger" or something similar. I doubt that spirits of anger exist. It seems to me that Galatians 5:16–25 gives us a clear contrast between what Paul calls "the works of the flesh" and "the fruit of the Spirit". Anger is clearly listed among the works of the flesh. For many of us, it is a real problem. We need the fruits of peace, patience, and self-control to help us work through a serious problem with anger. Treating anger as an evil spirit will normally be a dubious short cut; we are trying to evade responsibility for our own actions by getting a spirit cast out. As my friend Stanley Hotay, Bishop of Mount Kilimanjaro, wisely says, "You can't cast out the flesh or disciple the demons."

However, there is a passage in James 3:13–18, which I cannot ignore:

> *Who is wise and understanding among you? Let them show it by their good life, by deeds done in the humility that comes from wisdom. But if you harbour bitter envy and selfish ambition in your hearts, do not boast about it or deny the truth. Such "wisdom" does not come down from heaven, but is earthly, unspiritual, demonic. For where you have envy and selfish ambition, there you find disorder and every evil practice. But the wisdom that comes from heaven is first of all pure; then peace-loving, considerate, submissive, full of mercy and good fruit, impartial and sincere. Peacemakers who sow in peace reap a harvest of righteousness.*

This important text leaves the door open – bitter envy or jealousy, and presumably similar character defects, are devilish. That means, I suppose, that in extreme cases they allow evil spirits a foothold, which may necessitate some sort of deliverance ministry.

Once, in Argentina, I was praying with a lady who, herself, had experienced deliverance on account of her husband's Masonic membership. A woman came for prayer. She had a list of problems that seemed endless. She looked ill. She listed problems in almost every part of her body. We listened patiently but could see little prospect of effective prayer. She was enveloped in a cloud of despairing negativity.

Quite suddenly, my praying partner asked, "When you were about four, was a baby brother born into your family? Were you very jealous and angry?" The woman nodded. We explained that this root of bitterness (Hebrews 12:15) could affect her health. We led her through an extensive prayer of repentance. We prayed against all her illnesses, which seemed somewhat like a "spirit of infirmity" (see Luke 13:11). Suddenly, healing started to flow through her body. A few minutes later, she was largely free from pain and looked about fifteen years younger. The next night, she brought several friends to a healing service. I have no idea how complete her healing was, but certainly there was a dramatic improvement.

Was this a deliverance ministry? I don't know and it doesn't really matter. If she did have a spirit of infirmity or some other spirit, it was not like the evil spirits that I have described in earlier chapters. It exited quietly and with no fuss after my friend's inspired diagnosis, and her confession.

Deep spiritual problems

When people come for prayer, sometimes it becomes apparent that they are under a serious spiritual cloud. There are two main possibilities. Normally, you can hold a quiet, sensible spiritual discussion and decide, together, how best to approach the problem. Occasionally, as in some of the case studies I have mentioned, there is a violent reaction and you have to respond.

The main symptoms are those outlined in Mark 5 – attraction, yet also repulsion, at the presence of Jesus (and His ministers and holy places – particularly churches); speaking in strange tongues which are not under the control of the person seeking help; extreme physical strength; a desire for self-harm, especially suicidal thoughts and actions. To this we may add occult involvement – including possessing charms, amulets, books, or DVDs on the occult; unnatural bondage to sexual perversion, compulsive habits, unsought for blasphemy or mockery of God; any of these may be indicators of a demonic presence. Extreme fear – particularly of holy places – and an inability to pray are other signs. Frequently, people who are troubled by evil cannot say the Lord's Prayer. Also, as I mentioned earlier, you can tell a great deal by looking straight at people's eyes.

My main diagnostic questions are: first, have you been involved in any occult practices such as spiritualism, fortune-telling, crystal healing, tarot readings, seances? Second, are you aware of any of your ancestors, or partners, being involved in such things? Third, have you suffered any great traumas in the past – particularly any kind of physical or sexual abuse? Fourth, have there been any great tragedies in your life? Fifth, are you adopted?

Depending upon the answers, there are many different ways forward. We can offer direct physical healing with, if appropriate, the laying on of hands and / or anointing with oil. We can offer "inner healing", which is particularly appropriate if there are great hurts or traumas from the past, still affecting the person who has asked for help. We can offer "generational healing" if it is clear that there are ancestral problems – of the sort indicated in Chapter 6. Lastly, and in my case reluctantly, we can undertake some type of deliverance ministry.

Normally, I suggest that, at a future date, we go through a formal retaking of their vows of baptism. This, I explain, will involve a full renunciation of any dubious spiritual activities, a clear repentance, and a turning to Christ. For some this will be an initial profession of faith – a conversion. For others, already Christians, it will be a step of recommitment and hopefully a move towards a more fruitful discipleship. I will discuss the vexed question of, "can a Christian be demonized?" at the end of the book (FAQ 7).

In tune with John 14:17, we are mainly dealing with situations where a person is not actually demonized but has suffered from some severe spiritual attack. But sometimes, this approach is sufficient to deal with actual demons. The case of the marine who interrupted our dinner party was one such.

The procedure is simple, dignified, and straightforward. I find the service in the ASB particularly helpful. In the presence of a small number of witnesses (occasionally this is appropriate at a church service), the candidate is asked, "Do you renounce evil?" It is logical, and necessary, to take the vows in reverse order. He or she will reply, "I renounce evil, especially..." Then the candidate is asked, "Do you repent of your sins?" They will reply, "I repent of my sins especially..." Finally, he or she is asked, "Do you turn to Christ?" After an affirmative answer, the candidate can profess the Trinitarian faith, and can be anointed with oil. We can all then pray for a new infilling of the Holy Spirit. Any lurking demon will, almost certainly, show up at this time. Frequently, the candidate will express huge relief and experience a new joy and peace.

I find that this ministry is effective in about 95 per cent of cases of possible demonization. It has the advantages of being memorable for the person concerned, simple, and yet decisive. All bases have been covered! Such a ministry is definitely not a formal exorcism and does not usually require the permission of the authorities. In the case of the marine, I did both inform his doctor and ask the bishop's permission, as there was a real possibility of a violent confrontation – which happily didn't take place.

Demons manifest

Occasionally, the situation gets unexpectedly out of control. We have two main approaches – one is "to do nothing and to do it well", and the other is to try to get rid of the demons, preferably with the help and co-operation of the person concerned. In Gilbert and Sullivan's *Iolanthe*, there is a couplet, "Throughout the war the House of Lords did nothing in particular and did it very well." This apparently so incensed Queen Victoria that Gilbert was denied his knighthood until the next reign. Nevertheless, I think it is excellent advice for the deliverance ministry. It requires considerable self-discipline and faith "to do nothing and to do it well" but this is often the best approach.

When the African lady (Chapter 6, page 108) exploded into a demonic frenzy after recognizing the word that I had written down, I sat quietly with my startled praying partner. We had assumed that we were dealing with a problem of deep sorrow and an inability to forgive. We were not expecting a demonic exhibition. By sitting quietly, praying mainly silently, the demons expended their strength and departed. A confrontational ministry could have been lengthy and perhaps unsuccessful.

Here is an extract from my friend Alison Morgan's diary of her first trip with me to Africa:

Chibwika (near Mwinilunga NW Zambia) 29 July 1999

We've just had supper, after a fairly extraordinary day which began with birdwatching at the waterhole. The service started at 9, which actually turned out to mean 10.30. John preached and then we started to pray for people individually, which went on for ages. Delivered three people from demons, which was much easier and quite straightforward compared with the recent experience of dealing with Vicky – none went immediately, but none took more than about ten minutes. One woman began speaking rather incoherently in English, which I didn't pay much attention to, continuing to rely on Peter, the teacher who was translating for me. Peter began to look a little uneasy and explained that the woman didn't speak English. So it was the evil spirit – and the essence of what it said was, "I've gone!" Meanwhile I learnt to banish demons in Lunda, the local language – 'demon fuma!' is the required phrase, with reiterations of the name of "Yesu Christu". Will never forget the sad, light brown eyes of an elderly woman we cast a spirit out of; could almost see right down into her soul as I made her fix her eyes on mine as we prayed. Not a word in common; and yet I could see her agitation and her pain; and the weary relief which came over her as the thing went. I asked how old she was afterwards but she couldn't remember. Then a bunch of children, with the usual range of complaints – malaria, diarrhoea, headaches, stomach aches.

Then after lunch we had seminars with the leaders – Cesca and I did the women. Encouraged them they need to minister, taught from Ephesians 4 and 1 Corinthians 12, answered questions, then asked them to come individually for prayer if they felt they would like to offer themselves to be used by God in ministry. Asked each individually if she wanted to serve God in her church and then prayed for her. Not all of them wanted to do this – say fifteen out of twenty-five? Then they said they had various other prayer needs, so we got them all praying for one another in turn. They all said their pains, headaches, etc. went, except for two children. Either God was being very good, or they were being extremely polite; but they seem sincere in their affirmations of healing, particularly the ones who suddenly smiled or visibly relaxed as we prayed. The chief's daughter, resplendent in magnificent yellow, and contrasting with the grubby rags of most of the others, has been to the witchdoctor and she is spiritually closed.

She continues describing some of the ministry in a later sermon:

Well, let me just end by telling you what I saw when I went to Zambia. I went as part of a mission team. The first place we went to was in one of the remotest parts of the country. We travelled all day

179

down dirt tracks, and finally through the trees on a handmade road to a new mission station. We stayed there for three days, among some of the most underprivileged and unimportant people I've ever met. Education, medicine, and money have passed these people by. They live in mud houses and eat the maize and cassava they grow themselves. They have no safe water. They are nobody and they have nothing. But some of them have become Christians. So one afternoon, I and my colleague Cesca, gathered the women of the place together. We told them it wasn't just us who could pray for healing, they could too. One by one they came forward and shared their pain. One by one the group prayed for them. We started it off, then we just stood and watched them do it. We didn't even understand what they were saying. But we could see their faces. I will never forget one lady. She was old. She sat down on the ground. And she told us of her pain. She told it so clearly we could see it as she talked. She suffered from pain in her legs, pain in her arms, pain in her chest. You could see the despair and the pain in her eyes. Then they prayed for her as we had taught them. We watched. And as they prayed we saw her face change. Peace came all over it. She smiled. Her whole body relaxed. She stood up. Now, I don't know how that woman is today. She may even be dead. But as she was prayed for I saw her meet God, and something happened. Nobody in this world is less important than that woman. An old, illiterate peasant in a corner of Africa the world has forgotten. But God cares about her. And He cares about you. You don't have to be important. You don't even have to be good. Jesus came for the sick and the sinful. He came to heal and He came to save. So please come with your needs, whatever they are, and ask God to meet with you too. My experience is that whatever is happening in your life, if you throw yourself on the mercy of God, He will give you what you need.

One of my own abiding memories is of an old woman, probably the one mentioned above, wreathed in smiles and saying that her whole life had been transformed. In these rural areas, healing and deliverance are completely intertwined. One complements and completes the other.

My friend Peter Hancock[1] records that when he was in Zambia in 1993:

Archdeacon Tobias Kaoma was ministering deliverance in a church in Fuwela in Central Zambia. A young woman was rolling about on the floor and making a great deal of noise. Tobias was sitting quietly, apparently unconcerned, on a small table just watching her. I knew Tobias' high reputation for his ministry of deliverance and I remember thinking, "He knows something that I don't!" So I asked him why he was just sitting there. He told me that the spirits were great exhibitionists and that they like to make a great fuss so as to draw attention to themselves. When they had had their "go", he would then minister and cast them out in Jesus' name. He never seemed to get flustered or to shout at them. His ministry was the most powerful, and effective, that I have ever witnessed.

A man once came to see me from another parish about his spiritual problem. He declared that the main symptom was that "he was a menace in house groups". I nearly laughed – I could think of plenty in my own parish who would have fitted that description. However, he explained that many years earlier, before conversion, he had been involved in occult activities and had experimented in other ways. Subsequently, he had settled down to a good job, married, and become a Christian. He had suffered a severe breakdown but had been cured. And he couldn't share his faith with his wife – he felt that she had had too much to put up with. He thought he was "possessed". I explained that I couldn't pray effectively with him without someone else being present, so we went across to the church and I prayed a holding prayer – like a temporary dressing from a dentist! I suggested that he should come to the Wells Cathedral Healing Day, which was two days later.

During the service, I was greatly occupied with the organization of complicated prayer ministry, which involved over thirty pairs of prayers from different churches and different denominations, and several stations where anointing was to take place. A man came up to me – I confess that I didn't recognize him. He was my visitor from two days earlier. He looked quite different. "What has happened to you?" I asked. "Whatever it was left me last night," he replied. Evidently, the demonic powers recognized that they would stand no chance of survival in the cathedral. At the end of the service, I met his wife on the cathedral steps. She looked a bit shattered when

I tried to explain what had happened, and how important her own commitment to Christ would be. A short time later, I heard that she had turned to the Lord. It was a wonderful thing that God had released this man without any direct ministry, and then used it to bring his wife to faith.

In 1999, I was leading a service in Kitwe on Zambia's copper-belt. The church met in a school classroom. The service was quite difficult – I tried to have some silence so that we could call on the power of the Holy Spirit. Silence was virtually impossible as there was a Pentecostal congregation in the next-door classroom. At the end of the service, about a hundred people queued up for prayer. I asked my friend the pastor, "Where is the healing team?" "You are the healing team," he replied. I looked at my watch. I was on English time. In just over an hour I was due at the cathedral where I was trying (unsuccessfully as it turned out) to broker a reconciliation between the bishop and the cathedral leaders.

I quickly discerned a couple of deliverance cases. I sent them to the back of the queue as, if demons started manifesting, there would be no time for healing. Ministry was very brief and totally reliant on "the power of the Lord being present to heal" (see Luke 5:17). One woman said she had a stiff shoulder. She couldn't raise her arm. I commanded her to raise it "in the name of the Lord". It was that sort of day; there was no time for polite enquiries. Her arm shot up, and I thought no more about it. At the end, the two demonized people appeared and the demons departed very quickly. Amazingly, I was on time for my next appointment.

A week later, I was back in Kitwe. My friend contacted me. He told me the story of the lady with the stiff shoulder. She didn't normally attend church. But that Sunday, she had put on her finest clothes and taken some of the children with her. They had been amazed – they had never seen her raise her arm. As a result, her husband had called in my friend to cleanse the house. It was full of witchcraft remedies. The pastor described it as like a household conversion in the Acts of the Apostles. I was thrilled – and left wondering what would have happened, or not happened, if I had tried to minister first to the demonized at the head of the queue.

In earlier chapters, I have described some confrontational ministries. They never lasted very long and were, with a few exceptions, apparently successful. In Mutwe, I never discovered what happened to the demonized group of women, who included the one with the English-speaking spirit. I assume that many of them came for prayer the next day when there was little demonic interference.

I had a similar problem in Chipili on my final visit. A room full of high school children seemed to explode with demons. We were only able to help some of them. Demons, as Tobias Kaoma had remarked, are exhibitionists, and seem to gain confidence and power when they are present in some numbers.

As I have mentioned, even the most confrontational ministries are greatly helped if the person concerned tries to co-operate. If they can name the demon, call to Jesus, recite the Lord's Prayer, and tell the demon to go, the whole process is much quicker and much less abrasive. Sometimes, it is helpful to cut off what I would call "the controlling spirit". This is especially the case if there is a particular problem with the occult. At the end of the ministry, I think it is appropriate to anoint the freed person with oil. This is partly to emphasize that the Holy Spirit is now within them (assuming they have made a clear and credible profession of faith), and partly as a litmus paper test – any lurking demons should react to the oil.

I do remember once breaking my own rules. It was my final visit to Zambia in 2002. We were conducting a series of open-air morning seminars. We were in Chibwika, a large village with a thriving church. Chibwika is in the north-west corner of Zambia on the Angolan border. We had several seminars taking place simultaneously. Suddenly there was complete chaos. A woman attending the seminar next to mine was shouting and screaming. Everyone else stopped to watch. I felt decisive action was needed. I strode up to her and, speaking rather loudly, I told her to shut up in the name of the Lord. Mercifully she did, the demon left, and order was restored.

In Zambia in 1994, I worked with Revd Randy Vickers. He had a particular way of invoking the power of the Holy Spirit – here is a brief extract from my report:

When Randy arrived, I had just finished my teaching session. Randy had a session teaching about the Holy Spirit and then went through his procedure of invoking His presence. There was some spiritual reaction; but not the violent screams that I had witnessed elsewhere. Then we started to pray for the sick. Randy saw the dramatic healing of a baby who was suffering from chronic constipation. What I noticed, then and later, was that this gentle yet powerful approach seemed to disarm the demons. It was very instructive.

If you are involved in any prayer ministry where there is a possibility that demons will show up, it is necessary and wise to gain clearance from the Diocesan Deliverance Officer. It is necessary because the Anglican Church requires it, and it is wise because you will have some reliable prayer cover and a measure of protection if things go wrong. However, in many of the cases that I have described, things got unexpectedly out of hand. In those situations, you cannot sit around and await permission. It is, of course, important to report such cases.

Post-ministry care

After ministry, everyone needs care and attention. The person prayed for will usually be very tired. They will naturally be anxious that the demon may return. The story of Mary Magdalene and some teaching on Ephesians 6:10–20 should help. If they have been converted through the deliverance, they will need to join an Alpha course or an adult confirmation group. It is essential that someone responsible keeps a good pastoral eye on them. Potentially, they will be very useful members of the church. Often they will have a gift of discernment, which can be used to help others. Some of the people I have found to be the most useful members of deliverance teams were originally contacted because they had asked for help in this aspect of their lives.

Members of the team may also be very tired. In the early days of my ministry, I used to become very tired and rather bad-tempered about twenty-four hours later. Jane used to ask, somewhat wearily, "Who have you been praying with?" Michael Green used to feel that he hadn't done effective ministry unless there was a counterattack – rows at home, disturbed dogs. The only piece of theology that I ever taught him (he taught me much) was to apply Psalm 34:7 and to believe that "the angel of the Lord encamps around those who fear him".

If you have been covered by a prayer team, it is common courtesy to tell them, in outline, what has taken place.

Indirect attacks by the devil

Scripture also outlines Satan's general strategy. This includes lies (John 8:44 – perhaps the most persuasive in today's church, certainly in the West, is "I don't exist"). Detestable practices (Deuteronomy 18: 9–13) include spiritualism (very common today, especially sought out by many families after bereavement), any form of sorcery (healing through use of pendulums, etc.) and child sacrifice (allegedly practised in some forms of witchcraft). False accusation (see Revelation 12:10) is one of Satan's subtlest strategies to undermine the confidence of believers. Christians are often crippled by false guilt or a feeling that they cannot be forgiven for some past sin. This is one of Satan's most persistent, and successful, lines of attack.

Temptation (Matthew 4:1–11; 1 Corinthians 10:12–13) is a normal means of attack. Occasionally, people say they are in complete bondage to a temptation. Surfing the net for pornography would seem to be a modern problem. This could indicate a serious demonic issue. Obviously problems like alcoholism, compulsive gambling, or lack of sexual control are serious matters. However, I don't think they are demonic unless there is some other way, possibly generational, that Satan has got a direct foothold.

Tribulation and testing (Revelation 2:8–11) is a normal part of the experience of Christians working as missionaries or living in non-Christian cultures. The savagery of IS against professing Christians is a current example.

Paul says confidently, "we are not unaware of his schemes" (2 Corinthians 2:11). More importantly, as already noted, he also says, "Satan himself masquerades as an angel of light" (2 Corinthians 11:14). This verse warns us that Satan is at his most dangerous when practising deception. In *Thinking Clearly about Angels* (pages 226ff.), I describe a number of incidents involving serious deception. The opening story of Chapter 8 is about a serious deception that I was personally taken in by.

All of these matters will require prayer, and probably compassionate counselling, but they are outside the scope of this short book. The most important point I want to make is a simple one – listen carefully to people's stories, don't prejudge the situation, and reassure them (even if you think there is a natural explanation) that many others have had similar experiences.

To summarize the above:

MINISTRY TO BUILDINGS

(1)   Spend time with the people who are being troubled – it is best to visit with the local priest who can help with the follow-up. Listen to their story. With permission, take careful notes. Taking notes means you don't have to interject if a thought or a question springs to mind. Make a date for a return visit and explain what this will involve. Explain that you will be bringing another member of the diocesan team. Obviously, you may feel that there is no real spiritual problem. In that case, it is good to offer to bless the house.

It is also important to include some theological input. If, and only if, the resurrection of Jesus is a true historical event will this ministry be effective. It may be helpful to give some simple reasons as to why you believe this to be true.

(2)   For the second visit, unless it seems like overkill, there will be three people: the local vicar (essential for proper pastoral follow-up), yourself, and another member of the team. I prefer not to brief this person – they can then exercise their spiritual gifts unencumbered by previous knowledge. I also prefer not to robe and will probably bring nothing other than a Bible. I will leave it up to the person who has first asked for help to decide who else may be present. I don't encourage children to be there, but there are times when it seems to be necessary.

I will ask for a bowl of water, explain why I am using this, and make a simple prayer of blessing. I will also enlist the help of the occupants. If they see or feel anything, it is very important that they tell the team what they are experiencing. I don't make suggestions but such feelings may include a sense of extreme coldness, deep fear, a sense of something leaving.

We will then go round the building. I normally start at the top of the house. If necessary, I will climb a loft ladder into an attic. I will read from Scripture. Psalms 121 or 91 seem very appropriate. In each room I will sprinkle some of the water, praying "in the name of the Father, the Son, and the Holy Spirit" for any spiritual presence to depart and to go to Jesus. Other members of the team may add their own prayers. I will spend longer in places where there have been disturbances. Staircases often seem particularly troubled. After prayer, and a short period of silence, I will usually ask people if they felt anything or were aware of any presence.

When we have been around the whole house, and if necessary any outbuildings, we will sit down in the main room for a brief final prayer, discussion about the future, and the inevitable cup of tea. I will explain that this process will probably have been sufficient to bring peace and quiet to the building and the family. If necessary, I will return for a third visit, which will involve a simple service of Holy Communion.

(3) For the third visit, I will return with the same team. On this occasion, depending upon the family, I may robe. I will invite the household to take part in the service and receive the bread and wine (I realize that some team leaders will not feel comfortable with this). The service will be a simple Anglican rite, with an extended time of prayer for the household and the house in place of the intercessions. I do not usually repeat the prayers around the house except in places where there may have been a recurrence of trouble.

I have never found it necessary to make further visits, and rely on the local priest to provide appropriate ministry and pastoral care.

MINISTRY TO PEOPLE

I normally use a service which involves the renewal of baptismal vows. This can be found in *Common Worship*[2] on pages 150f. or, more helpfully, in *The Alternative Service Book* on pages 275f. The service can be conducted privately at home, in semi-public with a home group or in a church room, or as part of a church service. I prefer to do this in private with another member of the ministry team present. The person(s) will have been prepared. They will understand that they are going to make a full renunciation of any previous occult involvement. I always take the vows in the reverse order. It seems logical, especially in these circumstances, to first renounce evil before making a prayer of repentance and an affirmation of turning to Christ. It is important to make it clear that this is not an exorcism, but prayer to set someone free from any spiritual forces that *may* be troubling them, now or in the past. Once again, it is also important to emphasize the power of the cross as the means whereby evil forces are defeated, sins forgiven, and reconciliation offered by God. The risen Lord has complete authority over all the spirits that may be troubling them!

An alternative approach would be to make a clear renunciation of evil first and then follow the service in the formal ASB liturgy. It is useful to begin with the Lord's Prayer.[3] If someone is actually demonized, they will probably have difficulty saying this prayer – especially the important phrase, "Deliver us from evil".

The renunciation of evil should take the form, "I renounce evil, in particular my involvement with…" If there are ancestral issues, they can be dealt with in a similar way, unless it seems necessary to hold a separate service (see the end of Chapter 6). It is important to give the person time to consider, and probably write down, all the things which need to be renounced.

This session may include the removal and destruction of anything that could be construed as an idol (see Question 21 at the end of the book). It will certainly include confession (James 5:16) of any sin involving occult practices. Occasionally, the person will need reassurance that they haven't committed the unforgivable sin, "blasphemy against the Holy Spirit" (Mark 3:29). The context makes it clear that this sin involves accusing Jesus of exercising his authority to exorcise by the power of Satan. The person you are trying to help is highly unlikely to have done that!

At the end, provided that they seem to have made a clear profession (or recommitment) to the faith, I will often anoint the person with oil and pray for an infilling of the Holy Spirit. They will frequently join a follow-up group – adult confirmation, Alpha, or Emmaus are particularly appropriate.

In the unlikely event of a major spiritual reaction to the ministry (see Chapter 4, page 67 for some of the common symptoms), then stronger prayers for deliverance may be required. These will proceed with caution along the lines outlined earlier in the chapter.

Never tell someone they are demonized – certainly not possessed. Keep an open mind about the depth of the problem. Be confident that whatever prayers are offered in the name of Jesus will be effective.[4]

SPIRITUAL MATTERS – THE PAST AND THE PRESENT

(CHAPTERS 10–12)

CHAPTER 10

DELIVERANCE IN CHRISTIAN HISTORY

And let the prince of ill
Look grim as e'er he will,
He harms us not a whit;
For why? his doom is writ;
A word shall quickly slay him.

(Martin Luther, "A safe stronghold our God is still")

The church fathers

The writings of the church fathers, which include the testimonies of or about men such as Justin Martyr, Irenaeus of Lyons, Tertullian, Origen, Athanasius, and a host of others, all point to the importance of exorcism as a key weapon in the evangelism of the Roman Empire. The historian Ramsay MacMullen constantly alludes to this in *Christianizing the Roman Empire AD 100–400*.

The much disputed longer ending of Mark's Gospel includes the injunction: "And these signs will accompany those who believe: in my name they will drive out demons"(Mark 16:17). If these words are part of the original ending of Mark's Gospel, then the instructions of the risen Jesus are very clear. They are for all believers and for all time – not just for the apostolic age. If these words were added around AD 100, as most scholars believe, they must reflect the beliefs and practices of the church at the turn of the first century. Either way, this means exorcism was to be an important part of the church's witness. This was certainly the experience of the church in the next three centuries.

Justin Martyr (c. 100–165) has a number of reported comments, which suggest that the deliverance ministry was common in the early church. This is because demons were associated with pagan gods, and especially with food sacrificed to them (1 Corinthians 8 and 10:14–22). Exorcism, perhaps even more than healing, asserted the Lordship of Christ in a multi-faith world. He writes:

> For numberless demoniacs throughout the whole world and in your city, many of our Christian men, exorcising them in the name of Jesus Christ, who was crucified under Pontius Pilate, have healed, and do heal, rendering helpless and driving the possessing devils out of men, though they could not be cured by all the other exorcists and those who used incantations and drugs.[1]

MacMullen[2] has some very apposite quotations. Justin says, "How many persons possessed by demons, everywhere in the world and in our own city, have been exorcized by many of our Christian men?" Tertullian (160–220) issued the challenge: "let a man be produced by right before your court who, it is clear, is possessed by a demon, and that spirit, commanded by any Christian at all, will as much confess himself a demon in truth as, by lying, he will elsewhere profess himself a god". Cyprian (d. 258) declared that, "when [demons] are adjured by us in the name of the true God, they yield forthwith, and confess, and admit they are forced also to leave the bodies they have invaded, and you may see them, by our summons and by the workings of hidden majesty, consumed with flames."

Irenaeus of Lyons (c. 130–200) was another important early witness. As a boy, he had heard the famous martyr Polycarp speak. Irenaeus was a theologian, pastor, bishop, and possibly a martyr. In his writings, he makes a strong distinction between Christian miracles and signs performed by occult means (see 2 Thessalonians 2:9). He writes:

> Those who are in truth Christ's disciples, receiving grace from him, do in his name perform miracles... Some do really and truly cast out demons, with the result that those who have been cleansed from evil spirits frequently believe in Christ and join themselves to the church.[3]

He also mentions the healing of the sick. He states that all this is done by prayers to the Lord and not by means of angelic invocations or by incantations. He claims too that, in contrast to the partial or temporary cures affected by Gnostics and pagan magicians, the cures effected by this reliance on the name of the Lord Jesus Christ are both permanent and complete.

Origen (c. 185–254) is another powerful witness to the power of exorcism and healing in the name of Jesus. He makes much of this in his celebrated work, *Origen Contra Celsum*. Here are two examples (out of many in the text):

> *If the Pythian priestess is out of her sense and has not control of her faculties when she prophesies, what sort of spirit must we think it which poured darkness upon her mind and rational thinking? Its character must be like that race of daemons which many Christians drive out of people who suffer from them, without any curious magical art or sorcerer's device, but with prayer alone and very simple adjurations and formulas such as the simplest person could use. For generally speaking, it is the uneducated people who do this kind of work. The power in the word of Christ shows the worthlessness and weakness of the daemons, for it is not necessary to have a wise man who is competent in the rational proof of the faith in order that they should be defeated and yield to expulsion from the soul and body of a man.*

> *The Christian, the real Christian who has submitted himself to God alone and His Logos, would not suffer anything at the hand of daemons, since he is superior to them. And the reason that he would not suffer is that "the angel of the Lord will encamp round about those who fear him and deliver them" (Psalm 34:7), and his angel "continually beholds the face of the Father in heaven" (Matthew 18:10) and is always bearing up his prayers to the God of the universe through the mediation of the great High Priest. And the angel himself prays together with the man who is under his charge. Let not Celsus scare us, then, by threatening that we shall be hurt by daemons if we slight them.*[4]

What is striking is that Origen regards the work of exorcism as within the capabilities of ordinary Christians (Justin Martyr and

Tertullian make the same point). He is also absolutely confident of the protection that God provides to Christians in these circumstances. In Chapter 12, we shall see Gregory the Wonderworker spending the night in a heathen temple, to the astonishment, and conversion, of the Temple keeper and many others.

Minucius Felix,[5] writing at the beginning of the third century, gives a graphic description of exorcisms: "When they [demons] are driven out of men's bodies by words of exorcism and the fire of prayer"; he adds how they leave their victims: "reluctantly, in misery, they quail and quake".

Tertullian is clear that Roman society is indebted to the Christians for their spiritual protection. In a letter to an official called Scapula, he notes:

> *For, the secretary of a certain gentleman, when he was suffering from falling sickness caused by a demon, was freed from it; so also were the relatives of some of the others and a little boy. And heaven knows how many distinguished men, to say nothing of common people, have been cured either of devils or their sickness.*[6]

MacMullen[7] writes about Novatian (c. 200–258). He, although doctrinally orthodox, was a very controversial figure in the early church. He is thought to have become a Christian through his family calling in the local church's exorcists when he was gravely ill. There are various different accounts of this event!

Kydd writes most helpfully about the prevailing views of the spiritual battle:

> *In the midst of all the confidence and rejoicing there was more than a hint that confrontations with the demonic were not always simple. Bishop Cyprian sounded a cautionary note. Certainly ultimate victory was assured; he did not back away from the confidence expressed earlier. But sometimes dealing with the demons was a struggle. In one place, he talked about their deceptiveness. In another, he commented that when they were exorcised, they might leave rapidly or slowly. Cyprian thought this would depend on the faith of the sufferer "or the grace of the healer". Minucius Felix made exactly the same observation and offered the same explanation. These Christians*

were very conscious of the spiritual battle into which their faith in Christ had propelled them. To them the world of spiritual beings was no quaint abstract idea. They had to face its daily reality. Their experience of the power of Christ was a major source of confidence.[8]

The early fathers give an impressive witness to the continuation of the ministry of healing and deliverance long after the days of the apostles. Indeed, the clear impression is that many of them saw healing and deliverance as a quite normal part of the church's witness, and something which ordinary Christians would expect to be involved in.

However, after the dramatic conversion of Emperor Constantine (c. 312), the church suddenly became respectable and powerful. The miraculous faded somewhat. Augustine of Hippo (354–430) thought that Christians should not look for the continuation of the miraculous gifts. However, in his last book,[9] he completely changed his mind. He recorded that nearly seventy attested miracles of healing had occurred in Hippo. One of them, that of the healing of his friend Innocatius, he records in great detail. He also records[10] a dramatic "out of body' experience of a man called Curma whom he later baptized. He does not appear to have mentioned deliverance.

St Martin of Tours (336–397) was recorded by his friend and contemporary biographer Sulpicius Severus as having a remarkable effect when he emerged from solitude:

Many mad and possessed pagans thought they would be helped if they touched the old man, and fully as many became Christians in a few days as you would otherwise see in a year. He also exorcised the slave of Tetradius, a former proconsul, and the owner who was still a pagan, became a catechumen and before long received baptism.[11]

MacMullen makes a dramatic comparison between the powerful exorcisms performed by Antony (251–356), which were intended to demonstrate the Lordship of Christ (see Chapter 12, page 241), and the methods employed by the now politically powerful church:

Silencing, burning, and destruction, were all forms of theological demonstration: and when the lessons were over, monks and bishops, generals and emperors, have driven the enemy from the field of vision.[12]

A particularly horrid example was the lynching of the Neoplatonic philosopher, Hypatia, in Alexandria. In 392, she was dragged naked through the streets by a lynch-mob of monks who killed her and burnt her body. The murder, unbelievably, was approved of by monastic chroniclers.

> *Hypatia beguiled many people through her satanic wiles. After her murder all the people surrounded the Patriarch Cyril (who had instigated the mob) and called him the new Theophilus who had earlier destroyed the last remains of idolatry in the city.*[13]

Obviously the need for deliverance didn't completely disappear. MacMullen gives some evidence for the continuation of the deliverance ministry. In particular, in the fifth century, Theodotus in what is now Syria seems to have had a powerful ministry. William Dalrymple[14] writes about the influence of a number of people in pre-Muslim Syria. He is writing of his journey in 1994 nearly twenty years before the terrible civil war, which, among many other tragedies, has virtually eliminated the once very effective Syrian church.

> *Perhaps the holy man's most important task was to fight demons. The world was believed to be besieged by invisible agents of darkness, and to sin was not merely to err: it was to be overcome by sinister forces. Demonic activity was a daily irritation, and was believed to intrude on the most ordinary, domestic activities. A recently discovered papyrus fragment tells the story of the break-up of the marriage of a young Byzantine couple, a prosperous baker and the daughter of a merchant: "We were in time past maintaining a peaceful and seemly married life" they wrote in their divorce petition. "But we suffered from a sinister and wicked demon which attacked us from we know not whence, with a view to our being divorced from one another." The writer John Moschos (550–619), most notably of* The Spiritual Meadow, *tells the story of a nunnery in Lycia which was attacked by a troop of demons. As a result, "five of the virgins conspired to run away from the monastery and find themselves husbands".*[15]

Dalrymple also says:

Across the east Mediterranean that tradition still continues: to this day Christian monks are believed to be powerful exorcists, a talent they share with their Islamic counterparts, the Muslim Sufi mystics.

He tells of visiting a convent near Homs.[16] He attended a Christian service where the vast majority of the congregation were heavily bearded Muslim men. Apparently they came here mainly to pray for their wives to conceive. A nun told him of many answers to their prayers: "One Muslim woman from Jordan had been waiting for a baby for twenty-five years. She was beyond the normal age for childbearing, but someone told her... She came back the following year with triplets!"

I have read elsewhere of a church in Syria where Muslims would come quietly for prayers for healing or deliverance – tacitly acknowledging the power of Jesus without being able to take the risky step of confessing the faith.

At the end of his journey, Dalrymple visits the monastery of St Antony in the desert near Alexandria. The monks there seem to regard exorcisms, miraculous healings, and apparitions of long-dead saints as unremarkable.[17] Father Dioscuros illustrated his beliefs with this story:

This happened last week. The Bedouin from the desert are always bringing their sick to us for healing. Normally it is something quite simple... but last week they brought in a small girl who was possessed by the devil. We took the girl into the church, and as it was the time for vespers one of the fathers went off to ring the bell for prayers. When he saw this the devil inside the girl began to cry. "Don't ring the bell! Please don't ring the bell!" We asked him why not. "Because," replied the devil, "when you ring the bell it's not just the living monks who come into the church: all the souls of the fathers join with you too, as well as great multitudes of angels and archangels. How can I remain in the church when that happens? I'm not staying in a place like that." At that moment the bell began to ring, the girl shrieked and the devil left her. Father Dioscuros clicked his fingers: "Just like that. So you see that proves it."

An ancient seventh-century sculpted stone picture, from St Vigeans near Dundee, of a famous meeting between St Antony and St Jerome had intrigued Dalrymple. The saints were going to break bread but each deferred to the other. Eventually, they each held the bread and pulled it apart. Amazingly, Dalrymple was shown a very ancient framed picture of the same scene. The two saints are shown in St Paul's cave, sitting on a rock ledge. Clearly the artist knew the correct place. The Scottish illustration has the two saints breaking bread in exactly the same way but sitting awkwardly on high-backed chairs. For a long time, there has been evidence that the Celtic church had had contact with the Egyptian church. Perhaps Dalrymple had noticed another link in the chain.

It is to the Celtic church that we now turn. Cuthbert (see also Chapter 12, page 245) was also very much into deliverance ministry.

The Celtic saints

Chapter 15 of Bede's *Life of Cuthbert* is entitled, "How he exorcised the wife of a sheriff even before he reached her".[18] Hildmer was the name of the sheriff and he was a Christian, and he and his wife were much loved by Cuthbert:

> *His wife, though zealous in almsgiving and all the other fruits of virtue, was suddenly possessed of a devil. She was so sorely vexed that she would gnash her teeth, let out frightful howls, and fling her arms and legs about. It was terrifying to see or hear her.*

You can imagine this might have been a little inconvenient for a sheriff to have a wife gnashing her teeth and flinging her arms and legs about.

> *The convulsions gradually exhausted her and she was already at death's door, or so it seemed, when her husband galloped off to fetch Cuthbert.*

Hildmer tells Cuthbert how ill she is and asks for him to send a priest to give her Holy Communion and to bury her body in holy ground.

Bede adds, "He was ashamed to admit that she whom Cuthbert was used to seeing well was now out of her mind." Michael Mitton remarks, "It's those touching human comments that make me have little doubt about the historicity of these stories."

Bede continues that Cuthbert was ready to send a priest off to do what Hildmer asked, when:

> it suddenly came to him that she was in the grip of no ordinary illness: she was possessed. In the light of that discernment, Cuthbert decides to go to the wife and he and Hildmer go off, when there is another touching episode:
>
> As they were going along the sheriff began to weep. The bitterness of his anguish was apparent from his flood of tears.

Michael Mitton comments: Now why was he crying? "He was afraid that when Cuthbert found she was mad he might think she had served God up to now only in feigned faith." This is a surprisingly contemporary concern. We are very aware that we are in a spiritual battle. There has been, over the years, much discussion about whether or not a Christian can be afflicted by demons. For Cuthbert there was no doubt – Christians could be.

But also, this little story alerts us to that very normal human fear that if we become afflicted in some way by the demonic, whether it be some kind of sickness, or an addiction, or repeating pattern of sin, we must keep it hidden for fear people will doubt our spiritual integrity: "if he is afflicted with a demon in that way, he can't have been a very faithful follower of Christ".

This story of Hildmer's wife beautifully illustrates the fact that, for Christians who are troubled by the demonic and the spiritual battle, we can very easily have a sense of shame and failure. That sense of shame and failure can cause us to keep our affliction hidden, which means we fail to ask for help.

For Hildmer's wife, there wasn't much choice – her manifestation of the demonic was there for all to see, and clearly she and Hildmer were really anxious that people, and Cuthbert especially, would conclude she was a person of little or no faith. Cuthbert has no truck with this way of thinking:

Do not weep. Your wife's condition will not astonish me. I know, even though you are ashamed to admit it, that she is afflicted by a demon. I know too that before I arrive the demon will have left her and that she herself will come running out to meet us as sound as ever. She will take the reins, bid us come in quickly, and treat us with all her usual attention. It is not only the wicked who are stricken down in this way. God, in his inscrutable designs, sometimes lets the innocent in this world be blighted by the devil, in mind as well as in body.

Here is Cuthbert, full of prophecy and wisdom. He knows prophetically that this woman will be delivered, and what she will do when they arrive. But he also has the wisdom to know that the saints as well as the sinners can get afflicted by the demonic. He offers no theology really for this. Bede continues:

And as they approached the house, the evil spirit, unable to bear the coming of the Holy Spirit with whom Cuthbert was filled, suddenly departed. The woman, loosed from the chains of the devil, jumped up as though from a deep sleep, rushed out in gratitude to the saint, and caught hold of his bridle. She admitted quite openly that at the first touch of his bridle all trace of her affliction had vanished.

Cuthbert, in ways very similar to St Antony (see especially Chapter 12), himself knew some very personal attacks of Satan. He developed a deep love of extended times of prayer, sometimes whole nights without sleep, with work the next day. It was probably through these extended times of prayer that he developed his prophetic gifting.

Over the next centuries, there are few if any accounts of the demonic. The church was powerful politically, rich in money, but somewhat lacking in spiritual insight and power. In the thirteenth century, Pope Gregory X said to the great theologian Thomas Aquinas, "The church can no longer say, 'Silver and gold have I none.'" Aquinas replied, "No, nor can she say any longer, 'In the name of Jesus of Nazareth rise up and walk.'"

The Reformation and the Methodists

However, when the Reformation came, Martin Luther was well aware of spiritual warfare, as in his great hymn, "A safe stronghold our God is still". The third verse, with its words about overpowering the prince of ill, seems particularly appropriate.

And were this world all devils o'er,
and watching to devour us,
we lay it not to heart so sore;
they cannot overpower us.
And let the prince of ill
look grim as e'er he will,
he harms us not a whit;
for why? his doom is writ;
a word shall quickly slay him.[19]

Luther's life is full of spiritual conflicts – most notably the dramatic healing of his great friend Prince Philip Melanchthon.[20] When the Methodist revival came, George Whitefield and John Wesley both witnessed strange reactions to their preaching. Both were uncomfortable with these phenomena. Wesley, in his diary, notes many examples of people needing deliverance. Perhaps surprisingly, all of these seem to have sought out his help rather than having reacted to his preaching.

Here is one of the clearest examples (23 October 1739):

At eleven I preached at Bearfield to about three thousand. I was exceedingly pressed to go back to a young woman in Kingswood. (The fact I nakedly relate and leave every man to his own judgment of it.) I went.

She was about nineteen or twenty years old, but, it seems could not read or write. I found her in bed, two or three persons holding her. It was a terrible sight, anguish, horror, and despair above all descriptions appeared on her pale face. The thousand distortions of her whole body showed how the dogs of hell were gnawing at her heart. The shrieks intermixed were scarcely to be endured. But her stony eyes could not weep. She screamed out, as soon as words could find their way, "I am damned, damned; lost for ever! Six days ago you might have helped me. But it is past; I am the devil's now. I have given myself to him. His I am. Him I must serve. With him I must go to hell. I will be his. I will serve him. I will go with him to hell. I cannot be saved. I will not be saved. I must, I will, I will be damned!" She then began praying to the devil. We began to sing: Arm of the Lord, awake, awake!

She immediately sank down asleep, but as soon as we left off, broke out again with inexpressible vehemence, "Stony hearts, break! I am warning you. Break, break, poor stony hearts! Will you not break? What can be done more for stony hearts? I am damned that you may be saved. Now break, now break, poor stony hearts! You need not be damned, though I must." Then she fixed her eyes on the corner of the ceiling and said "there he is: ay. There he is! Come just now. Take me away. You said you would dash my brains out: come do it quickly. I am yours. I will be yours. Come just now. Take me away."

We interrupted her by calling again upon God, on which she sank down as before, and another young woman began to roar as loud as she had done. My brother now came in, it being about nine o'clock. We continued in prayer till past eleven, when God in a moment spoke peace into the soul, first of the first tormented, and then of the other. And they both joined in singing praise to Him who had "stilled the enemy and the avenger".[21]

Other examples included a ten-year-old girl who frequently attempted to throw herself into a fire or out of a window. She would try to tear up the Bible, utter oaths and blasphemies, and rage against Wesley. Nearly a year later, her symptoms suddenly ceased. There is a very lengthy account of a woman called Elizabeth Hobson who could see people when they had just died. She eventually inherited a house from her grandfather, described as an exceedingly wicked man. This caused her endless spiritual and legal problems. Finally, she was delivered through the prayers of some of Wesley's friends. Another account is of a woman who had what Wesley described as a spirit of pride and lies. She decided she didn't need to read the Bible, or to pray, as she was good enough. Eventually, after several sessions of prayer, she received true peace.

Wesley also had many experiences of divine protection when

mobs, or even bulls, were let loose to attack him. On one occasion, a theatrical troop who were mocking him were thrown into confusion when the stage collapsed beneath them.

George Whitefield had this experience in Philadelphia in 1740. His biographer, John Pollock, reports:

> *He had called together a "society" composed of young white women, and on Saturday May 10th, he went to organize it. As he entered he heard them singing with a fervency that delighted him. He began a brief prayer before addressing the assembly but to his own astonishment couldn't stop. Petitions, praises, raptures poured from his lips: "A wonderful power was in the room". Soon the girls were sobbing and confessing and weeping for sins. His prayer was drowned by cries which, he was sure, could be heard a great way off. When he ceased to pray no one noticed for every girl in the room was totally absorbed in prayer and confession, an amazing medley of sound. "They continued in prayer for above an hour, confessing their most secret faults; and at length the agonies of some were so strong that five of them seemed as affected as those who were in fits".*
>
> *George crept away. He wondered, how much was the work of the devil trying to disrupt the Gospel, how much was genuine, unfathomable power of God. He had two profitable encounters with people who had recently been converted. But at midnight, he was summoned back to a young woman in unspeakable agony of body and mind. He prayed and talked with her. Her distress abated. George now felt sure that the devil caused the fits, as with the boy in Mark 9 who was thrown headlong when Jesus rebuked the evil spirit.*[22]

Pastor Blumhardt

Another minister whose ministry was greatly changed by an exorcism experience was J. C. Blumhardt (1805–1880).[23] The great twentieth-century theologian Karl Barth regarded him as one of his mentors. Blumhardt had, for some time since his installation in 1838, a quiet, effective ministry in the small village of Mottlingen in the heart of the Black Forest in Germany. He was known as a diligent Lutheran pastor; many people were healed and he was much in demand.

A decisive battle began in December 1841 and amazingly lasted two years. In her youth, Gottliebin Dittus had come into contact with witchcraft through an aunt. The demonic played a growing influence upon her life until in desperation she turned to Blumhardt for help. For a while, Blumhardt had tried to avoid being involved. A doctor who attended her was completely bewildered. He said, "Is there not a clergyman in this village who can pray? I can do nothing for her."

Then some of the brethren, who had heard Blumhardt preach confidently about faith, came to him saying, "If you do not wish to shake our belief in your preaching you cannot retreat from the evil one." After a moment's thought and silent prayer he answered: "You are right; but to be in accord with the word of God you must unite with me in supplication according to James 5:14." He, always accompanied, prayed regularly for her. She endured the most excruciating agony.

Trying to cope with the angst of not being able to achieve complete victory, he sought the counsel of a Professor Stern, who reminded him of Mark 9:29. That prompted Blumhardt to give more attention to fasting. The climax was reached at about 2 a.m. on 28 December 1843. Blumhardt was praying for Gottliebin when he perceived that her sister Katharina had also come under demonic influence. He turned to pray for her when suddenly she shrieked, "Jesus is victor! Jesus is victor!" and fell silent. Blumhardt recorded that her screams were so loud that half the village was able to hear them. At that moment both women experienced complete healing.

This dramatic healing changed Blumhardt's whole cosmology. He continued a quiet healing work. But a professor of medicine at Tubingen University was impressed by the many letters that he received from people who had been healed. He set up a house of healing which acted as an inspiration for many houses of healing that were set up in England in the following century. The whole village was deeply touched spiritually. Nearly all professed faith. One notorious sinner came to ask if it was possible for him to be saved. Blumhardt told him of God's mercy. Immediately his countenance was changed and he left, full of joy, to go from cottage to cottage to tell everyone what he had experienced.

But the key experience which transformed the power and depth of Blumhardt's ministry was the deliverance of Gottliebin and her sister. Without that decisive experience of the power of the name of Jesus, his preaching about faith would have become ineffective. In Chapter 12, we shall see something very similar in Irian Jaya.

More recent experiences and conclusions

While writing this book, I was given a copy of *Anna Hinderer: Pioneer Missionary*.[24] In 1853, Anna travelled with her husband, David, to Nigeria. They were stationed in Ibadan which is about 100 miles north of Lagos. They served there until 1869. Anna died in England the next year. During their time, they saw many conversions. Their church recorded ninety-six communicants in 1867. Typically their converts had much opposition from their families, which could include considerable violence. Invariably, they had worshipped idols, which they usually brought to be destroyed.

Anna realized that there was a great deal of contact with ancestors, especially in a fearful ceremony called "the Feast of Egungun", which could last a whole week. They made friends with the local king. When he died, before great feasting, four men (an unusually small number) were put to death and forty-two of his wives poisoned themselves.

They suffered a great deal from illness – especially yellow fever. This must have contributed to Anna's early death. David had trained local leaders and he was able to revisit Ibadan in 1874 and see that his churches were flourishing. One of his local leaders Daniel Olubi, who was ordained in 1871, died at the age of eighty-two in 1912.

Anna and David seem to have been widely respected by the non-Christians. They suffered greatly during incessant local wars and had periods when they were almost starving. Anna supported a household of about thirty and brought up many local children. One king, whose territory lay between Lagos and Ibadan, was seriously impressed when he failed to kill David, who was too ill to travel between the two places.

This very moving story raised one serious question for me: why did all these baptisms take place completely unhindered by evil spirits? There would seem to be a number of possibilities.

(1) There were no actual evil spirits to worry about.

(2) The authority of David Hinderer's teaching was such that the evil spirits removed themselves before the baptism. The actual service, according to the BCP, would have included the decisive question, "Dost thou renounce the devil and all his works?"[25]

(3) They lay dormant – managing not to disclose themselves.

(4) The native Christians knew about them but didn't dare mention them to David, particularly as it probably wouldn't have been part of his teaching.

I incline to (2). I think the spirits knew when they were going to be defeated and didn't want to disclose the power and the hold that they had on the non-Christians. Anna noted that those who came for baptism seldom referred to their past and just started a new life with a new name. By way of contrast (see Chapter 5, page 84), my friend David Ridge certainly encountered the power of the demonic forces some one hundred and fifty years later in Jos in central Nigeria.

In 2006 and 2008, I was able to visit the Chaco region in northern Argentina where some of the few indigenous tribes live. They have their own (Anglican) church, their own bishop and church leaders. One of the present-day missionaries (this account is from Christobal Wallis who works under the authority of the present bishop, Nicholas Drayson) has given me this account of the evangelization of the region:

> The pioneer Anglican missionary in the Chaco region was Wilfred Barbrooke Grubb, who wrote several accounts of his work in the Paraguayan Chaco, starting in the year 1890. There is a fairly extensive anthropological literature on the different indigenous peoples of the Chaco, but with few exceptions these don't reveal much about missionary thought and practice. What this literature does often demonstrate is the hugely significant presence for the indigenous people of diverse "spirit beings", the shamanic practices employed in relating to them, and the centrality of healing in both traditional shamanic and Christian practice.

Here it must be understood that most illness or the absence of wellbeing is generally believed by both the Wichí people and other indigenous groups in the Chaco region to be the consequence of some "spiritual" intervention and the search for cures is equally directed towards the assistance of spirit beings. It is not surprising, then, that healing ministry (whether shamanic or Christian) be ubiquitous and in many cases barely distinguishable, in practice, from deliverance ministry.

It can safely be said that the early Anglican missionaries to both the Paraguayan Chaco (as from 1888) and the Argentine Chaco indigenous peoples (as from 1911) had a thoroughly rationalistic world view and considered that Christianity meant overcoming superstition and the belief in all the spirits that inhabited the indigenous peoples' world. If the Amerindians lived in fear of the spirits and saw these as the cause of their ailments of one kind or another, the task of the missionaries was to enlighten the people so that they no longer would give credence to such superstitious beliefs.

The principal means for combatting superstition was twofold: ridicule and medical treatment. On the one hand, the pioneer missionary Barbrooke Grubb took every opportunity he could to expose "witchcraft" as pure superstition and quackery. His view of the shamans, whom he called "wizards", was that "the greater part of their art is pure deception. Yet they are to a considerable extent the victims of self-deception themselves..." He further remarks that "much of their witchcraft is pure trickery; a few of them have the rudiments of the conjuror's art, although, as a rule, their deceptions are very clumsy. The people are so credulous and unsuspicious that the wizards do not find it necessary to acquire any great skill."

In his attempt to demonstrate that the people were being duped by their wizards he himself performed conjuring tricks to first astonish his audience only then to reveal to them the secrets of his own trickery.

To Barbrooke Grubb's mind everything, even unusual occurrences, had a rational explanation. So, for example, dreams which for the Chaco Indian are considered revelations of the spirit world, should be explained as caused by recent events, hidden fears, or simply by indigestion.

In the early days of his missionary work it was considered unwise to introduce a strong medical programme. One of the principal reasons being that any successful healing would simply be taken as another form of witchcraft, since the native idea was that almost every physical trouble was caused by evil spirits and witchdoctors and so, similarly, any cure was equally "spiritual" rather than physical.

However, in the long-run it was the introduction of scientific medical treatment that was seen as the major antidote to superstition. So, Richard Hunt, Barbrooke Grubb's closest colleague, would write after returning from long years of missionary work in both Paraguay and Argentina of the benefits recognized by the Indian people of a doctor and a dispensary. "In the course of a few years the medical missionary had won the people, and the charming of the sorcerer gradually ceased and his power waned."

"Enlightenment rationalism" imbued the work of these early missionaries and so Barbrooke Grubb would write towards the end of his life that one of the great achievements of the missionary work had been to release the indigenous peoples from their belief in spirits. "The fair-minded reader will, with very little effort, be able to understand what an inexpressible relief it must be to an Indian to have his mind enlightened to such an extent that he no longer lives in a state of constant supernatural dread. This relief, among others, it has been one of the Mission's privileges to bring to him." According to this frame of mind there can be little scope for a ministry of either "deliverance" or even "healing", since the spiritual dimension of sickness and health is not recognized as significant.

Many years later in the late 1950s, a Mennonite missionary among the Toba Indians (also in the Argentine Chaco), Elmer Miller, who eventually left his work as a missionary to become an anthropologist, expressed a similarly rational viewpoint. "Praying for the sick always represented something of a dilemma for me. While I did not consider prayer inefficacious, the notion of laying on of hands with the expectation of a miracle was over and beyond my standard of faith. I was particularly uneasy when the sick were removed from the protective walls of their homes into the heat or cold so that the church leaders could lay on hands and pray for healing... In contrast to Toba preachers, I consistently recommended clinics and medicine."

In Miller's opinion it was not just his attitude that down-played the supernatural dimension of faith, but was characteristic of Protestant missionaries in general. In an article based on his experience in the Argentine Chaco, entitled "The Christian Missionary, Agent of secularization" (Anthropological Quarterly, Volume 43, No. 1, January 1970), Miller writes that "naturalistic beliefs form the organizing basis for the missionary's comprehension of the vast majority of day-to-day events and experiences. Rather than reinforce or expand traditional supernatural beliefs, the missionary, in fact, supports the many naturalistic orientations Westerners tend to impose on non-Western cultures... Missionaries actually assign supernatural beliefs and actions a minor role in describing and explaining everyday experiences of human existence." Whereas the Tobas would tend to seek other-than-natural explanations for occurrences, the missionary would give a natural cause and effect explanation. In particular, whereas illness and healing for the Toba fundamentally involved spirit beings, for the missionaries it was more a question of germs and the right scientifically-based medicine.

In the reports of the Anglican missionaries there are also accounts of situations where possibly one might have expected a response similar to a deliverance ministry, but in practice there is no sign of such a reaction. In Paraguay during the years 1912 to 1913 "a strange new cult" developed in the Lengua (now called Enxet) church, that was clearly syncretistic and bordering on what are commonly called "cargo cults". A kind of spirit possession was one of its features and the cult attracted a number of those who were professed Christians along with others. While the cult was taken to be "an assault by the Adversary against the progress of Christianity", as far as we can see no attempt was made to challenge the leaders or the spirits involved at a spiritual level. Rather, the leaders and their followers were challenged publicly by presenting in a rational manner the truth of the Gospel and the deception of the cult's teaching. We may safely assume that the missionaries did pray earnestly over the issue, in the same way as they recommended that SAMS followers should pray for the apostates.

In the year 1927, two years after the founding of the Mission station San Andrés among the Wichí people, in the present-day Province of Formosa (Argentina), the missionaries were surprised by what they called a "regular epidemic" of suicides. The epidemic seemed to be led by a girl called Monteya, who led girls off into the forest to consume a deadly poisonous fruit. Many of those involved whose lives were saved reported that "they felt impelled by some mysterious power to eat the fruit" and accordingly witchdoctors were called in to deal with the spiritual forces attacking the people. Once again, while the missionaries considered that this was "an attempt of Satan to wreck the work of the Gospel before it had time to take effect" (H. C. Grubb, The Land Between the Rivers, 1965, p. 7), and Grubb explicitly quotes Ephesians 6.12, the response was work and prayer rather than counterattacking with some form of deliverance ministry.

There has been a Pentecostal influence among many of the indigenous groups of the Chaco, going back in some cases to the 1930s. Pentecostal emphasis on the power of the Holy Spirit, power to heal and transform, power over all other spirits has generally found ready acceptance in many indigenous people, whichever denomination they may adhere to. Indigenous concepts of illness and healing which are framed in terms of the influence exerted by different spirit powers are fertile ground for receiving the message of the power of the Holy Spirit over and above all other powers. Praying for healing and praying to cast out evil spirits – both by individuals and in groups – is now common practice in nearly all churches, although the style may vary according to the denomination.

During the 1980s a missionary nurse from Australia, who worked with the Anglican Church, developed what can surely be called a "deliverance ministry" among the indigenous people and was greatly respected by the people as this ministry, as our current Bishop once wrote, "scratched where it itched". However, I am not sure that today it can be said that there are either missionaries or indigenous pastors that have a specific deliverance ministry. It is just common practice for a person to ask for prayer for release from illness or an evil spirit. And the ensuing prayer may be by an individual or, more commonly by a group. We are asked again and again for prayer and just in the past few weeks two young people came to us asking for prayer as they felt spirits were attacking them. I would not, however, consider that I have a deliverance ministry (in Spanish called "Ministerio de Liberación").

In some cases, we suspect that more "magical" ideas have crept into this area of ministry, such as using the Bible as a talisman and pressing it on the affected part of the body, or repeating endlessly the "Name of Jesus" or the "Blood of Jesus", as if these words of their own have a magical power. In the last ten to fifteen years there has also been a steady extension of electricity into rural areas and the growing involvement of the indigenous peoples in a monetary and consumer economy has led to many families acquiring televisions. Many watch with delight "tele-preachers", especially the more sensational ones who specialize in casting out demons and their ways are then copied by Indians, whether they be pastors or not. Young "prophets" have sprung up all across the Chaco, who may also dabble in casting out evil spirits.

So, while recognizing the value of this ministry and the importance of taking into account the indigenous people's own experience of spiritual dimensions, this whole area is liable to perversions and requires great discernment.

I find this account fascinating. The rationalism of the early missionaries has gradually been somewhat replaced with a more spiritual approach. Obviously, this can lead to some of the excesses (devils everywhere) that we have discussed elsewhere, but it seems much more scriptural than the "devil goes missing' approach of the Victorian and early twentieth century. Certainly my own brief visits to northern Argentina suggest that the deliverance ministry is needed, and appreciated, among both the indigenous and the local people.

There is a very obvious difference between the amount of deliverance ministry experienced in the first four centuries of the church and that recorded up to the beginning of the twentieth century.

With the exception of the experiences of the Celtic church and the ministry of John Wesley and J. C. Blumhardt in the eighteenth and nineteenth centuries, accounts are few and far between. Then, with modern medicine and the insights of psychiatry, it is somewhat surprising to find a considerable increase in the last hundred years.

Tentatively, I would offer these reasons. First, for many centuries, England was a nominally Christian country. This gave the spiritual opposition much less room for manoeuvre. Anyone suffering the symptoms of demonic possession was unlikely to seek help – they were far too likely to be accused of witchcraft and suffer terrible penalties. Secondly, there was no "deliverance" ministry for those practising such things – trial by ordeal and execution, by burning, were a far too common outcome.[26] Thirdly, it would seem that the ministry of deliverance continued throughout the centuries in churches in the Middle East.[27] Fourthly, the missionary movement, mainly from the nineteenth century onwards, undoubtedly in some places faced the problem of evil spirits.[28] Fifthly, in the twentieth century, there was a much greater expectation and experience of the work of the Holy Spirit. This brought the demonic much more into the open. At the same time, the decline in Christian belief and morality in Europe meant that there was a considerable rise in occult activities and psychic healing. If you walk down Glastonbury High Street, almost every shop is selling something psychic. Such open practice would have been impossible in earlier years.

Wherever there is powerful movement of the Spirit, especially in missionary situations, there is likely to be a conflict with the powers of darkness. The early church was well equipped to deal with this until it reached political power and respectability. The Celtic saints, in their battle to evangelize all parts of the British Isles, needed this power. Interestingly, Augustine of Canterbury, coming up from the south and with a different theological direction, also saw many miracles. He even received a mild rebuke from the pope and was told not to rely on signs and wonders. The pope quoted from Luke 10.[29]

Then, more recently, the extraordinary evangelistic ministry of the Wesleys was accompanied by many signs. The decisive ministry of George Whitefield, especially in New England, was accompanied by many signs – though few exorcisms appear to have been reported.

The ministry of J. C. Blumhardt developed from a quiet village ministry into something that touched the whole German church, mainly after the exorcism of the two sisters.

What can we learn from Christian history?

The overall picture is somewhat patchy. My impression is that where there is no expectation, or understanding, of evil spirits then there is much less likelihood of spiritual conflict. The Hinderers were, I think, fairly typical in dismissing the worship of idols and the influence of ancestral spirits as of little significance once conversion was professed and baptism received. Paul dismisses idols with the comment, "we know that an idol is nothing at all in this world" (1 Corinthians 8:4). Anna Hinderer comments, "It is remarkable in the African character, but one hardly sees anything of sorrow for the past, nor are we able to draw from them that they feel any." This is a powerful witness to this viewpoint.[30]

Similarly, in Chapter 12, we shall see that Jacques Teeuwen is startled and completely unprepared when a candidate for baptism, who has been suitably prepared and examined, is obviously overtaken by an evil spirit. After this first confrontation, evil spirits were often encountered. David Lithgow also has his eyes opened on the Woodlark Islands when a man commits suicide. David realizes that he was demonized and not psychiatrically ill as he had first thought.

Paul says, "For we not unaware of his schemes" (2 Corinthians 2:11). But perhaps the early missionaries were somewhat unaware. As a result, Satan chose either to lie hidden or to remove his troops before the ordeal, for them, of Christian baptism.

We may conclude that, throughout Christian history, almost whenever the gospel was preached with power and conviction, then deliverance was needed. But, as the final chapter of this book will show, there were always some places where the power of the devil was more obviously apparent.

CHAPTER 11

CULTURAL CONSIDERATIONS

Satan trembles when he sees
The weakest Saint upon his knees.

(William Cowper, "What various hindrances we meet")

Africa needs God

We return to Matthew Parris' article in *The Times* entitled, "Africa needs God".[1] He recounts how he travelled to Malawi. He had travelled to see the work of a small Christian charity called "Pump Aid", which was included in *The Times* Christmas Appeal. Its aim was to provide much needed clean water for small rural communities. Such work is important.

My second daughter, Susie, learnt a great deal from spending a gap year teaching in a rural school near Kabale in southern Uganda. For months, she had to walk for twenty minutes down a precipice to collect water. This was followed by a longer, difficult climb bringing the water back to her small dwelling place. The advent of clean water from a newly installed well, built on this occasion by Tearfund, transformed her daily routine.

My mother-in-law at the age of sixty felt called to move to western Kenya. She set up a rural development project near Oyugis. Spring Protection schemes, designed to bring clean water to communities, were one of many successful projects. Thirty years later, aspects of her work still flourish – notably JAM. JAM began as "Jesus and Me", which was a youth evangelism project named by my eldest daughter,

Rachel. It has morphed into JAM, "Justice and Mercy" – a project run by Kennedy Okoth, whose education my mother-in-law sponsored, and which supports about 1,200 people who are mainly HIV widows. It brings hope and healing to the poorest of the poor. One of their greatest needs, as they work in local groups, is for a local well.

Parris was impressed by Pump Aid. He wrote, "It inspired me, renewing my flagging belief in development. But travelling in Malawi refreshed another belief, too: one that I've been trying to banish all my life."

He explains that he was convinced of the enormous contribution that Christian evangelism makes in Africa, which he sees as sharply distinct from the work of secular NGOs, government projects, and international aid efforts. He asserts that, "In Africa Christianity changes people's hearts. It brings a spiritual transformation. The rebirth is real. The change is good."

His main thesis is that, while mission hospitals are good, it is the faith that is essential. Faith liberates African people from fear. It helped people stand tall. He describes his travel aged twenty-four into many parts of sub-Saharan Africa: "Whenever we entered a territory, worked by missionaries, we had to acknowledge that something changed in the faces of the people we passed and spoke to: something in their eyes, the way they approached you."

On his return to Africa to visit the Pump project, Parris observed the honesty, diligence, and optimism of the project workers. He noticed their quiet, unostentatious faith. He noticed, too, that they were greatly influenced "by a conception of man's place in the Universe that Christianity had taught". In addition, he noticed something about African tribal beliefs and practices:

Anxiety – the fear of evil spirits, of ancestors, of nature and the wild, of a tribal hierarchy, of quite everyday things – strikes deep into the whole structure of rural African thought. Every man has his place and, call it fear or respect, a great weight grinds down the individual spirit, stunting curiosity.

He concludes that Christianity, with its teaching of a direct two-way link between the individual and God, smashes through the spiritual framework of subservience and fear.

Removing Christian evangelism from the African equation may leave the continent at the mercy of a malign fusion of Nike, the witchdoctor, the mobile phone and the machete.

It is interesting, and moving, that Parris, the staunchly eloquent atheist, acknowledges the reality of the rebirth that Christianity brings. He sees the release from fear of evil spirits, ancestors, and the malign power of the witchdoctors. Presumably, for him, this power must be cultural.

Many people would agree that witchdoctors have obtained their position through some medicinal knowledge, through fear, through an unwritten hierarchy, which all must acknowledge. Ancestors can still influence people. Living people seem to live out their lives in fear of offending the dead. Evil spirits dominate people's dreams, feed their fears, and at times control their actions.

Evil spirits – products of culture?

At this point, we must ask and attempt to answer the crucial question: is this malignant power a reality or a cultural myth? If it is a reality, then the transformation that Parris acknowledges that Christianity brings is not only effective in bringing freedom and dignity, but it is also essential in freeing people from a reality of evil and fear.

Presumably, those who see mention in England of evil spirits as "medieval mumbo-jumbo" must deny their reality in Africa. They are cultural spirits, which have affected people's thinking for generation upon generation. People are so taken over by fear, which passes from one generation to another, that they act as if completely in bondage to this fear. The ancestral world is writ large in the DNA. It is a reality only because people believe in it. There are, however, at least two major difficulties with this type of thinking.

First, evil spirits know no cultural boundaries. Evil spirits encountered, by me, in sophisticated Oxford, rural Somerset, working-class Leicester, rural Zambia, other parts of East Africa, Argentina, Papua New Guinea, and reported to me by many others whom I respect in different parts of our globe, act in identical fashion! There was little difference between the marks of the first evil spirits, which I unexpectedly encountered in Oxford, and those

I encountered in Mutwe Wa Nkoko in rural Zambia. There is little difference between those that I have met in Leicestershire and those that I have heard about, and experienced, in PNG.

The five marks, which I outlined from the story of the Gadarene man (Mark 5:1–20) were present in part, or in total, in all situations. The primitive spirits encountered by David Lithgow[2] in the Woodlark Islands were no different to those encountered in pubs, factories, offices, and homes in England, which I have been called into.

Read the stories in this text, or any other similar book, and you will inevitably conclude that these evil powers, real or not, display their wares in the same way throughout the world. They are also dealt with effectively through prayer in the name of Jesus. The sons of Sceva may try other methods; they may achieve partial freedom. But in the end Jesus, and only Jesus, will set people and communities free.

As we have seen in Chapter 10, the ministry in the early church was similar. There are no discernible cultural differences in the writings of Justin, Tertullian and Cyprian, who all present evidence of regular exorcisms, with one case leading to the conversion a future bishop. The accounts by Athanasius of the ministry of his contemporary, St Antony, by Gregory of Nyssa about Gregory the Wonderworker, and Sulpicius Severus about St Martin of Tours, all speak of their power as exorcists and their effectiveness as evangelists.[3]

There are at least two other areas where a malign spiritual influence can be seen to be independent of cultural boundaries. In Chapter 6, I outlined some work and theology in the area of generational healing. The seminar I conducted in Tucuman in northern Argentina, in 2004, led to much prayerful ministry in this area. The concerns outlined, which included spiritualism, gambling, sexual licence and abuse, Masonic influence and alcoholism, were similar to those I have encountered in England. The ministry was similar; the occasional manifestation of spirits was similar, as was the generally beneficial effect.

A second area of ministry which proved to be necessary in both England and Africa was where spouses had been adversely affected by their husbands' spiritual activities. Once, in Kitwe in northern Zambia, I was praying for a group of people. All responded positively except for one young woman. She was showing all the familiar signs of demonic trouble. Our prayers, unusually, were having no effect. We could not discern how an evil spirit could have entered her, or why it was proving so difficult to free her. Eventually, I asked her about her husband. Evidently, he had strong connections with tribal witchcraft – I forget the details. Once she had confessed on his behalf, she was quickly set free. Paul reminds us (1 Corinthians 6:16) that sexual union makes two people into "one flesh". This seems to permit evil spirits to cross over from partner to partner.

The experience (see Chapter 6, page 115) of the wife of the convinced Freemason who, despite a strong Christian profession and involvement in ministry, needed considerable and extensive ministry, is an example of the same phenomenon in England. Once again, there is no discernible cultural difference. The troubled wife in Leicester and the troubled wife in Zambia had exactly the same problem and the same symptoms. Each appeared to have indwelling demons; each had good, loving husbands who had opened themselves by some spiritual disobedience to evil powers. In one case it was tribal witchcraft, in the other Freemasonry. The results were the same. However, I would readily acknowledge that opening yourself to any form of witchcraft virtually guarantees a spiritual problem, whereas opening yourself up to Freemasonry *may* be relatively harmless.

Some cultural differences

In Africa, there is a more intuitive belief in the supernatural and a great expectation that God will intervene. There is a much greater belief in the possibility of curses. This is especially true in the areas of healing and deliverance. Here is a testimony from an intelligent, educated member of the team at Neema Crafts[4] based in Iringa in Tanzania:

My name is Paulina. I am a Masai and I teach business and entrepreneurship to people with disabilities at the Neema Crafts Centre, Iringa, Tanzania. I have had three big health issues in my life, each of which I believe have been connected to curses used against me within my own family. The first happened when I was four years old. I was born healthy and had no problem walking, running and jumping. One day I woke up with a pain in one of my legs that was so bad I just kept crying and I couldn't walk. When I went to hospital they said it was polio. My bad leg is now a couple of inches shorter than the other, the heel is thick and the front of my foot has shrunk. My mother and father both said it had been caused by a curse against me. I didn't walk for two years after this, but when I was six I began to be mobile again.

Immediately after I started to walk, I broke out in spots and boils all over my body. Some family members told my mum just to let me die as I was already crippled and no use to anyone. But my mother and uncle took me to the local herbal doctor first and then to the government hospital in town. Here they gave me some medicine and operated on the worst of my boils and they slowly reduced. Some of the boils have left marks on my skin that you can still see today.

In 2011, while I was in Zanzibar, I began to develop an issue with my heart and at the bottom of my stomach. When I went to hospital they couldn't find any problem, but they gave me an injection and I felt better. Then I developed a problem with the left side of my body. My arm, body and hand were all experiencing numbness. The following year I returned to Iringa and I went to get an ultrasound to check whether there was a problem in my chest – my side was very tender and I couldn't sleep. Unfortunately, they couldn't see any problem, but they gave me some medicine to try to help.

When I later became pregnant my stomach issue started again, but I also began to feel dizzy and my heart was racing. I couldn't sit or rest easily and I felt there was something moving up and down my chest. I felt awful. My mother said that I should go to a herbal doctor and she gave me some local remedies for both my heart and stomach. After I gave birth however the problems continued.

The pain was not a continuous thing, but I would have episodes when I felt the sickness descend on me. The pain would start around my heart and move through my left arm as a sort of numbness. Then I would feel dizzy in my head and I would begin to find even breathing difficult. I went to many doctors about this problem but they couldn't find anything wrong with me. During one bout of sickness I asked the Neema Crafts chaplain to pray for me and the problem reduced, but after a week it started up again. The fits were so bad I had to leave my desk and sit in a room on my own shaking and shivering. I was very scared.

When John came out to visit his daughter Katy, he was able to sit with me and listened to my story. He held my hand and looked into my eyes for a sustained time. We then began to pray and he used some Scripture to pray against any specific ancestral issues particularly connected to witchcraft. Since this time, I praise God that I have never had any relapse of these issues but have been perfectly healthy!

I believe there is a spiritual cause at the bottom of all of these problems. My father is married to three wives and my mother is his second wife. Ever since I was born, my father's first wife (my step-mother) has hated my mother and each of her seven children – we are four boys and three girls. She has been particularly jealous of us because my mother sent us all to school – my father didn't give us even a shilling to go.

In Masai culture if a child shows that it is particularly gifted or intelligent then it can be poisoned, cursed or left to die simply because the child may upset the status quo. I have been told that as a child I was particularly "mtundu", which means mischievous and clever, and so probably attracted more of the wrong type of attention from my stepmother and other villagers. I know that she has been to the witchdoctor to put a curse on our side of the family and she told my father just to let me die when I was sick. My brother Paul also suffers from epileptic-type fits, which we believe are connected to curses. Although I have forgiven her for these things, even now, we don't like to go back to the family home because she stirs up so much trouble against us.

To Western ears, this may seem far-fetched. But when I went with the chaplain, my son-in-law Ben, and Mim who was head of the physiotherapy department, Paulina, as she has described, was in a bad state. Her health problems were affecting her work and her home life. We spent about an hour listening to her story and praying. The chaplain, a local Anglican priest, was particularly helpful in explaining the cultural issues and giving Paulina confidence.

Our prayers were gentle. There was no strong spiritual reaction – just a sense of peace. I said that I would return the next week. When

I came back, Paulina looked quite puzzled. She was feeling so much better she had forgotten that we were returning for another prayer session! I am certain that her remarkable change in health was due to lifting the curses placed upon her and releasing the fear that they had induced.

Curses can happen anywhere, but I think much more rarely in England. Here is a powerful testimony from an Anglican vicar, John Widdas, first published in *ReSource* magazine[5] in November 2006:

> *In 1986 the then Bishop of Wolverhampton, Christopher Mayfield, asked me to consider becoming the next Vicar of Tamworth. "I know I'm taking a risk," he said! I agreed. I was a liberal catholic who had been baptized in the Holy Spirit while at St Chad's Lichfield and now I was a catholic, evangelical charismatic! St Chad's was pleasantly full most Sundays and I think the Bishop was now hoping for similar results at the 1,000 seater St Editha's Tamworth.*
>
> *I had been a curate there from 1966–1969 and the people expected the same as before. On the other hand, the Bishop was hoping for rapid growth before most of the present congregation died. In this he was correct. We held over 70 funerals for church members in the first 18 months!*
>
> *As Lent came round we held a Tuesday evening Eucharist in the crypt. We had a couple of hymns and I did a talk. Gradually we introduced well known choruses and I introduced John Wimber style talks which evolved into times of related ministry afterwards. This was enthusiastically supported by the curate Robert Latham. There were requests not to stop at Easter so we carried on. It involved more and more and people came forward for the release of the Holy Spirit in their lives which in turn released the Gifts of the Holy Spirit in them. We saw amazing things in the ministry afterwards.*
>
> *Robert moved on to be a vicar and we were joined by Peter Mockford and family. His creative contributions added much to the event. Eventually the crypt was overfull so radical decisions had to be taken. We moved the Sunday Sung Eucharist with excellent organ and choir to 9 am and brought in a Family Communion with music group, overhead projector, large screen and a nave altar at 10.45 am. It was well publicised and 150 people came to the first service. We were delighted that a similar number continued to*

arrive week after week. They were very largely people who did not come to the Sung Eucharist so mercifully the move had little effect on other services.

We developed systematic preaching with a resumé of the sermon handed out on a single side of A4 on arrival. There were healing teams available every Sunday in the Side Chapel and people moved from receiving Communion to the healing ministry. The people who came were largely in response to the Words of Knowledge which were, in turn, the result of prayer before the service led by the church secretary and my wife. The healing team of the day kept a log of: the Words of Knowledge, whether there was a response, what the result was. There was usually a forest of ticks on the page. Things were going from strength to strength.

Then it happened. Services that had been prayed over, well prepared for and should have gone well fell like a damp squib. The leader got a blinding headache just before the service and was afflicted with memory loss and unaccountable weakness. Church members sat in the pew full of expectation and were unaccountably hit with terrible rage and jealousy. Feuds and factions broke out. The whole church and especially the Family Eucharist was falling apart. Peter and I met to pray. "What on earth is going on?" we asked the Lord and each other. It became clear we were under intense satanic attack presumably from a local group.

Over a period of many months we wrestled with each problem in prayer and the Lord led us on step by step until we worked out a strategy of spiritual warfare. At last the corner was turned and the church was again growing. It was not easy and not without cost. Peter and I wrote Lightning from Heaven *for Kingsway explaining how we dealt with the situation. It sold quite well considering it was a specialist subject dealing with demonic attack.*

Shortly afterwards a church member turned up at the door. She was a kindly person who kept in the background at church. We had worked together on supplying local soldiers in the Gulf with decent desert boots and some of the luxuries of life and prayed for them each lunch-time.

"John", she said, "I need to tell you something. I have been sent by the local satanic coven to destroy the growing church in the centre of town. Your worship is destroying our activities within a three

mile radius. However, over the past many months of the struggle I have come to realize that the power of Jesus is much greater than the power of Satan. I want to leave the coven and become a Christian."

It was an awesome moment. Yet I was suspicious. Was this yet another trap? One day she arrived at the vicarage thinking I was alone and told me she had been "called in" to meet the regional leader in Hopwas Woods. She said he had carved the Baphomet on her back with a razor blade (a star, with two points uppermost). I called my wife. The woman was startled. "Take her to the bathroom and look at her back and tell me what you see," I said to my wife. She returned and confirmed her story. Now I was reasonably assured she was on the level. This was further confirmed when a social worker involved with her daughter's care came to Christ through her witness. They are both still faithful followers attending another church. When the book was published I asked her to read it and tell me what we got wrong. "Nothing, that was what we were trying to do to you," she said as she returned the book.

John, aged sixty-eight, died soon after this article was published. It is clear that the powerful praise of the church and the incantations of the coven were, in very different ways, disrupting their opponents.

Here is another example of a curse affecting someone in England.

Some years ago, I was asked by a doctor to see one of her patients. He was a young businessman, still able to work, but crippled physically by ME for seven years. ME is a curious illness, which baffles the medical profession but leaves its sufferers physically exhausted and in great disarray. We had a long conversation. It was clear that he had some psychic experiences dating back to his childhood. Eventually I asked the obvious question: "What happened seven years ago?" The reply was quite surprising. "Seven years ago, I started dating a young woman. Eventually, I discovered that she believed she was a witch. I stopped going out with her. She warned me that she had cursed a previous partner and that my fate would be same. It was."

About two days later, I went with a friend to pray through the young man's house. There were a number of disturbing features. He was clearly quite psychically aware, which probably made him more vulnerable. Then we prayed for the man. We cut off the effect of the curse. He said he felt better. In fact, he was so much better that he was able to restart his workouts in the gym the next day. His doctor was impressed! He joined an Alpha course and expressed a considerable interest in the faith. He has remained in excellent health.

John Wesley, whose journal is remarkably level headed, records (13 August 1746) the case of a woman who had suffered great torments for nearly seven years. She had fallen out with a neighbour who had then apparently paid fourteen shillings (serious money in those days) to a man "to do his worst for her". Since then, she had been in endless trouble in both mind and body. However, quite suddenly (Wesley doesn't say how), she had experienced release and praised God in a way that Wesley had scarcely ever heard.

These beliefs can create difficulties. There are many dubious ministries in Africa. In Tanzania, I was frequently asked by clergy and lay leaders, "If people pay more, are they more likely to be healed?" I heard horrendous stories of people, often young teenagers, being spiritually blackmailed and threatened with curses, to pay faith healers vast sums for cures which weren't happening. This was going on in relatively sophisticated cities like Arusha, not in the much poorer rural areas. Faith healing and magic become intertwined. Clear, authoritative, Christian ministry which is given freely is very necessary!

In general, I encountered many fewer evil spirits in East Africa than in rural Zambia. Obviously, I haven't sufficient data to form more than a superficial impression. However, I think the East African revival of the 1950s could well have been responsible. In the very rural areas of Zambia and Malawi that Matthew Parris writes about, they are probably very numerous.

They also appear to be very numerous in Fortaleza in north-eastern Brazil, where a friend of mine works among the drug addicts, the prostitutes, and the occupants of the city slums. This account by Andy Fanstone paints a vivid picture:

One day as I sat on the steps of the project house in the slum, one of the main drug dealers came up wanting to talk with me. We had had several conversations before and this guy was genuinely open and searching for God. I remember one day even walking into his house and he was sitting there reading the Rick Warren book, The Purpose Driven Life. *However, he was not quite ready to give up his car, riches and lifestyle of "comfort" that the money gained from drug dealing gave him in exchange for Christ, the forgiveness of sin and eternal life. He was called Fabinho and as we sat on the stairs of the project, he started recounting with a half excited and half embarrassed smile on his face what had happened the night before. He had been walking past the next-door neighbour's house on Sunday evening, and as he passed by, he heard some raised noises as if there was a commotion going on and so he went in to see what was happening. When he entered the house, to his surprise the mother of another of the main drug dealers who lived in that house was manifesting a demon and speaking in a different voice in quite a violent manner. He said he ran out and went to try and find some Christians to pray for her, but since it was Sunday and they were all at church he couldn't find any, so he went back into the house. He put his hand on her and started praying. He prayed, "I know I have no power or authority, but I know Jesus does and so in the name and authority of Jesus Christ I command you to leave." And the demon did, but then it jumped into the aunt. So Fabinho prayed the same prayer over her too, putting his hand on her shoulder; "I know I have no power or authority but Jesus does and so in the name and authority of Jesus Christ I command you to leave." Once again the demon left and once again went into another family member and started manifesting in her. Fabinho said this happened a total of four times and then quietness and peace returned to the house once more. Without trying to look too taken aback I said, "I told you Jesus had power", and subsequently asked if he was ready to give his life to Jesus now. He still said he was not ready as he was not quite ready to give up all that Jesus required of him. This unsaved drug dealer perhaps might not have understood the theology of what had just happened to him, but understood the power and authority of Jesus better than most Christians. Thankfully, two weeks after this, Fabinho did give himself to Christ, and went on to marry his girlfriend, get a job, and opened up small groups in the slum which many of the drug dealers subsequently started attending.*[6]

This is very revealing about the prevailing culture in the city. It is also interesting that the drug dealer, as yet uncommitted, was rather more successful than the sons of Sceva in Philippi! With a little more knowledge, he would have commanded the spirit to leave and go to Jesus. Then it would have been unable to enter any of the other members of the family. Nevertheless, this account and many others in my friend's book demonstrate that the demons in north-eastern Brazil behave in just the same way as the demons in rural Zambia or Oxford.

In England, while I certainly met people troubled by evil spirits, they were small in number when compared with the problems people encountered in their houses. In Africa, I didn't spend long enough in any one place to be invited into many houses. Those where I was entertained, with amazing generosity, were usually owned by the clergy or the more well-off lay people.

These apparent differences don't alter my general conclusion that the demonic forces we encounter are essentially the same throughout the world. The five marks that I mentioned in the account of the Gadarene demoniac (the attraction and repulsion to Jesus, the strange voices, the physical strength, self-harm, wild eyes – see Chapter 4) apply universally. There is absolutely nothing cultural about them.

Principalities and powers

The Greek word εξουσια occurs over a hundred times in the New Testament. It is usually translated as power, sometimes as authority. A typical passage is Colossians 1:15–16:

> *The Son is the image of the invisible God, the firstborn over all creation. For in him all things were created: things in heaven and on earth, visible and invisible, whether thrones or powers or rulers or authorities; all things have been created through him and for him.*

What is Paul referring to? Commentators have various interpretations. Those of a more liberal persuasion tend to see the powers and authorities as institutions like multinational companies, philosophies such as apartheid, capitalism, communism; those of a more conservative viewpoint tend to see them as demonic spiritual forces. Certainly Jesus gave His disciples this authority over evil spirits (Matthew 10:1; Mark 6:7; Luke 9:1). He Himself was observed to exercise this authority (Mark 1:28 and Luke 4:36).

Green[7] offers eight uses of the word – the realm of illness (Luke 13:16); in history (Pergamum where Satan's seat is according to Revelation 2:12–13); in nature (the Galatians in bondage to elemental spirits, Galatians 4:8); in the Law (which, according to Romans 7:10–14, instead of freeing its Jewish adherents bound them into spiritual death); within the church when false apostles disguised themselves as servants of righteousness (2 Corinthians 11:13–15); as the force behind human sin (Romans 7:15); as a negative influence on the state (compare the portrait of the state in Revelation 13 with Paul's view in Romans 13 – something authorized by God has become corrupted by Satan); and lastly as the means of death – the power of death (Hebrews 2:14), which is seen here as in the hands of Satan.

The word εξουσια is certainly capable of different cultural interpretations. But behind the culture there is one ultimate evil authority – Satan. Sin manifests itself in many different ways. In our culture, sexual liberty, the pursuit of wealth, and the denial of any absolute truth are among the many different ways in which Satan has moved us away from God. In Africa, the use of witchdoctors, the corruption, especially of the political elite, poverty and disease are ways in which Satan's hand can be clearly seen. In today's world, the atrocities and the merciless government pursued by Islamic State are a terrible example of the misuse of εξουσια. In recent history, Nazi Germany, Stalinist Russia, Maoist China, and apartheid South Africa have had a similarly baleful influence on their citizens. Their philosophies may have been very different but the force behind them was the same. They are all examples of Oscar Cullman's statement (see Chapter 2, note 7) that:

The devil is bound to a line, which can be lengthened even to the point where, for a while, Satan can make himself independent and has to be fought against by God.

Two hundred years earlier, Christians saw slavery as another example of a terrible misuse of power by the European nations and in the American continent. Its removal involved a titanic parliamentary struggle in England and a terrible civil war in America. John Wesley and the early Methodists were among its strongest opponents.

John Wesley's final letter, written in February 1791, to William Wilberforce began:

> *Unless the Divine Power has raised you up to be as Athanasius, contra mundum; I see not how you can go through with your glorious enterprise in opposing that execrable villainy which is the scandal of religion, of England and of human nature. Unless God has raised you up to do this very thing, you will be worn out by the opposition of men and devils; but if God be for you, who can be against you? Oh be not weary of well-doing. Go in the name of God and in the power of his might, till even American slavery, the vilest that ever saw the sun, shall vanish away.*

Wesley saw the true spiritual nature of the evil powers and the true possibility of Divine Power.

Occam's razor and the balance of probabilities

There are two intellectual arguments. The first is provided by Occam's razor. William of Occam (c. 1287–1347) taught as follows: the principle in philosophy and science is that assumptions introduced to explain a thing must not be multiplied beyond necessity, and hence the simplest of several hypotheses is always the best in accounting for unexplained facts.

By far the simplest explanation for the many phenomena that I have recounted is that they were in accord with Scripture, that evil forces exist and that, in certain circumstances, they can show up in political institutions, buildings, and in people. Any other explanation is contrived and difficult to fit with all the facts. Apart from concluding that we are all deluded idiots or deliberate liars there is no rational explanation.

The second argument is based on probability theory. The event in Mutwe recorded in Chapter 1, where an evil spirit, or something inexplicable, spoke through a woman's voice in perfect English has a probability of occurring of virtually zero. I know a small number of sane, cautious people who have had similar encounters. However, there is no rational, or indeed psychological, explanation for such an event.

Returning again to the opening chapters of Mark's Gospel, if these accounts (almost certainly first hand from the apostle Peter) are true, then what happened in Mutwe is still unlikely but it is explicable – it becomes possible. Probability theory, using Bayes' theorem[8] suggests the probability of Mark's account of evil spirits being true is hugely increased by the confirmatory Zambian experience. Alternatively, if we are able to accept Mark's account as historically accurate, then such a strange event becomes explicable.

At least three other people working with me have witnessed this strange phenomenon. In Chibwika, Laurie White, who was a recent convert and on his first mission in Africa, was somewhat sceptical. But on his first morning of prayer ministry, teamed with Alison Morgan, a spirit spoke distinctly in clear English (see Chapter 1, page 19). Similarly in Mwenda (see Chapter 1, page 27), Father James Chungolo heard a powerful spirit speaking in French. Also Andrew Fanstone[9] records a difficult exorcism of an illiterate street boy in Fortaleza. Two hours of effort speaking to him in broken Portuguese proved fruitless. Andrew became so tired that he began to speak in English. To his amazement, the boy answered all the questions as though he was fluent in the language! These apparently inexplicable events demand an explanation!

There is no *via media*. We have to choose – perhaps the devil is indeed missing. Perhaps he is a convenient myth made up to explain the many disasters in a fallen world. The alternative is that he does indeed exist. He is, as the Bible teaches, a malevolent spiritual being who opposes the will of God.

I have alluded briefly to angels.[10] Some of the stories I have recorded elsewhere about angels are equally persuasive. Both the existence of the positive (angels) and the negative (evil spirits) drive us inexorably to accept the supernatural. If we accept the existence of a supernatural world, Christianity provides by far the most credible explanation of the phenomena that a surprising number of people encounter. It also provides a means of dealing with occurrences which cause great fear and distress.

Our world can be adequately explained by science – save for this one thing. Many people recognize that they are spiritual beings who belong to a spiritual universe. It is particularly interesting that more primitive societies (as we would arrogantly call them) are much more aware of the spiritual world (Australian Aborigines, for example). Where have these beliefs and experiences come from?

Science cannot explain or even address this issue, although, as I've said above, I think that probability theory can help us. Evil spirits are not a cultural phenomenon; they exist, are marshalled, and ordered in some way. This surprising claim we shall consider in the final chapter.

To sum up: Satan uses many different cultures in many different ways; but in the end, he is the source of one and the same evil power. In particular when people, whether in darkest Africa or sophisticated Oxford, are taken over by a demon, the manifestations and marks are strikingly similar. Evil spirits are *not* a product of culture!

CHAPTER 12

SPIRITUAL WARFARE: BONFIRES FROM EPHESUS TO NEW GUINEA

The Son of God goes forth to war,
a kingly crown to gain;
his blood-red banner streams afar:
Who follows in His train?

(Bishop Reginald Heber)

Scripture from Genesis to Revelation portrays a long conflict between mankind and the forces of darkness. Scripture is quite clear that God can always penetrate the darkness (Psalm 139 and John 1:5, for instance) and yet there are places where darkness seems to rule and cause chaos. The high places (see below) are places of constant spiritual disobedience. Sodom is a place so wicked that not even ten righteous people can be found. Paul has a powerful vision of the spiritual battle (Ephesians 6:10–20 and Colossians 2:9–15, for instance). Peter (1 Peter 5:8) likewise sees that the enemy prowls around seeking whom he may devour. Jesus refers to Satan as "the prince of this world" (John 12:31). In the temptation narrative (Matthew 4:1–11, for instance), Satan makes great claims as to his power and authority over the world. Human history suggests that there are, and were, places of exceptional darkness – some well known, some quite obscure.

In my rectory garden in Somerset, at the right times of year, if I was patient I could always see a few Holly Blue butterflies flitting across the garden wall towards the tall holly trees in the Shepton churchyard. One year, 1998 in the spring, instead of the usual one or two, I could easily see ten or twenty at once. A little later, it was not difficult to find some small caterpillars on the fresh green berries of the holly tree. I also captured a small wasp, Listrodomus Nycthemerus, flitting around seeking "whom it could devour" – although in this case the devouring was accomplished by the next generation emerging inside the caterpillar from eggs laid by the vicious parasite. Estimates as to damage vary, but some writers reckon that up to 90 per cent of caterpillars are destroyed in this way. Occasionally, the predator has several bad seasons. Then the numbers of butterflies can build up dramatically. It doesn't happen very often; but the results are spectacular. Indeed, as the predator depends on its victims for its own life-cycle, if it is too successful then it will have no victims and it will die out. The reverse is not true. If the predator disappeared, the butterfly, which can use many breeding plants, will inexorably flourish.

This always seems to me to be a parable about spiritual warfare. Dismiss the tiny, well-hidden wasp, and the number of butterflies will multiply rapidly. Discern and disarm the enemy and evangelism will flourish. Sometimes this is accomplished by powerful preaching, as for instance with George Whitefield in America in the 1740s or in Irian Jaya (see below); sometimes it is accomplished by a demonstration of God's power and authority, as in Egypt with St Antony or in the Woodlark Islands (again, see below).

Paul had an extraordinary second visit to Ephesus. After a brief stop during his second missionary journey, he returned around AD 53 and stayed for over two years. Much of the time was spent in teaching but signs followed – in this case, healings and deliverances accomplished through his hands and also through handkerchiefs which he had touched. His fame spread. Others, notably the sons of Sceva, tried to copy his methods with disastrous results. The name of the Lord Jesus was exalted, many believers confessed to magic practices and brought their books to be burned in a dramatic bonfire. In a way, it was too good to last. The cult of the goddess Artemis (Diana) suffered. The silversmiths, who profited from selling her images, complained. They argued that Ephesus was a great city dedicated to her worship and that their income and the city's importance were being greatly diminished. A riot took place. The town clerk calmed them. He spoke of the greatness of the goddess and claimed that the men, that is Paul and his companions, were neither sacrilegious nor blasphemers against Diana. That is quite surprising! I cannot imagine that Paul or anyone else thought that the cult of Artemis could coexist with discipleship to Jesus.

Paul left, and the church flourished. A few years later, Paul visited nearby Miletus, summoned the Ephesian elders and gave them a powerful sermon, which is summarized in Acts 20:18–35. In his later letter, written sometime afterwards probably from Rome, Paul concludes with a famous passage about spiritual warfare. As we read these verses (Ephesians 6:10–20), it is easy to imagine the captive Paul recalling some of the great battles against the powers of evil he had experienced some years earlier in Ephesus.

Christian tradition suggests that Paul's young disciple, Timothy, who acted as his representative in Ephesus (1 Timothy 1:3), became bishop there and was reputedly martyred in AD 97 for opposing licentious festivities devoted to Diana. It would seem that the cult of Diana flourished despite Paul's successes. The book of Revelation also suggests that, by the end of the first century, the church at Ephesus had "forsaken" its first love (Revelation 2:4).

In Chapter 3, I mentioned four possible power encounters recorded in Acts. These took place in Samaria, Cyprus, Philippi, and Ephesus. In the first three, the opposition centred round individuals – Simon the Sorcerer, Elymas, and the slave girl (or perhaps more correctly her owners). In Ephesus, the spiritual opposition was deeper. The cult of Diana was renowned throughout the province of Asia and beyond. This was a serious spiritual battle. It is fashionable in some circles to talk about "territorial spirits". Neither Luke nor Paul mentions them but certainly they are both aware of principalities and powers opposed to the spread of the gospel.

The idea that certain areas could be deeply influenced by negative or perhaps positive spiritual forces is found both in the Old Testament and the Gospels. Naaman's strange request to take some earth back from his visit to Elisha was sanctioned by the prophet (see 2 Kings 5:15–19). Elisha was also surprisingly generous when faced with Naaman's request for forgiveness when he attended the House of Rimmon on official duty.

As we discussed in Chapter 7, the high places were a constant source of spiritual disobedience. Godly kings and energetic prophets were always seeking to destroy them; ungodly kings were always restoring them. Moses (Numbers 33:52) had instructed that all stone figures and metal images were to be destroyed along with the high places in which they were found. Most of the rulers of Israel and Judah did the exact opposite.

The godly Hezekiah even had to destroy the famous bronze serpent (made by Moses as an antidote to the venom of the fiery serpents – see Numbers 21:4–9), which had become associated with a cult for Asherah. It shows how easily people are led astray when something, which was later used by Jesus as an illustration of his death on the cross (John 3:14), could become so desecrated that it had to be destroyed.

One of the most remarkable spiritual encounters takes place in Daniel, chapters 10–12. His angelic visitor (10:4–9) had been delayed for twenty-one days by the Prince of Persia. He arrived after help from the archangel Michael. Many writers use this passage to illustrate the idea that spiritual powers can control territories. As there are no parallels elsewhere in Scripture, we would be wise to proceed with caution and not to build elaborate theories on one obscure passage of Scripture. It is worth contrasting this encounter with the spiritual battles of Nehemiah which are carried out at a more normal level. Prayer, wisdom (surveying the scene at Jerusalem by night), overcoming determined and deceitful human opposition, understanding the causes of social unrest, bringing the people to sincere repentance and rejoicing when the wall of the city was rebuilt were the order of the day.

In the Gospels, we get a strong indication that evil powers could be associated with places. In Mark 5:10 (see Chapter 4), the legion of devils begged not to be sent out of the country with which they were familiar. They asked, instead of being banished, to be allowed to enter the herd of pigs. The law of unintended consequences led to their swift destruction.

Powers dispossessed by the early church

In the writings of the church fathers, Origen clearly believed in the reality of regions controlled by evil spiritual powers.[1] He thought there were places where the demons exercised considerable spiritual power, especially "supposed holy places" where curious spells were used when they were originally set up. Origen also saw the real possibility of demons controlling whole regions of the universe to rule "those who have subjected themselves to evil".

One of Origen's pupils took this very seriously. Gregory the Wonderworker[2] effectively evangelized a whole area by leaving a demon in a heathen temple stripped of its power. This leads to the conversion of the temple warden who eventually succeeds Gregory as a bishop. Later Gregory performs an exorcism on a youth with the memorable words:

> *"Not I is it that commands you, but Christ who flung the swine into the sea: Quit this youth!" As the demon heard the name of the divine majesty, he cried out loudly saying "Alas for me, for Jesus! Alas, for me, on account of his disciple."*

And the devil himself, being enraged by the territory conquered from him by the bishop where once both countryside and chief city were in the grip of the demons, inspired a woman to defame Gregory. She is a prostitute and accuses him of being one of her lovers, but he exorcises the spirit from her and protects his reputation.

At the end of all this, in a region where there had only been a handful of Christians, there were now only a few left unconverted. Effective evangelism was preceded by spiritual warfare which released both buildings and people from demonic control. Once again, the original text indicates that the evil spirit had a territorial interest both in the temple and in the countryside.

Even more important was the witness of St Antony. Not only was he a remarkable holy man who performed many healings and exorcisms, but he was also a great defender of orthodox Christianity against the Arians. His teaching, and life, greatly influenced Athanasius, whose efforts towards the end of the fourth century were crucial in protecting Christian doctrine. He lived most of his life in the Egyptian desert and was subject to many deceitful and direct attacks by demons. They engaged in a ferocious warfare to disrupt one of the key holy men at a time when the church might have completely lost its direction. His life is an interesting case, where Satan seems to have recognized his exceptional importance and, in consequence, subjected him to a continuous spiritual assault. The demons also complained, more than once, that the monks were taking their territory, certainly powerful evidence which confirms the thesis of this chapter.

One dramatic occasion is recorded as follows:

> But those of his acquaintances who came, since he did not permit them to enter, often used to spend days and nights outside, and heard as it were crowds within clamouring, dinning, sending forth piteous voices and crying, "Go from what is ours. What do you even in the desert? You cannot abide our attack." So at first those outside thought there were some men fighting with him, and that they had entered by ladders; but when stooping down they saw through a hole there was nobody, they were afraid, accounting them to be demons, and they called on Antony. Them he quickly heard, though he had not given a thought to the demons, and coming to the door he besought them to depart and not to be afraid, "for thus," said he, "the demons make their seeming onslaughts against those who are cowardly. Sign yourselves therefore with the cross, and depart boldly, and let these make sport for themselves." So they departed fortified with the sign of the Cross. But he remained in no wise harmed by the evil spirits, nor was he wearied with the contest, for there came to his aid visions from above, and the weakness of the foe relieved him of much trouble and armed him with greater zeal. For his acquaintances used often to come expecting to find him dead, and would hear him singing, "Let God arise and let His enemies be scattered, let them also that hate Him flee before His face. As smoke vanishes, let them vanish; as wax melts before the face of fire, so let the sinners perish from the face of God"; and again, "All nations compassed me about, and in the name of the Lord I requited them."[3]

This encounter is instructive. We should note that the demons were complaining that Antony had invaded their territory (the desert), his robust use of Scripture (following Jesus' example in the temptation narratives), and his effective teaching given to his followers as to how to cope with spiritual attack.

On another occasion, Athanasius writes of a visitation by Satan who complains:

> I have no longer a place, a weapon, a city. The Christians are spread everywhere, and at length even the desert is filled with monks. Let them take heed to themselves, and let them not curse me undeservedly. Then I marvelled at the grace of the Lord, and said to him: You who art ever a liar and never speak the truth, this at length, even against your will, you have truly spoken. For the coming of Christ has made you weak. He has cast you down and stripped you. But he having heard the Saviour's name, and not being able to bear the burning from it, vanished.

Once again, the spiritual forces of evil are complaining that their natural territory has been taken over. There has been no specific warfare prayer, but the powerful presence of Antony and his followers has greatly discomfited the enemy.

Another encounter shows how he, like Jesus, strengthened the faith of others:

> When therefore he had retired and determined to fix a time, after which neither to go forth himself nor admit anybody, Martinian, a military officer, came and disturbed Antony. For he had a daughter afflicted with an evil spirit. But when he continued for a long while knocking at the door, and asking him to come out and pray to God for his child, Antony, not bearing to open, looked out from above and said, "Man, why do you call on me? I also am a man even as you. But if you believe in Christ whom I serve, go, and according as you believe, pray to God, and it shall come to pass." Straightway, therefore, he departed, believing and calling upon Christ, and he received his daughter cleansed from the devil. Many other things also through Antony the Lord did, who says, "Seek and it shall be given unto you" (Luke 11:9). For many of the sufferers, when he would not open his door, slept outside his cell, and by their faith and sincere prayers were healed.

Towards the end of his life, Athanasius records a dramatic confrontation with a group of philosophers:

> *"And these signs are sufficient to prove that the faith of Christ alone is the true religion. But see! You still do not believe and are seeking for arguments. We however make our proof not in the persuasive words of Greek wisdom 1 Corinthians 2:4 as our teacher has it, but we persuade by the faith which manifestly precedes argumentative proof. Behold there are here some vexed with demons"; – now there were certain who had come to him very disquieted by demons, and bringing them into the midst he said – "Do you cleanse them either by arguments and by whatever art or magic you choose, calling upon your idols, or if you are unable, put away your strife with us and you shall see the power of the Cross of Christ." And having said this he called upon Christ, and signed the sufferers two or three times with the sign of the Cross. And immediately the men stood up whole, and in their right mind, and immediately gave thanks unto the Lord. And the philosophers, as they are called, wondered, and were astonished exceedingly at the understanding of the man and at the sign which had been wrought. But Antony said, "Why marvel ye at this? We are not the doers of these things, but it is Christ who works them by means of those who believe in Him. Believe, therefore, also yourselves, and you shall see that with us there is no trick of words, but faith through love which is wrought in us towards Christ; which if you yourselves should obtain you will no longer seek demonstrative arguments, but will consider faith in Christ sufficient." These are the words of Antony. And they marvelling at this also; saluted him and departed, confessing the benefit they had received from him.*

Ramsay MacMullen[4] is duly impressed by this. He contrasts this dramatic approach saying that silencing, burning, and destruction were forms of theological demonstration which he sees as all too apparent after Christianity became the official religion of the empire.

Powers disconcerted by the Celtic saints

Moving on in time, the writings of the Venerable Bede[5] indicate that spiritual warfare was a major component in the evangelism of England. Bede (673–735) was the first historian of the English church. His writing contains reports of significant miracles and spiritual battles both from the life of Augustine of Canterbury and local English saints. He writes of the mystical conversion of King Edwin, the realization of his chief priest that "the religion that we have hitherto held has no virtue or profit in it". He tells of Cedd (c. 650) building a monastery in a place of ill repute which he cleansed by prayer and fasting throughout Lent. Thus the famous monastic site of Lastingham came into being.

Similarly, he records how Cuthbert (d. 687) chose a deserted barren place where he wished to build a hermitage. First he drove out the evil spirits; then he started to cultivate the land, and prayed for water to be provided. Through prayer the soil, previously barren, proved fruitful, and his hermitage became a place of pilgrimage. Eventually, he was summoned to become a bishop. He did his uttermost to refuse, but was compelled to come and respond to the call. His life was full of miracles.

Bede records a number of battles with fire (see John Paton below). He cites Canterbury and Bamburgh being saved by the prayers of Miletus, Bishop of London (c. 610) and Aidan, Bishop of Lindisfarne (c. 645), and how Cuthbert's evangelism of Melrose was interrupted by what he describes as sheets of false fire. While he was at Melrose he was frequently out on preaching trips. On one such occasion, a huge crowd gathered to hear him and, while he was speaking, Cuthbert became aware that "the ancient enemy, the devil, was present, come to hinder his work of salvation". Bede tells us that Cuthbert then exhorted the crowd to be on their guard against the devil's attacks, for, Cuthbert explained, "he has a thousand crafty ways of harming you". Cuthbert was under no illusion that the enemy was real and dangerous. But he also was utterly confident of the power of God. There was no Dualism in his thinking. As Cuthbert continued to preach, the devil sent down "mock fire" to a nearby house.

Bede relates:

Sheets of flame, fanned by the wind, seemed to sweep through the whole village, and the noise of their crackling rent the air. Cuthbert managed, with outstretched arms, to restrain a few of the villagers, but the rest, almost the whole crowd, leaped up and vied with each other in throwing water on the flames. But real water has no effect on phantom fire, and the blaze raged on, until through Cuthbert's prayers the father of lies fled, taking his false fire with him into the empty air.[6]

The crowd were naturally astonished, but also felt ashamed that they did not trust Cuthbert who was encouraging them to pray rather than pour water on the phantom flames. Bede tells us the crowd then appreciated that "the devil did not cease for even an hour in his warfare against man's salvation". It's all an insight into how commonplace Cuthbert perceived the spiritual battle to be.

If this all seems a bit far-fetched, I have included a note[7] about much more recent events in Bougainville.

Powers not dethroned

After the conversion of England, there was no obvious reason for attempting spiritual warfare of the sort undertaken by Gregory the Wonderworker. Witchcraft was quite widely practised and suspected witches were executed rather than exorcised. The Salem witch trials in early seventeenth-century America showed the worst side of a fanatical version of Puritan Christianity. The great missionary movement of the nineteenth century certainly encountered some fanatical opposition. As far as one can tell from the records, this was usually encountered by medicine and healing rather than spiritual warfare. However, as we shall see, there were some notable exceptions.

Sadly, in the last hundred years there have been many examples of places, nearer at home, where Cullmann's theology of Satan apparently making himself independent of God (see Chapter 2, page 37) seems all too true. Some of the most obvious examples include the Holocaust, the Rwandan genocide, and the current activities of IS in various Middle Eastern countries.

There is some evidence, considerably disputed, that many of the leading Nazis were influenced by the occult. Himmler, architect of the final solution, seems to have been particularly influenced in this way. The Rwandan genocide was probably the product of extreme Hutu nationalism. A leading Catholic was so shocked by the barbarity that he said something to the effect, "these people need to be baptized again". However, there is little evidence of any direct negative spiritual influences. IS is a distortion of Islam. As I have written elsewhere,[8] ultimately the beliefs of Christianity and Islam are incompatible; but a peaceful dialogue based on the higher moral teachings of the Quran and the Bible should be possible. The beliefs of IS, Al Qaeda, Boko Haram, and similar fanatical cults are obviously satanically inspired and as dangerous for the Christian faith in the twenty-first century as, say, emperor worship in the first.

Powers defeated in distant lands

However, in recent centuries where the church, through intrepid missionaries, has expanded into hostile territory, it has witnessed many more of the type of spiritual battles which were seen in the first few centuries. Examples I would cite are from the New Hebrides, a Chinese offshore island, Irian Jaya, the Woodlark Islands south-east of Papua New Guinea, and Fortaleza in Brazil.

Watchman Nee has a dramatic story. In the 1930s, he was trying to evangelize a Chinese offshore island:

The locals were quite uninterested. "We worship Ta Wang and it is his festival in a week's time on 11 January." A young member of the team, Brother Wu said "I promise you that it will certainly rain on the 11th." Everyone laughed. The Christians retreated. Had the young man spoken out of turn? Had they been presumptuous? Or had they spoken as "fools"?

As they prayed they received a word: "Where is the God of Elijah?" (See James 5:17–18). They felt that they shouldn't pray any more, but continue to preach. The weather remained very fine. "No stir in the air, no stir in the sea." Ta Wang's diviners knew about the weather. On the morning of the festival, Watchman Nee and his team got up very early to pray. They felt that they could now remind the Lord of his promise. Very quickly it started to rain; then it poured. They found the luckless Ta Wang floating down the street and his followers soaked in the rain. Some of the village elders, bareheaded and without umbrellas, were in serious difficulties. Divination was made. "Today is the wrong day. The festival is to be on the 14th with the procession at six in the evening."

The Christians responded by asking for fine days and then for rain to come at six o'clock on the 14th. We had a good response to our preaching. The 14th was another perfect day but again they reminded God of his promise. Torrential rain appeared at the appointed time. The next day Watchman Nee's team had to leave. Other workers took over the mission; but no longer was Ta Wang an effective opponent. Many were converted. Ta Wang's power was broken.[9]

A similar example of direct divine intervention is provided by the Victorian missionary to the New Hebrides, John Paton. In 1862, after a few years of dangerous ministry amid the cannibals on the island of Tanna, he and two other missionaries, Mr and Mrs Mathieson, were under attack. A group of natives, armed with clubs, had set fire to the fence surrounding the mission house. John went out, taking an unloaded revolver, to confront them and beat out the flames. He was surrounded by the natives, none of whom dared to strike the first blow. His friends remained inside, deep in prayer. John said:

"Dare to strike me and my Jehovah God will punish you! He protects us and will punish you for burning his church, for hatred of his worship and people, and for all your bad conduct. We love you; and for doing good you want to kill us. But our God is here to protect us and punish you."[10]

In the midst of all of this, there was a mighty roar. Every head turned, and they all knew that a tornado was coming. First there was wind, which drove the flames away from the mission house; then the wind was followed by torrential rain, which put them out.

The natives fled in terror. John Paton returned to the mission house, and his companions said, "If ever in time of need God sent help and protection to His servants in answer to prayer, He has done so tonight."

The next morning, they were still in great danger. Friends warned them that an attack was about to be mounted. Then a second providential event occurred. A sail was spotted, a rare event indeed, and the ship came to rescue them. They left Tanna. Soon afterwards, John returned to the nearby island of Aneityum where his ministry bore much fruit over the next twenty-five years.

Andy Fanstone, as previously mentioned, is a missionary I know. His work, as we have seen (Chapter 11), among the drug addicts in Fortaleza in north-east Brazil often involves direct spiritual conflict. He writes:

One of my early encounters with the street children I had which was a steep learning curve for me was when we went out to one of the central squares in Fortaleza. We had gone out with our backpacks full of games, first aid kits, colouring pencils, and Bible stories to spend time with the children who lived there. Claudia, one of the staff members (whom I was later to marry) and I were seated on one of the benches, talking to Fransico, one of the street boys. The conversation was going well when suddenly Fransico reached forward and snatched at Claudia's watch, pulling it off her wrist. In my poor Portuguese I said, "Fransico don't do that, we are your friends and are here to help you." However his appearance changed and his eyes looked vacant and he replied in a very rough, deep and coarse voice. "My name isn't Fransico, it is Ze Pilintra." I thought he was playing some silly joke on us and so insisted, "This is not funny Fransico, stop playing games and give me the watch back." Claudia however, who is slightly more perceptive than myself nudged me with her elbow and whispered quietly, "Ze Pilintra is a name of a spiritual entity here, he is demonised, start praying."

Fransico then continued talking in this unusual rough Darth Vader type voice saying, "You know these boys are mine and you will never take them out of my hands." As he said this, he leant forward and picked up a stone from part of the broken concrete pavement. I was now catching on and starting to understand this was getting quite serious and the other street children who also saw what Fransico was doing in turn picked up stones to threaten him in our defence so he would not throw the stone at us. I explained to them everything was all right and that they could put their stones down as we would resolve this with Fransico. Claudia and I were now praying quietly in tongues in our Spirit and every time we did Fransico would lower the rock and look away. After a short time of this stand-off, Fransico turned and started walking off. I and Peter, another staff member, followed him. Fransico crossed a main road, walked down a block and then jumped over a broken-down wall into an abandoned piece of land. He walked forward about ten paces and then turned around and just stared at us with a fixed glazed look that seemed as if he was looking right through us rather than at us. He stood there in this trance state for a minute or so while we took it in turns to try and talk to him. Fransico then suddenly started swaying a little bit back and forth and from side to side and then suddenly as though he was woken up by a little electric shock came back to his senses. Immediately he came walking over to us and climbed back over the wall to meet us. He seemed a bit unsure of what had just happened, and so I explained and asked him to return the watch he had stolen from Claudia. He insisted he had not stolen a watch and would never steal anything from us as we were there to help him. I asked however if I could look in his pockets and as I did, to his complete amazement and embarrassment, the watch was there. He swore he had no recollection of taking it and apologised for what had happened.

When I arrived back at the house I went to my room and closed the door. This was not in the script of Oliver Twist. "What just happened and how can I possibly help these kids?" I thought to myself. My theory of just providing some Bible stories, food, a nice shower and a bit of care as a remedy to all their problems was starting to look a bit shaky. Yes, I had read in the Bible about demons, but with them on the pages of my Bible they were at a safe distance and made quite interesting reading. But with them up close and personal things did not feel quite so comfortable. I called out to God asking for help and understanding and Matthew 12:29 dropped into my heart. I looked it up and it said, "Or again, how can anyone enter a strong man's house and carry off his possessions unless he first ties up the strong man? Then he can plunder his house." Having read this, the sentence the demon that spoke through Fransico then came back to mind: "These boys are mine and you will never take them out of my hands."

That day God gave me important insight as to what had just happened and the importance of spiritual warfare in the rescue and restoration of the street children. I had come against the "strongman" that was holding these boys captive, in slavery to a life of drugs and squalor on the streets. I could not expect to just walk up and take away his possessions without a fight. First in the spiritual realm I needed to bind the strongman so I could then go and take these boys away from his hands. If a ferocious dog is bound on his leash, he can growl and bark as much as he likes, but it is easy for me to come and take away his big juicy T-bone steak that is just out of his reach, for he is bound. "For our struggle is not against flesh and blood, but against the rulers, against the authorities, against the powers of this dark world and against the spiritual forces of evil in the heavenly realms" (Ephesians 6:12).[11]

Power encounter in Irian Jaya

When I visited Argentina in 2004 and 2006, my first hostess was Priscilla Breekveldt. Her husband, Hans, was a leader in the Anglican church in Salta and was ordained deacon in 2015. She worked for Latin Link. Priscilla was a very gifted, enthusiastic translator. She also told me about her childhood in Irian Jaya (then Dutch New Guinea until 1962). She had arrived aged two with her parents, Jacques and Ruth Teeuwen, who were working for RBMU (Regions Beyond Missionary Union). I remember her saying quite simply, "In the village where I grew up, we witnessed every New Testament miracle!"[12]

The coastal regions had been evangelized for many years, but it was not until a US airplane was lost in 1945 that the Baliem Valley mountain regions of the Central Highlands were explored in 1957. Living there were large tribes of pygmy-type people who were completely unknown to the wider world. The Teeuwen family were sent to the village of Kanggyme, which literally means the place of death, in the autumn of 1961. Very soon they were on their own, surrounded by almost naked, largely unwashed bodies, covered with terrible tropical ulcers and sores. Their dictionary consisted of a word-sheet with six useful phrases! Their greatest gift was Liiru – a needle which brought incredible healing to festering bodies.

Sometimes, they unwittingly upset people. An obnoxious man, with a pig tusk through his nose, an ostrich feather sticking out of the net bag covering his hair, and bracelets of shells on his arms, tried to jump the medical queue. He was sent back and walked away. He turned out to be the local chief.

Jacques became uneasy. He was always expecting a pre-dawn

attack. He listened to a cassette where the preacher spoke about "the bondage unto fear" (Romans 8:15, AV). He felt convicted. He prayed for deliverance from fear and slept soundly.

The medical work enabled Jacques and Ruth to gain the confidence of the local people. Then they heard a strange phrase, "Nabelan Kabelan" – which they, as others had earlier, discovered meant eternal life. The people told the missionaries that they were afraid of death and they wanted to live for ever. Their forefathers had told them that the snake possessed the secret – the empty snakeskins were proof of it. But the snake was elusive and never came to tell them.

The Holy Spirit had prepared a way for the gospel message to be heard: "Jesus Christ truly holds the secret of Nabelan Kabelan!" The good news swept through the whole Swart Valley which had a population of about 25,000.

After six months, they were relocated to the village of Mamit. Jacques made slow, but determined progress, teaching the gospel message. People began to understand about the Creator, about sin and about Jesus. There was a breakthrough when they realized that God loved their enemies as well as them. Tribal warfare had been a way of life. One well-respected man stood up and said he had killed seven people – people whom God had created and loved. A tear rolled down his cheek as he spoke.

Soon afterwards, a local chief addressed his tribe. Beside him was huge pile of weapons – bows, arrows, ten-foot spears, war jackets, shields, and bone daggers. Now that they understood, and had received Nabelan Kabelan, these weapons were not needed. A huge bonfire was lit. The people sang. The words "Wa Jetut" (Thank you, Jesus) soared into the heavens. The prophet Isaiah who had foretold a great time of evangelism would have approved: "They will beat their swords into ploughshares and their spears into pruning hooks" (Isaiah 2:4).

Soon afterwards, the local chiefs gathered. They told Frank Clarke, a longer-serving missionary, that "we want to go to our enemies". At first, he was appalled. He thought that they were going to make war. But they insisted they were going unarmed to tell their enemies about Nabelan Kabelan. They gathered on a high rock. This was a place from which they would normally hurl insults on the nearby villagers as a prelude to a vicious attack. This time their message was completely different. They raced down the hillside, crossed the river and climbed up to Panaga. The villagers, armed to the teeth, were terrified. One of the visitors spoke about their mission. A miracle took place. The villagers listened intently. There was no bloodshed, a great welcome, and a commission for these villagers to go into the mountains to tell others.

All kinds of evidence of God's grace were manifest. People confessed to stealing. People came to have all their filthy hair cut off. They believed they could use their long hair, unloosed, to please and to worship evil spirits.

Even women, who had a very degraded and low place in the Dani culture, were allowed to testify. Women suspected of witchcraft were subjected to a test which would almost certainly lead to their being killed in a brutal way. They lived separately from the men and were continually ill-treated. Daughters or young girls could be sold for a couple of pigs. They were just another form of goods and chattel.

Two years after Jacques and Ruth had arrived at Mamit, the first baptism took place. Fifty-eight carefully-tested believers were baptized. About five thousand people came to watch. Soon afterwards, the local church chose three indigenous leaders. Many more people requested baptism. All were examined. Most, including a deaf and dumb man, were accepted. One proud young woman was unanimously refused by the local leaders. The revival spread. Hundreds were baptized; thousands professed what appeared to be genuine faith.

Then one day, there came a crucial test. Jacques writes:

Shortly before Angginonukwe was due to be baptized, the three elders came to see me about her. "Angginonukwe has gone funny," they announced in a matter of fact way. "We think she has an evil spirit."

Something inside me raised alarm. Could a Christian be possessed by an evil spirit? "Tell me about her." I was more than curious.

"Well, it all started as soon as you passed her to be baptized," one of the elders began. I seemed to sense a hint of sarcasm in his voice. "She has taken off her grass skirt and is running around in the forest. She has not eaten or slept for days."

251

"Try to catch her and bring her here so that I can talk to her," I decided abruptly. The men took off as if they were going on an exciting hunt. Soon – much too soon for my liking – a procession came to a halt in my front yard. The elders were carrying Angginonukwe and unceremoniously dumped her on the ground. The wicked expression on her unwashed face reminded me of the state many Dani women had been in prior to conversion. Her eyes rolled wildly, flashing with a strange mixture of hatred and terror. When I came near, she began to claw ferociously, her mouth spitting out vile language and foam.

Although I had no experience whatsoever in this area, I was certain that this was some kind of demon possession. *"She has an evil spirit,"* I declared, perhaps more to myself than to the onlookers.

A hush fell over the crowd. Suddenly I was overcome by a wave of loneliness as the implications of what I had just said imprinted themselves on my mind. I knew that everyone saw the connection between her desire to be baptized and her present condition. The powers of darkness were presenting a terrifying challenge. And if I did not meet it and overcome it in the power of Christ, we might as well pack our bags and go home. Who would want to be baptized if it meant becoming subject to the wrath of evil spirits? If our work among the Dani was to continue at all, the Lordship of Christ needed to be established very emphatically. The significance of the occasion was crystal clear. I had to take action.

"Angginonukwe has an evil spirit," I reiterated. It was old hat to the crowd. They had been sure of it before I was. What interested them was to see how I would handle it. No one stirred. Tension mounted.

"Jesus Christ is stronger than evil spirits." I spoke loud and clear, expecting to break the tension. Nothing happened. Nobody moved. The people required more than just words. Turning to the elders, I said, *"Do you believe that Jesus is stronger than evil spirits?"*

What had never happened before happened at that moment. The elders very deliberately let me down. They were not prepared to commit themselves with the stakes as high as they were.

Tuwanonuwa spoke for the others: *"You told us He is."*

I felt like backing out myself, but I couldn't. *"Do you believe that Jesus Christ can cast out this spirit?"* I repeated. All three elders *answered this time, but only to verbalize the doubt I could read in their eyes. "You told us He can."*

"Do you believe that Jesus can do it now?" I was growing more and more anxious.

"You told us he can."

"Let's pray," I announced tersely.

All present dutifully bowed their heads and closed their eyes. In the name of Jesus, I commanded the evil spirit to come out of Anggionukwe, to leave her alone and to depart from our area.

As soon as I opened my eyes, I saw that she was different. Her facial features were relaxed. Her eyes had lost their wild glare. When I spoke she reacted. "Say 'Thank you Jesus'," I ordered.

"Wa Jetut," she responded in her native tongue.

I could have jumped for joy and expected her to do the same. But I was in for a surprise. As soon as she said "Wa Jetut" she closed her eyes. For a terrifying moment I thought she had died. She had merely fallen asleep. Sound asleep. For days on end the evil spirit had tortured and exhausted her. She hadn't eaten, she hadn't slept. Now she was free. Free to sleep in peace. That was evidently what she needed most.

The elders picked her up and carried her to her hut, where she slept for more than twenty-four hours. When she woke up, she was ravenous. She ate so much that she upset her stomach and was unable to attend the baptismal service. Anggionukwe was baptized during the next service. When we left the field ten years later, she was still in fellowship.

This experience did much to bolster the faith of the Dani believers. Many sick were healed. Evil spirits, some in visible shapes, were cast out, and the dead were raised.[13]

Jacques gives a detailed account of an elder in another village, who had already reached a good age in a society where life expectancy was about thirty-seven. The elder had died and the Dani understood death. I know of only one man for certain, but there were rumours of two or three more which I could not confirm.

"He was very, very sick. Then he died. We all cried very much. Even though we would see our brother again in God's yard, we

cried. We loved our brother. We still needed him. He was a good elder. 'If we still need our brother, why don't we ask our heavenly Father to make him alive again?' someone suggested. And someone else said, 'Jesus was dead and became alive again. And He rose up Lazarus too, and the widow's little boy!' After that, everyone agreed that we should ask Jesus to rise up Lenwarit. The hut was full of men. Lenwarit lay dead stretched out on the floor. For a long time, we asked Jesus to make our brother alive again. We all prayed very hard. But nothing happened."

Leenggwa, my informant, shook his head thoughtfully, reliving the battle that had taken place.

"Nothing happened," he repeated, "we prayed all night, but nothing happened. At dawn some of the younger men got up. 'Our heavenly Father will not answer our prayers this time. We will get wood to cremate our brother.' I said we should pray once more. When we did, Lenwarit began to move. He sat up! Then he looked around and said 'I am very hungry. Are there any potatoes?' He had become alive again. He was not sick any more. Tonight I will bring him here for you to see."

Later, Lenwarit arrived. "I am the dead man," he said cheerfully!

And so the revival continued. A college (also a Bible school) was set up. Future leaders were trained. But there were setbacks too. Two missionaries were murdered in another nearby area.

Jacques stayed, serving different areas, for another ten years. The original leaders, and converts, remained faithful. As he was leaving Karubaga to serve with Brother Andrew in Open Doors, Jacques remembered that, when he was leaving Mamit for his first furlough, he had asked a group of leaders who were sitting around a fire:

"Did you ever want to kill me?"

Though we have no secrets from each other, the men enveloped themselves in an embarrassed silence. A young fellow tried unsuccessfully to suppress a snicker. He decided to speak. "Sure," he said. "Then why did you never do it?" I persisted.

Their amazement was genuine. "We don't know really... We just never got round to it."

All along God had been in charge. He had prepared the way with Nabelan Kabelan. He appears also to have prepared the way with a dream. Jacques told me that, when he had been there some time, an old man casually told him that he had dreamt that "people with white skin would come to us with some good news".

God brought an extraordinary change in people's spiritual and physical lives. He had inspired bonfires of weapons. The dramatic exorcism of Angginonukwe lifted everyone's faith. Miracles abounded. And the little girl, Priscilla, who arrived in the land of the Dani aged two along with her siblings, became a missionary. This wasn't spiritual warfare in the jargon, twenty-first-century sense. It seems much more like the revival in the future USA inspired by the preaching of George Whitefield. But it was certainly one of the most remarkable harvests of all time and, as Jacques understood at the time, the deliverance of Angginonukwe was the key to future progress.

Power encounters in Papua New Guinea

One of my most moving overseas expeditions was in 1995, answering a call to speak at the SIL (Wycliffe Bible Translators) biennial conference at Ukarumpa in Papua New Guinea.

The conference – part spiritual input, part offers of counselling and prayer, part intensive business – was attended by all the translators from PNG and the surrounding islands. We met amazing people and heard amazing stories, some already told in this book: Bible translators and local Christians protected by angels from bullets and other dangers in Bougainville; a little girl who was comforted by angels when she found herself underwater after a car crash on a river bridge; the teenager who reluctantly admitted to her parents that she had encountered demons in her subterranean bedroom for many years; a serious-minded Lutheran translator whose children had been attacked by evil spirits – but he didn't dare tell his home churches in Germany for fear they would think him mad; the translators who had great difficulty with Luke 11:11 as the locals liked eating snakes and disliked fish; a local driver who took us to lunch in his village – casually remarking as we arrived, "By the way, my grandfather knew the taste of human flesh!"

Added to this, we tried to meet many prayer needs as the brave and gifted translators unburdened some of their inner fears and physical problems.

But for me, the definitive experience was reading *Not in the Common Mould: The Life of Dr David Lithgow*.[14] David was born in 1928 and died, comparatively young, in 1994. After training as a doctor, he worked in mission hospitals in Fiji. Then his wife, Daphne, gave him a book which pointed him towards Bible translation. He gave the rest of his life from 1961 to serving a group of offshore islands – the Dobuan group – which were quite close to Alotau, on the eastern tip of PNG, and the even more remote Woodlark Islands. David quickly became a gifted translator – revising the Dobuan Scriptures and helping in new translations of a number of other remote languages.

Brought up as a Bible-believing evangelical, David had experienced something of the power of evil spirits when working in Fiji. On the Woodlark Islands, David noticed that the local churches, which were well attended, never mentioned magic, witches, spells, or the local pre-Christian beliefs. The early missionaries had told their converts never to talk about these things. They assumed that they would just fade away. However, after reading *The Sorcerers of Dobu* (published in 1932), David knew that sorcery was deeply embedded in the local culture.

During a period of recuperation in Australia, David encountered, and received, an empowering experience by the Holy Spirit. He was in the midst of a huge crisis. He was trying to produce a better, more accurate, and more culturally understanding version of the Dobuan Bible. He was encountering huge opposition from prominent people who, rather like lovers of the BCP in England, treasured their language and their traditions far above its potential usefulness.

One afternoon, a man, known to be mentally disturbed, entered their house armed with a long knife shouting, "You're the destroyer of our Book." David said, "I'll pray for you." The man responded angrily, "Don't you pray for me!" The police arrived and took the man away. Several months later, the Lithgows heard that he had killed himself.

David suddenly realized that the man had been taken over by an evil spirit – the menacing voice that he had used was not his own. This was a watershed moment. David knew that he had to speak out. One Sunday, he knew the time had come.

He had been asked to lead a service in Dobu. He felt very ill. Daphne prayed for him. As he rose to speak he felt as if strong powers were trying to stop the words from coming out. People listened with rapt attention. "Jesus has greater power than evil spirits, which we name as Satani, and the devil, but which you call Tamudumudulele." As that dreaded word was uttered publicly in church for the first time, one could have heard a pin drop. Four more times, David felt the same forces trying to stop him from speaking but after that they gave up. Others started to speak out in a similar way. It was as though spiritual floodgates had been opened. Gradually a revival seemed to start.

On his last evening of one tour, a woman was brought into a farewell feast. She was obviously resistant to prayer. The local pastor prayed "in the name of Jesus". The woman screamed and stiffened, gabbling in a loud voice. David took authority: "Evil Spirit, in the name of Jesus, I command you to go." The local pastor asked, "Do you believe that Jesus can heal you?"

"No," she replied defiantly. "A witch has put something on my shoulder, in my thigh and down in my stomach."

David knew that he had to pray in the unknown tongue that he had been given some years earlier. He and the local pastor prayed in the local language. The woman slumped forwards. Then, in a normal voice, she agreed that Jesus could heal her. Many people were watching and witnessed how she was now able to believe in Jesus as Lord and Saviour.

Over the next few years, David and local pastors experienced many meetings which included repentance, healing, deliverance, destruction of magic tools, baptisms in the sea, and a general sense of the Lord's leading. Coming ashore at Budibud, a small island to the east of the Woodlark Islands, David spoke about magic and sorcery. He urged people to forsake these things and turn to Jesus. As he sat down to pray, he heard the sound of footsteps coming down the aisle. A great crowd were saying, "God has spoken to us; we want to obey Him." Some had brought wood, gum, ginger, stones, and bones, which were the tools of their magic.

That afternoon, there was a huge bonfire, reminiscent of Paul in Ephesus, on the beach. All the precious possessions which had been handed in that morning were consigned to the flames. Many children, and sixteen adults, were baptized in the sea. Whereas this seems to have provoked great opposition in Ephesus, here it produced great joy and peace. This was the first of many such demonstrations of God's saving grace. David and others were filled with a sense of awe.

As they tried to reach a remote village, a storm threatened to disrupt a crucial meeting. Suddenly bold, David said, "The Lord wants to show his power now, and Satan is causing a storm to stop it. We will pray the storm to go." He prayed, and the wind subsided.

On one occasion, a local witch came forward, very shyly, for prayer. David invited the local leaders to help. They all prayed that the spirit of witchcraft would leave her and the Holy Spirit would pour His life into her. Then she slumped down as though lifeless. When she had recovered, she was helped to walk away – free. David felt an extraordinary sense of unity and awe. The transcendent presence of God was wonderfully present.

All this came at great cost to David. In 1979, he had been diagnosed with an abnormality causing Bence-Jones protein in his urine, which could at any time develop into bone cancer. He had experienced physical healing a number of times. On one occasion he needed tetracycline capsules to treat Golden staph infection. He was on a remote patrol. He records in his memoir:

> At the beginning of the treatment, I had only ten capsules, but I hoped to get more at aid Posts along the way. In this I had no success. One night there were only two left. I shook them out into my hand, took one, and put the other back in the bottle. Next morning I took hold of the bottle to take the remaining capsule. I opened the bottle and shook into my hand twelve capsules, enough to complete the cure. They looked brand new – as they were – from the hand of God. I was overwhelmed, wondering why He would do such a thing just for me.[15]

In 1994, David became very ill. He returned to Australia. A clear diagnosis confirmed that he had only a few months to live. He didn't seek healing, although doubtless many prayers were offered. He didn't seek chemotherapy. He enjoyed time with his family. His condition didn't deteriorate greatly until, some five months after the diagnosis, he lapsed into a coma and died. In his obituary notice, *The Brisbane Courier* referred to "his greatest translation".

To me, this wonderful story told in David Lithgow's biography (and there must be so much that is untold), is one of the clearest illustrations of the power of a territorial spirit and the right way to confront it. By refusing to name Tamudumudulele, the missionaries had allowed witchcraft to prevail, and only a shallow form of Christianity. Once named, the power of evil was wounded and then broken. The battle was taken up by the locals and many were freed from bondage, fear, disease, and demons.

During my visit to PNG, it was a great joy to meet one of David's sons – a pilot for SIL. Soon afterwards, I was also thrilled to hear that the teenager who'd had demons in her bedroom had professed faith, and been baptized shortly after her bedroom was cleansed.

These examples, all from obscure and largely unknown parts of the globe, make a strong case for the reality of spiritual warfare and the effectiveness of serious prayer. Whether we are called to actively seek out the underlying roots of the evil powers, or whether we are wiser to wait and to react to any knowledge obtained, is less clear.

Power needed

Surveying the scene in our own country, the church faces an ever growing challenge to survive. There are many places where great work is being done and the number of disciples is growing. On the other hand, there are many places where the gospel witness has been virtually extinguished. Many new converts will have had contact with occult ideas – spiritualism, various forms of healing, tarot readings and the like. They need help to renounce these things as I have described earlier.

A far greater problem for the church is that, "The god of this age has blinded the minds of unbelievers" (2 Corinthians 4:4). Many people see no need of a spiritual life, they see no evidence for a spiritual life, and they cannot see what difference it would make if they discovered it. Like the citizens of the Roman Empire, about whom Ramsay MacMullen has written so persuasively, their eyes will probably only be opened by signs and wonders – healings, exorcism and the like. I think St Antony had it right when, instead of arguing with the philosophers, he astonished them by exorcising several people "very disquieted by demons".

Then there is a third group of people that the church must take into account. There is a growing band of vociferous atheists. I get the impression, with a few honourable exceptions[16], that they are largely beyond argument. We must make our case to them. I, despite many attempts, have had few serious conversations. The most hopeful avenues would appear to be the evidence for the resurrection, the evidence from signs, and the demeanour of Christians facing persecution or death.

Active spiritual warfare is part of the calling for some Christians. Understanding of its reality should be part of the understanding of all Christians. Paul said, "We are not ignorant of his devices." The more that is true of every church member, the more effective will be our witness to a largely unbelieving and disinterested world.

For me, the experience in Mutwe Wa Nkoko (Chapter 1) was key. Not only did it affect so many other people, but writing about it in *Renewal Magazine* led to contact with Tony Collins and to the beginning of my long relationship with Monarch. Prayers spoken aloud in public against the prevailing spirits were heard. Doubtless much more needed to be done and is still being done there. But that afternoon in May 1992, when I heard the hollow, mocking laughter of the local crowd, opened my eyes, for ever, to the deeper spiritual battle.

The evidence from Scripture and Christian experience would seem to support the idea that evil powers can dominate some places. When there is effective evangelism, these powers seem to emerge from the shadows and are invariably vanquished by the cross of Christ. Scripture doesn't offer any particular strategy for dealing with these situations, but gives us the confidence that, once identified, the hostile powers will be defeated and expelled. I find it deeply moving, and strangely encouraging, that sophisticated Ephesus in the first century, and the primitive Woodlark Islands at the end of the twentieth century, should experience the public burning of many valuable possessions used for the practice of sorcery. The devil was certainly not missing in either Ephesus or the Woodlark Islands, or in the many places we have cited on this long journey.

We need to pray that the many who see their buildings, or

themselves, released from dark forces become effective disciples. *Deliverance is not an end in itself.* But when the Gadarene man, "clothed and in his right mind", becomes an obedient witness, then we may rejoice.

I think Scripture should have the final word:

> *He [Christ] disarmed the rulers and authorities and put them to open shame, by triumphing over them in it [the cross].*
>
> (Colossians 2:15, ESV)

> *The seventy-two returned with joy and said, "Lord, even the demons submit to us in your name."*
>
> *[Jesus] replied, "I saw Satan fall like lightning from heaven. I have given you authority to trample on snakes and scorpions and to overcome all the power of the enemy; nothing will harm you. However, do not rejoice that the spirits submit to you, but rejoice that your names are written in heaven."*
>
> (Luke 10:17–20)

POSTSCRIPT:

FREQUENTLY ASKED QUESTIONS

We argued the thing at breakfast, we argued the thing at tea, and the more we argued the question, the more we didn't agree.
(William Carleton, *Farm Ballads*)

1. How can I believe this sort of thing when I've had no experience of it?

In the introduction, I mentioned adders and Purple Hairstreak butterflies. I cited them as natural creatures which, although quite common around my house, are seldom seen. We all know that electricity exists, but we cannot see it. We can see, and feel, the effect of the wind, but we cannot see the wind itself. Scientists know there are "black holes" but they cannot see them.

Bishop J. C. Ryle, writing about Mark 5:1–20 in his *Expository Thoughts on the Gospels*, comments:

No doubt there is much in the subject of Satanic possession which we do not understand. But let us not therefore refuse to believe it. The Eastern King who would not believe in the possibility of ice, because he lived in a hot country and had never seen it, was not more foolish than the man who refuses to believe in Satanic possession because he never saw a case himself and cannot understand it.

Also, very unusually I think for a Victorian, he comments:

Let us beware of supposing that Satanic possession was entirely confined to our Lord's time and that there is no such thing in our own days. I believe the opinion of not a few eminent physicians is clear and decided, that Satanic possession still continues, though cases are exceedingly rare.

2. Will the spirits attempt to return to the person/building from which they have been removed?

Jesus, in Matthew 12:43–45 and Luke 11:24–26, warns us that this alarming possibility can occur. That is why we need, as far as possible, to help those who have been released to turn to Christ. They also need careful follow-up and instruction in the faith. This is also true for people living, or working, in disturbed buildings. Anyone freed from the tentacles of evil spirits has seen the power of God in their own lives or surroundings. They have evidence which should make them believe. They are most unwise if they "ignore so great a salvation" (Hebrews 2:3). The words of Jesus should remind those of us who minister that we are engaged in a very serious matter.

3. Who should/should not undertake this ministry? What precautions should be taken? What follow-up is required?

The witness of Irenaeus, Cyprian, and Tertullian (see Chapter 10) is that in the early days of the church, many people undertook what was regarded as a straightforward ministry. Nowadays, we would be wiser to read James 5:13–20 and see this as a ministry for the "elders of the church". Within the Church of England, each diocese has a diocesan advisor (usually with a strong team of clergy, lay people, and medical people) who acts under the direct authority of the bishop.

While this might seem irksome, it is a great relief to know that we are covered both by the prayers and the authority of those whom God has placed in charge of us. In the fairly unlikely scenario that an obvious evil spirit shows up when we are praying with someone, we should make a holding prayer (like a dentist with a temporary filling) and seek help.

When undertaking this ministry, we should never act alone. Jesus, advisedly, sent His disciples out in pairs. James commanded that the elders should be called. We should, within the proper bounds of confidentiality, seek prayer cover.

We should ensure that there is no blockage between us and the Lord – if there is it is liable to be uncomfortably exposed during the ensuing ministry. We should be open to the gifts of the Spirit. Pictures, scriptural texts or words of knowledge may come into our minds. I have found, in this ministry particularly, they are invariably helpful. We need to be people of prayer. Many people find fasting helpful. In Mark 9:29, after the disciples ask an unusually sensible question, "Why couldn't we do it?" Jesus replies, "This kind can come out only by prayer (and fasting)." The words "and fasting" are not found in the best texts. However, fasting was an important practice in the early church and this practice has left its mark on much of the manuscript tradition.

We need to be sure that the ministry takes place somewhere quiet where we will be undisturbed. This is not easy in Africa where children, and others, see deliverance as a form of "spectator sport".

Afterwards, *we must continue in contact* with those we have ministered to. Failure to maintain contact with those we have prayed for is grossly irresponsible. Sometimes, we are offered payment. It is best to refuse (in total contrast to mediums who can ask for payments as large as £500). If the person insists, let them donate something to their local church or some other good cause. It is reasonable to accept travelling expenses but quite wrong to ask for them.

4. Are those engaged in the ministry of deliverance liable to experience a counter-attack from the forces of darkness?

Psalm 34:7 teaches us, "The angel of the Lord encamps around those who fear him, and he delivers them." We are unlikely to experience serious counter-attack unless we are, consciously or subconsciously, expecting it. In my early days of ministry, about a day later I would experience extreme tiredness, show more than my usual irritability, and sometimes succumb to headaches. Gradually, I learnt that, protected by the armour of God, the prayers of others, and a measure of faith, this need not happen.

My friend David Prior, sometime vicar of St Michael's Chester

Square, writes: "the one perspective to mention is the way I am alerted (in counselling and in general) to the presence and/or influence of the demonic. I am suddenly overwhelmed with a deep fatigue and I have to claim full deliverance for myself before proceeding. That is normally the start, not the end, of any ministry."

Christine, the woman who had come to my house "to complain about the social services" (see Chapter 4, page 71) acquired some spiritual intuition. An American woman, who I think worked at the Pentagon, was set free from various spirits. Christine warned Michael that he would be attacked by her. Later that night, the American tried to assault Michael Green and David Watson (two of the country's leading evangelists) with a knife. They, totally unused to Anglo-Catholic ways, made the sign of the cross. It was as though they were protected by a ring of steel. The attack subsided and calm was restored!

5. What does the Bible mean by being demonized (possessed)? Is there a less serious state involving demonic interference?

The Greek word δαιμονιζομαι (daimonizomai) occurs thirteen times in the New Testament. Often it occurs in individual stories (notably the Gadarene man in Mark 5, etc.); also the dumb man (Matthew 9:32), a blind and mute man (Matthew 12:22), and on a number of occasions where multiple healings took place (Matthew 4:24, for instance).

A number of people are said to have (or have had) devils – notably Mary Magdalene (Luke 8:2). The words "unclean spirit" Greek ἀκάθαρτος (akathartos) occur about twenty-five times in the Gospels and Acts. The most notable usage is in the opening clash between Jesus and powers of darkness in the synagogue in Capernaum, recorded in great detail in Mark 1:21–28.

There does not appear to be any significant difference between the two words.[1]

The word "possessed", which occurs in some translations (AV and NIV notably), leads people to think of absolute possession, whereas the Greek word δαιμονιζομαι (daimonizomai) allows for a wide variety of demonic influence. Absolute possession arguably is virtually impossible (except after the exceedingly rare unforgivable sin), since we are all made in the image of God and must retain traces of the divine maker. Some demonization is sufficiently serious to require prayers of exorcism when actual demons are expelled from the person.

Demonic interference, rather than full possession, seems to occur. The people Paul consigned to Satan (see Q7 below) would, if they wanted to return to fellowship, have needed to repent of their sins and, presumably, be set free from Satan's influence.

Paul was "stopped by Satan" from revisiting Thessalonica (1 Thessalonians 2:18). He was also tormented by "a messenger of Satan". No one knows what form this tormenting thorn took. Much ink has been wasted on it. The most absurd suggestion I read in a book about healing was that "if Paul had had more faith" he would have been set free!

Peter (Luke 22:31) was warned by Jesus that, "Satan has asked to sift all of you as wheat". The next verse is very interesting. Jesus continues, "But I have prayed for you, Simon, that your faith may not fail. And when you have turned back, strengthen your brothers."

Reading the first half of the verse, it looks as if Jesus prayed unsuccessfully. But the second part makes it clear that Jesus foresaw Peter's repentance and restoration.

In my experience, few people seem to have indwelling evil spirits. Most are set free by a clear, and unequivocal, renunciation of any evil practices which they, their partner(s), or their direct ancestors have been involved with. Most are set free quietly and without any spiritual fireworks. Most are set free very quickly. Jacques Teeuwen's encounter (see Chapter 12, page 253) seems a model of effective ministry – particularly wonderful as he hadn't encountered evil spirits previously.

6. Can you distinguish between demonic and psychiatric illness?

This is a very difficult question – the gift of discernment is vital. It is unwise to attempt any sort of deliverance ministry with someone with a known psychiatric problem without consulting their psychiatrist. Some psychiatrists are quite open to the possibility of demonic troubles.

Using the five diagnostic tests, which I highlighted in Chapter 4 when considering Mark 5:

- Psychiatric patients are less likely to react adversely to the name of Jesus than demonized people. A good test is to ask them to say "Jesus is Lord" or to pray the Lord's Prayer with you.

- Psychiatric patients often hear voices telling them to do dangerous things. On the other hand, they are much less likely to speak in strange voices in the way that people with demonic problems frequently do. Once, when playing chess as a prison visitor, I was cornered by a man who engaged me in a bizarre conversation which ran as follows: "Vicar, my name adds up to 666 – the number of the beast in the book of Revelation. This makes me think of canine, which is dog, which is God backwards. I'm enjoying this conversation, are you?" Despite the religious overtones, the man was clearly ill and needed psychiatric help. The conversation, although very strange, was not inspired by evil spirits!

- Displaying great strength can be a sign of either psychiatric or demonic problems.

- Self-harm, especially suicide attempts, are features of both types of problem.

- Wild and disturbed eyes also occur in both situations.

In other words, the first two tests are the most helpful in trying to determine the problem. The woman (Chapter 4) who came to complain about the social services helps to make the case: she was diagnosed with a "personality disorder", yet after deliverance ministry she improved greatly and has led a nearly normal life for forty years. She certainly fulfilled the first two tests. Failure to minister to her would have left her without much hope in this world or the next.

That, I think, is the clearest justification for our ministry of deliverance. People need our help. We must have the courage, and the faith, to offer it. As more and more young people turn to doubtful methods of healing, seek help from tarot cards, use drugs which open their minds to unknown spiritual forces, this ministry will become increasingly important. The church would be wise to equip itself properly for the task and forget all this nonsense about the non-existence of the devil!

By contrast, the moving testimony I have alluded to at the end of Chapter 8 shows how misdiagnosing a psychiatric case as demonic can cause terrible harm. We should be very cautious and, where possible, consult with psychiatrists and doctors.

7. Can a Christian be demonized?

Some of the problem concerns terminology. The New Testament usages include being affected by an indwelling demon ("my daughter is demon-possessed" (Matthew 15:22)); having an unclean spirit (Mark 5:2); having a spirit of infirmity (which had crippled a woman for eighteen years (Luke 13:10–17)).

The word "possessed", which occurs in some translations (AV and NIV notably), leads people to think of absolute possession. Whereas the Greek word δαιμονιζομαι (daimonizomai) allows for a wide variety of demonic influence. Some demonization is sufficiently serious to require prayers of exorcism when actual demons are expelled from the person.

In addition, the forces of the enemy can attack the believer. Hence we read Paul's instruction to "take up the shield of faith, with which you can quench all the flaming darts of the evil one" (Ephesians 6:16). Paul himself suffered from Satan's direct influence. Apart from his celebrated thorn (2 Corinthians 12:7) he was also prevented, directly by Satan (we are not told how), from visiting the Thessalonians (1 Thessalonians 2:18).

Satanic influence ranges from external prevention of a Christian's plans, right through a spectrum which ends with internal demonization that, in the case of the Gadarene man, was so strong that he lived a completely wild, uncontrollable life. The woman crippled by a spirit falls somewhere in the middle; she was spiritually alert enough to attend the synagogue. Jesus describes her as a "daughter of Abraham" and it is unclear at what level, apart from her physical state, that Satan affected her.

Traditional biblical teaching is that the Holy Spirit and an evil spirit cannot coexist. Many texts support this (1 Corinthians 6:10; 2 Corinthians 5:17; Romans 6:3–4, etc.). Nevertheless pastoral experience does suggest that it is possible for people to believe and to profess faith, and yet to be severely troubled by evil spirits. The main reason for this would seem to be that either they received inadequate teaching at the time of their conversion, or that inadvertently they, or their partner or ancestors, have touched something deeply occult.

It is often stated that there are no biblical examples of believers needing deliverance. Actually, we have very few scriptural examples of any ministry to believers. The sad cases of Ananias and Sapphira (Acts 5:1–11) are obviously exceptional. However, we might note that Peter asks, "Why has Satan filled your heart?" Also Paul several times handed rebellious disciples over to Satan. In 1 Corinthians 5:5, it seems to be implied that the immoral man will be excluded from the church and handed over to Satan, so that his spirit may be saved. The phrase "handed over to Satan" is also used in 1 Timothy 1:20, with the aim of teaching better ways. It would seem likely that Hymenaeus and Alexander, together with the sexually immoral Corinthian, would need some kind of deliverance if they repented and returned to the church.

Romans 6:3 presents us with the ideal – the past is buried in baptism. Yet some professing Christians remain deeply troubled by sin. Alcoholics, despite professing faith, struggle to remain free. People involved with witchcraft feel a huge pull back to the occult. Compulsive gamblers continue to struggle. Depressives are still liable to fall back into the "Slough of Despond".

In the same way, some Christians remain troubled by demons which lie dormant until they try to move forward into ministry or under the power of the Holy Spirit.[2] I have prayed prayers of deliverance with many professing Christians. I am unwilling to think that all, or indeed any, of them had made a false profession of faith. Their problem was probably caused by inadequate ministry teaching at the time of conversion or confirmation. One bishop[3] used to get all the confirmation candidates and their godparents to specifically renounce evil. His confirmations had a dynamism which can be lacking in more normal circumstances!

I think 1 Thessalonians 5:23 may help cut through this Gordian knot. Paul writes: "May your whole spirit, soul and body be kept blameless."[4] This distinction between soul and spirit, uniquely expressed here, may well be important. The soul is the place where our mind, our will, and our emotions are rooted. These are places where perhaps an evil spirit may reside – even in believers. Damaged emotions, especially caused by abuse or rejection, can open a pathway to dark powers; a mind subjected to pornography or other very unhelpful thoughts could be so damaged as to open a pathway; a will which is not subjected fully to Christ may also open the way. These are areas where a spirit may influence, or even reside, in believers.

Having said this, we need to be very cautious. Suggesting to believers who are depressed, troubled, or ill that they may be being troubled by evil spirits is irresponsible. If this is the case, it will become quite clear when they are prayed for.

The huge difference when praying with believers in this area is that they always co-operate. They are puzzled and surprised, as we are, but they long to be free. This makes the ministry much more straightforward.

8. Doesn't Ezekiel 18:1–4 invalidate generational healing?

These verses from Ezekiel make it clear that "the one who sins is the one who will die" and that the children cannot hide behind the sins of their fathers. However, generational healing is about releasing people from negative things that may have been passed down the family line (spiritual DNA). Recently the BBC *Ten o'clock News* reported a particularly brutal murder carried out by girls aged twelve and thirteen. It was reported that the older girl, who was in care, had visited her mother on the day of the crime. It was alleged by the girl that her mother had sent her away with a bottle of cider and some pills, and the suggestion that she could kill herself. While such appalling parenting doesn't absolve the teenager from guilt, it may help to explain her brutal behaviour.

Generational healing is a gentle ministry designed to release people from negative things which have travelled down the generations. Occult "gifting", compulsive gambling, suicide, adultery, depression, migraines, and abusive behaviour are among many things that I have prayed for people to be released from.

Jesus (John 9:1–3) seems to countenance this possibility. In response to the disciples' question, "Rabbi, who sinned, this man or his parents?", Jesus replied, "Neither this man nor his parents sinned." He did not say that this was a stupid question; merely that it was the wrong question on this occasion.

9. "Deliverance is a form of abuse" – please comment.

Once, when appearing on *The Big Question*,[5] after I had given some examples of the deliverance ministry, one of the audience said that all deliverance is a form of abuse. I don't deny that occasionally it can be. There are some very distressing stories on the Internet. That is why I wrote Chapter 8. However, most deliverance ministry is carried out in a prayerful, careful, compassionate way. Many people are extremely grateful. For those undertaking the ministry, it is spiritually challenging, tiring, and occasionally dangerous. However, that is part of our calling.

10. How long should deliverance sessions take?

I believe that an hour is quite long enough. It is useless to go on praying when nothing is being released. On one occasion, Michael and I had five sessions with a person. The first three were fairly fruitless; on the fourth occasion the spirit manifested powerfully in church; on the fifth there was a remarkable release. If the opening session seems to have been unsuccessful, we should obtain the maximum possible prayer cover, particularly at the time of any subsequent meetings.

Normally, I would expect to meet the person once to try to understand the problem, and on the second occasion to pray for release. Do try and keep a sense of proportion. Humour helps; the devil hates being laughed at and it helps people relax.

11. Can spiritual warfare influence evangelism?

In Chapter 12 (page 238), I mentioned the occasional abundance of the Holly Blue butterfly, which appears to correspond with times when its enemy, a parasitic wasp, is scarce. There are reports of effective evangelism following times of intense spiritual warfare.[6] In Chapter 12, the stories of Watchman Nee and David Lithgow illustrated this. Equally important, the deliverance achieved by the authoritative prayer of Jacques Teeuwen was essential in order to maintain the power of the revival. But throughout history, other revivals do not appear to have needed such prayer. Doubtless, Wesley and Whitefield were supported by much prayer – but not in the modern usage of warfare prayer.

12. What do I say to someone who says, "I have a friendly ghost in my house"?

"My friend, there is no such thing as a friendly ghost." Even if it doesn't trouble you, it will trouble other people who visit or stay in the house. We do not really know what such entities are (see Chapter 7) but they are not helpful spiritually. They need, with quiet authority, to be "sent to Jesus for whatever purpose he may have for them". We do not have the right to send them to hell.

13. I have psychic powers – they both frighten and intrigue me. What should I do?

Once a month, in Shepton Mallet, we had an evening communion service with an emphasis on the possibility of receiving prayer for healing. After one service, a young man came up to me and said, "I go to a spiritualist church in a nearby town. I have a gift of healing which I use there. My wife does not like me attending the spiritualist church – could you use me?"

I took a deep breath and prayed quietly. Then I replied saying something like this: "I must tell you we are not in favour of spiritualism. But if you join our church, take part in our discipleship course (Alpha), and are able to renounce spiritualism and turn fully to Jesus, God may give you back a gift of healing which we may be able to use."

To be honest, I expected a sharp and negative reaction. However, he agreed to all my conditions. Both he and his wife professed faith and he, eventually, became a useful member of our ministry team.

I have met many people who claim to have psychic powers. Most are frightened by them. They often seem to have received them from a grandparent. They are usually willing to renounce them and to pray for them to be removed. That is by far the wisest course of action.

14. I have been involved in spiritualism (or reading tarot cards or something similar), does that mean that I am "possessed"?

"If I attended a party where someone had scarlet fever; I wouldn't necessarily catch the disease." By attending a spiritualist session, or by receiving a tarot reading, or something like crystal healing, you have done something unwise. But, nearly always, it will be sufficient to repent and renounce your involvement.

When people have played with Ouija, or had their fortunes told, I always ask, "Did anything happen? Did anything come true?" If the answer is "yes", then a more careful and comprehensive ministry is needed. If the answer is "no", it is usually sufficient for them to pray along the lines that I have just indicated.

15. I have been healed by someone using psychic power (crystals, Reiki, spiritualism, black boxes, etc.). Surely this shows that these powers can be used for good?

In Chapter 5, page 90, I recounted the story of the "pendulum and the black box". That should act as a sufficient warning. Jesus was quite clear that people could achieve false miracles. "For false messiahs and false prophets will appear and perform great signs and wonders to deceive, if possible, even the elect" (Matthew 24:24). Paul says much the same: "The coming of the lawless one will be in accordance with how Satan works. He will use all sorts of displays of power through signs and wonders that serve the lie"(2 Thessalonians 2:9).

Some years ago, a parishioner who practised aromatherapy and various other forms of healing was dramatically converted. She researched, with great care, her various practices. She quickly realized that Reiki was opening people up to "universal energy", which could lead to all manner of spiritual black holes. Consequently, she discarded Reiki, but continued to practise aromatherapy and various other therapies, which seemed, like normal medical practice, physically beneficial and spiritually neutral. She began to offer to pray with many of her patients. For the most part, whether they were believers or not, they were very grateful. It seems to me that her natural healing gift has been deepened and she is able to offer help in a far more profound way.

Just because someone is healed by some alternative therapy, it doesn't mean that it is beneficial. In fact, it is quite the opposite. If you are healed by a "black box", you are likely to seek physical and spiritual benefit from all manner of strange practices and to be drawn further away from the kingdom of God.

16. Why do we need to bother about these matters? Surely Christians have more important things like the state of the world, the counter-Christian culture in this country, the ineffective witness of the church, evangelism, etc. to worry about.

> *When you enter the land the Lord your God is giving you, do not learn to imitate the detestable ways of the nations there. Let no one be found among you who sacrifices their son or daughter in the fire, who practises divination or sorcery, interprets omens, engages in witchcraft, or casts spells, or who is a medium or spiritist or who consults the dead.*
>
> (Deuteronomy 18:9–11)

If we want our nation to prosper, we need it to be spiritually healthy. When I wrote *Encounters*, Richard Atkinson, now Bishop of Bedford, wrote a powerful piece about his ministry in a very rough estate in Sheffield. He used the text, "But let justice roll on like a river, righteousness like a never-failing stream" (Amos 5:24). We need both social justice and spiritual health. The spiritual health of the early Methodists brought much more social justice to our country. The spiritual vision of William Wilberforce helped to remove the slave trade. Equally, a just society will be more open to the gospel.

Besides, I believe that an effective ministry in the areas I have been writing about will help proclaim the gospel. Try an experiment: ask ten neighbours or friends if they or anyone they know well have had any strange psychic experiences. I am sure you will get some affirmative answers which can then be a gateway to more profitable spiritual conversations. A friend of mine told me that he was being interrogated by two sceptical reporters. He turned the table by asking them if they had experienced any psychic phenomena. Rather sheepishly, they both answered positively.

When buildings are cleansed or people are set free; it is a wonderful witness to the resurrection of Jesus of Nazareth. Peter said as much in Acts 4:10 and again in Acts 5:31–32. Paul demonstrated this in many places – notably in Ephesus. If an almost visible force leaves a building (see Chapter 7) or a person (Chapter 3, page 59), there is no possible psychological explanation. If prayers are offered in the name of Jesus, then if Jesus is not risen from the dead, these prayers are futile (see 1 Corinthians 15:14). On the other hand, if there is a clear and unequivocal change, then this is evidence for the truth of the resurrection. This evidence is not nearly as important as the evidence of the empty tomb, Mary Magdalene, John, Peter, James the Lord's brother, and many others in the apostolic age – nevertheless it is evidence to present to a sceptical disbelieving world.

17. Can you comment on the tension between recognizing the spiritual battle that we live while, on the other hand, not giving the devil credit, respect or attention he doesn't deserve?

When I was struck by lightning (Chapter 2, page 33), an experienced clergyman about to lead a mission in the parish said, "That was the devil trying to disrupt the mission." In my view, that sort of statement gives far too much power to the devil.

We need to recognize the presence of evil, we need to confront it, but we do not need to give it respect or too much attention. Ultimately, the devil is under God's permissive authority.[7] We may not understand that, but it is what Scripture, and above all what Jesus, teaches.

Take the powers of darkness seriously, but not too seriously. Satan hates being laughed at. He hates being reminded that he is defeated. He hates the cross and the resurrection. *Christus Victor!* "Christ is risen! He is risen indeed."[8]

18. Some people have more spiritual awareness than others – do you agree?

It seems obvious that many so-called primitive societies have far greater awareness of the numinous than most people in the "sophisticated" West. Aborigines in Australia have remarkable telepathic understanding; many Africans have an extraordinary sensitivity to the world of their ancestors.

In our society there are, I think, three groups of people who have, or who acquire, unusual spiritual sensitivity. Some seem to be born with a greater awareness of the spirit world. I have met people who can see auras. They are usually very uncomfortable with this as sometimes it means they claim to be able to foresee a forthcoming death. Some have an ability to foretell the future by reading palms, turning tarot cards or whatever. Some have a natural healing ability – their hands react to pain, their touch can bring relief. Some can "heal" using black boxes, crystals, pendulums or whatever. Some seem to see ghosts or angels. Some speak in strange tongues – one person whose story I have told earlier said that, as a small boy, he spoke in strange languages. He was adopted and knew little about his natural parents. One little girl that friends of mine knew said she could astral-plane at night.

These "gifts" are usually inherited. They are set deep in the spiritual DNA. Most of the recipients are uncomfortable with them; some glory in them. Some people genuinely try to use them for good; others are terrified by their strange abilities.

There is a second group of people who come into contact with these people. They are encouraged to "develop" their own natural gifting (see for instance the Glastonbury story, Chapter 5, page 88). They are attracted to this strange "other" world and the power that it seems to bring. Some are quick learners and can be used in a variety of ways. The man who wanted to join my church, who at the time attended a spiritualist church and who was used there as a healer, was one such (see Q13 above).

We need to remember that the devil cannot create anything. These "gifts", like those of Pharaoh's magicians, are counterfeits of the gifts of the Holy Spirit. In *Encounters*,[9] Howard Barnes told how in Bushenyi, in Western Uganda near Lake Edward, 250 pastors and 600 believers gathered for a great rally. All was well, until the prayer march passed the house of a witchdoctor. Howard was told, "He is a very powerful man, he controls this area." Howard was furious. He entered the garden of the man. The witchdoctor came out to meet him. Howard embraced him. He said, "Jesus doesn't want you to do all this stuff." The man was delivered; his power was released.

In the deliverance ministry, the gifts of knowledge and "distinguishing between spirits" (1 Corinthians 12:8–10) are particularly valuable. I have already given many examples. Jordan Ling (see Chapter 7, page 140), among others, was particularly gifted and helped me on a number of occasions. This third group of people tend to be very sensitive. They are immensely useful in any frontline ministry but are often reluctant to take the lead. They feel vulnerable to spiritual counter-attack.

I don't have much gifting in these areas. My ministry, such as it is, depends upon listening carefully to the Lord, asking the right questions, listening to the troubles of the person I am trying to help, and listening to my praying partner.

19. You frequently quote Paul, "For we are not unaware of his schemes" (2 Corinthians 2:11): What are his main schemes?

(1) Persuading people that he doesn't exist.

(2) Appearing to be more powerful than he actually is.

(3) Tricking people into trying out psychic experiences – tarot, Ouija, fortune-telling, healing that involves spiritual or psychic powers.

(4) Lying dormant within souls that he has managed to enter.

(5) If people seek help, directing them to spiritualists.

(6) Implanting false guilt.

(7) Frightening people with psychic signs and force.

Let me expand on these a little.

(1) If ministers don't believe in the devil's existence, their ability to help troubled people disappears. If people don't believe in his existence, they are more likely to experiment with dangerous spiritual matters. Ouija boards, spiritualism, curious forms of healing, all can seem very attractive – particularly if the idea that dabbling in these matters could open the door to some malign spiritual force is thought to be just an inconvenient myth.

That is why for the most part, as C. S. Lewis suggests (see Introduction, page 16) – *The Screwtape Letters)*, evil spirits prefer to lie dormant.

(2) Negative spiritual experiences can be very frightening. People often think that there is no way to be free. Jesus said, "If the Son sets you free, you will be free indeed" (John 8:36). Also, read again the answer to the last question.

(3) Psychic phenomena can be very attractive. Sometimes (see Chapter 5, page 86, 88 and Chapter 6, page 125) predictions can come true. In *Macbeth*, after hearing that a prophecy to Macbeth has come true, Banquo says, "What! Can the devil speak true?"[10] In Scripture, on a number of occasions the evil spirits speak the truth. In the synagogue in Capernaum (Mark 1:24), the evil spirit recognizes Jesus for who He is. This recurs in Mark 1:34 and Mark 5:7. The fortune-teller in Philippi, Acts 16:17, also spoke the truth, as did the spirit raised by the Witch of Endor – albeit in a most unhelpful way.

As I was doing the final revision for this book, I read a strange report in *The Times* of a man who went into a shop in Brighton for a tarot reading. Out of ten cards selected from a pack of seventy-eight, the first was the "blasted tower", which indicated a serious quarrel; the second was the emperor, which indicated a dominant male; the third was the devil, indicating serious trouble. The reader also picked out cards representing death and justice. The man then confessed to murdering his flatmate who was a spiritualist. The tarot reader called the police. Not unnaturally, the police thought it was a joke but eventually arrived and the murderer was brought to justice. The murder had taken place ten days earlier. Obviously, the body would have eventually been discovered and the flatmate would have been the prime suspect.

How these readings work is a mystery (see again the story about Madam Zelda, Chapter 5, pages 86). The fact that the victim was also a psychic may have sharpened the spiritual connection. But one positive result does not justify a procedure which can bring great fear and which is clearly forbidden by such texts as Deuteronomy 18:10; Leviticus 19:26b and 31; Isaiah 2:6, 8:19, 44:25, 47:12–13; Jeremiah 27:9 and Zechariah 10:2. In addition, the account of Paul's dealings in Ephesus (Acts 19) makes it clear that when the Lord's name is honoured, people turn away from such things. Revelation 21:8 states that those who practise such things are excluded from the new Jerusalem.

(4) In Chapter 4, page 70, I gave an example of a dormant spirit, which emerged when the person concerned tried to make

spiritual headway. This can occur if proper instruction is not given at baptism, confirmation, profession of faith, or when someone is called to new ministry or seeks a deeper experience from the Holy Spirit.

(5) Spiritualists, usually at a price, are glad to help. They, even if there seems to be an improvement, will ultimately make matters worse – for the simple reason that they are taking people further away from Jesus and thickening the veil that Paul says is over the mind of unbelievers (2 Corinthians 4:3–4). If someone is healed by a black box (Chapter 5), it is almost inevitable that they will recommend this course to others. People can be physically healed by all manner of dubious practice (see Matthew 24:24).

(6) In Revelation 12:10, Satan is described as "the accuser of our brothers and sisters". He will often endeavour to implant false guilt and sometimes, even the very extreme idea that we have committed blasphemy against the Holy Spirit (see Mark 3:29). Mark's account makes it pretty clear that this sin is caused by attributing Jesus' works to the devil. A possible modern equivalent would be to say that Hitler was a good person and to deny the reality of the Holocaust.

(7) Sometimes psychic forces can be very powerful. Dreams and other experiences can be terrifying. We need to help people by first calming them down, then praying against the experiences, and then by putting suitable protection in hand. Of course, *the only complete protection* is for the person to turn to the Lord and put on "the full armour of Christ".

20. What did Jesus mean by a "spirit of infirmity" (Luke 13:11, NKJV)?

And a woman was there who had been crippled by a spirit for eighteen years.

(Luke 13:11)

The Greek reads, "pneuma eckousa asthenias" (πνεῦμα εχουσα ἀσθενείας). The phrase is translated "having a spirit of infirmity" in most English Bibles. The word "asthenias" occurs twenty-three times in the New Testament and is usually translated by the word "infirmity" – only once, here, do we have a "spirit of infirmity". What did that careful writer Luke mean? Clearly, Jesus saw that Satan (Luke 13:16) was particularly involved in this woman's long illness. The healing took place in two quick stages – a word of command (see Mark 1:41) and then the laying on of hands. Nowhere does Jesus exorcise a spirit with the laying on of hands.

I think we may conclude that while, in some unknown way, Satan had got involved with this woman's life, unlike the boy with the epileptic symptoms (Mark 9:14–27; Matthew 17:14–18; Luke 9:37–42), she did not need any form of deliverance. This supports what I have written above in Q7.

Fred Smith[11] gives three examples of dealing with smoking. In one, he thinks that he saw a "demon of nicotine" leave. In the second, when he was "filled with the Holy Spirit" he instantly lost the desire to smoke. In the third, after five years, he had surreptitiously started to smoke a pipe. This led to lying, guilt, and shame. When Fred confessed this (he doesn't say to whom or if he was praying on his own) he was delivered.

When my friend John Knight[12] tried to give up smoking each Lent; the result was disastrous. His family begged him not to attempt this as his bad temper made their lives unbearable (Isaiah 58:4 has something similar to say about the wrong sort of fasting). Later, after a new experience of the Holy Spirit, he was challenged as to whether his smoking was "of the flesh or the spirit". He knew the answer. Instantly his desire to smoke disappeared and there were no angry side effects.

One of my Shepton parishioners, Ivy Batt, was bereaved in 1984. She confided that she was increasingly addicted to nicotine. This was understandable at a time of intense sorrow. I prayed for her to give up smoking and that the taste of cigarettes would become unpleasant. Now, thirty years on and aged over ninety, she reminds me in nearly every phone conversation, that she no longer smokes.

I would beg to differ from my great friend Fred. I don't think there is a demon of nicotine. But I don't doubt that Satan uses nicotine to ruin people's health and waste their money. This is a spiritual issue. In that sense, I suppose we could write about a "spirit of nicotine".

When it comes to cancer, there are many ways of praying. Fred invariably saw cancer as caused by an evil spirit. He had some amazing successes. I remember being present in Oxford Town Hall when a man went forward for prayer – he was yellow with cancer, presumably connected with the liver. A few minutes later, he left. He looked a picture of health. I spoke to him as he left and telephoned him some weeks later – he was still perfectly well. By contrast, Agnes Sanford believed that cancer should be cursed. She used the fig tree in Mark 11:12–25 as a model. That makes sense. Radiotherapy and chemotherapy are used to attack (curse?) malignant cells. Most Anglican clergy would use "the laying on of hands" or "anointing with oil". I think that God blesses all these approaches. There is no one right way. What is needed is faith – the gift of faith – as Jesus explained to the disciples after the fig tree had withered and after the boy (Matthew 17:20) had been healed.

What we all need is to be people of prayer (Mark 9:29) and to be given the gift of faith (Mark 11:22 and 1 Corinthians 12:9). The actual method of praying is far less important. God, I believe, honours faith not technique.

21. Can an idol have power over me or my household?

There are plenty of examples. Michael Green[13] records that, during one deliverance session, the team had to smash to pieces an idol brought from a far country. Certainly magic, occult, and pornographic books need to be destroyed (Acts 19:19). I have been asked to destroy Masonic regalia. I have had to break up and burn a Ouija board. Nevertheless, we need to exercise wisdom. Paul (1 Corinthians 8:4 and 10:19) implies that an idol has no power. I believe that an idol has no power unless we invest power in it. However, it is better to be on the safe side. If you are worried about some object, book, CD, or video, it is far better to be without it. I think this is in agreement with Jesus' teaching in Matthew 5:29. I gave an example (see Chapter 9, page 184) of a household in Zambia who, after the dramatic healing of the mother, had a considerable cleansing of witchcraft remedies.

22. Why did the Pharisees accuse Jesus of driving out demons by the power of Beelzebub? (Mark 3:20–30; Matthew 12:25–29; Luke 11:17–22)?

Mark describes a situation where Jesus is at the height of his popularity. He is so busy that He doesn't have time to eat (Mark 3:20). Curiously, he faces two types of opposition. His family think that "he is out of his mind" (verse 21) and want "to take charge of him". The Pharisees attack him theologically, "He is possessed by Beelzebul! By the prince of demons he is driving out demons" (verse 22). The reason for the Pharisees' attack is plain. Jesus was a huge threat to their authority. Lane[14] says they may have been part of an official delegation from Jerusalem who came to examine Jesus' miracles with a view to declaring Capernaum a "seduced city" – one taken over by an apostate preacher.

Jesus deflects his family (verses 31–34) and disarms the Pharisees. He tells them it is ridiculous to suppose that Satan would drive out Satan (verses 23–27). He also asks a telling question: "If I drive out demons by Beelzebul, by whom do your followers drive them out?" (Luke 11:19; see also Matthew 12:28). This retort is important. It is unanswerable but it also teaches us that Jesus acknowledges that other people, probably his opponents, can remove demons. This has far-reaching implications for the work of exorcists from other faiths. However, judging by the amazed reaction of the crowd (Mark 1: 27) and the incompetence of the Jewish exorcists in Athens, Jesus' power and authority was rightly seen as far greater than that of the contemporary exorcists. Also, in His most famous sermon (Matthew chapters 5–7), Jesus warned his followers in no uncertain terms:

> "Not everyone who says to me, 'Lord, Lord,' will enter the kingdom of heaven, but only the one who does the will of my Father who is in heaven. Many will say to me on that day 'Lord, Lord, did we not prophesy in your name and in your name drive out many demons and perform many miracles?' Then I will tell them plainly, 'I never knew you. Away from me, you evil doers!'"
>
> (Matthew 7:21–23)

These are sobering words – not least for your author! Jesus makes it clear that He is looking for obedience (Matthew 7:24) and lives which are fruitful (Matthew 7:17). Effective exorcism is not necessarily a mark of true discipleship. I wonder if Judas Iscariot, who certainly performed exorcisms (Mark 6:7), heard those words.

23. What do I do if I think I have a problem?

If the problem is in your house, it would be useful to discover whether the previous owners had any problems and whether there is any history of spiritual problems in the neighbourhood. If you know your neighbours reasonably well, it would be helpful to ask them whether they have experienced any problems. It is also useful to write a chronological list of any strange happenings.

If the problem is with you, or a member of the family, it is important to consider the family history. Were there any similar problems, psychic experiences, suicides, tragedies, or compulsive behaviour (gambling, alcoholism) in previous generations? Once again, it is useful to write down the symptoms and events that are causing you anxiety. This information will be very useful to those who come to help you.

Keep calm! You are not the only person who has experienced strange happenings. Get in touch with your local Diocesan Office or a local church. Quiet, effective help will arrive! You will be surprised how seriously your concerns are taken. You will be surprised that your problems can be solved. The services of the churches are confidential and "free at the point of deliverance".

24. How can I be sure that someone needs deliverance ministry?

We cannot be absolutely certain. Paul says, "We live by faith, not by sight" (2 Corinthians 5:7). He also teaches us that one of the gifts of the Spirit is that of "distinguishing between spirits" (1 Corinthians 12:10). In all situations, we act by faith taking account of all the evidence that we can gather. We act reverently, cautiously, but with authority.

We can be certain that people who seek our help need to renounce any occult involvement of themselves, their ancestors and any partners. Usually, when they are prayed for everything is calm and peaceful. But sometimes they will display some, or in extreme cases, all five of the diagnostic symptoms that I outlined in Chapter 4:

(1) An attraction and repulsion towards Jesus, holy places, holy things, holy people. They want help but something is trying to prevent them from getting it. They will often be unable to pray through the Lord's Prayer, especially the words, "deliver us from evil".

(2) Speaking in a voice that is clearly not their own. This may be in a demonic tongue (easily recognizable by its unpleasantness), a language which is not known to them or, most commonly, in a voice which is clearly not theirs (the woman in Chapter 4 who came to complain about the social services spoke in the voice of an old man when the demon took over).

(3) Extraordinary physical strength (a comparable physical situation occurs sometimes when people are having an epileptic episode). Sometimes this takes the form of acting in a way that is completely inappropriate and out of control – such as slithering across the floor like a snake or making lurid sexual gestures. There are other physical phenomena which occur, for example, unexpected deafness, mocking laughter ("you can't help me"), severe shaking, inability to speak (especially the words "deliver us from evil"), inexplicable fear, retching, uncontrolled coughing. All these can be pointers towards some kind of demonic interference or indwelling.

(4) Threatening or undertaking self-harm. Attempts, or threats, to commit suicide are the most common forms of self-harm connected with demonization. As I have said earlier, most self-harm *has nothing to do with demons* and is caused by a terrible lack of self-worth often caused by sexual, physical, or emotional abuse.

(5) Displaying strange eyes – people who are demonized often cannot look at those who are praying for them. Their eyes are sometimes clouded, sometimes strangely bright. Such people will seldom look you full in the face.

When faced with some of these phenomena, if we are confident through the discernment of those who are helping that the problem is demonic, we need to take action. We pray, with quiet authority, to cut off any controlling spirits. Our prayers are decisive – not, "if it be thy will…" We may command the spirit to reveal its name (the person we are trying to help often knows the name of the spirit). We may enlist the help of the person themselves – they may be able to call upon Jesus to set them free. We command the spirit, in the name of Jesus, to leave and go to Him. The person will usually know when they are free. It is then generally helpful to have a pause for reflection and perhaps a cup of tea. They will feel very peaceful and relieved; their eyes will look different and they will be able to pray naturally and without any sense of interference.

Then we can make sure there is nothing else that needs to be addressed, that the person can make a clear profession of faith, and finally we may anoint them with oil. This is a powerful sign of God's healing presence and also a useful litmus test that the spirits have all left. We can then arrange for suitable discipleship and careful pastoral oversight. We can also remind them of Bishop Stanley Hotay's maxim: "You cannot cast out the flesh or disciple the demons." Now that *the devil has gone missing*, discipleship can begin.

ENDNOTES

Introduction

1. *The Times*, 8 February 2014.

2. Ramsay MacMullen, *Christianizing the Roman Empire* AD 100-400, Yale University Press, 1984.

3. C. S. Lewis, *The Screwtape Letters (Letters from a senior to a junior devil)*, Letter VII, Fontana, 1955.

Chapter 1

1. One morning shortly afterwards, at St Peter and St Paul's Shepton Mallet, I was leading our midweek communion service. A retired priest, Canon Theo Wetherall, was attending with his wife, Caroline. I noticed a strange light around his face. At the end of the service, somewhat embarrassed, I said to them, "Theo's face was shining – like the lady who saw an angel in Zambia." The next day, his wife rang up: "Could you come round? I think Theo has just died." When I reached their house, Theo was sitting, clearly dead, in his chair, with a seraphic smile on his face. Caroline was so glad I had mentioned his shining countenance when they were worshipping in church the day before.

2. Some years later, I visited Worldwide Butterflies to ask if I could photograph a Blue Charaxes butterfly, similar to those I had seen on that day. I said to Robert Goodden, the founder and proprietor, "You'll probably think I'm mad, but I want to photograph the butterfly because in the same village where I spotted it, someone saw an angel." Robert smiled and said, "My wife had her life saved by an angel on the A303." They told me the story (which I've included in *The Grand Surprise*). We became good friends.

Lest my interest in butterflies should be regarded as an untimely diversion, when on active service, I would remark that, on Radio 4, I heard the lepidopterist Major-General Lipscombe describing how, in the midst of a military operation above Caen in the summer of 1944, he noticed a fine colony of Chalkhill Blue butterflies flying in the nearby hills. He was an expert concerning the many variations in wing colours and patterns that can be found in this particular species!

3. John Stott in *The Message of Acts* (IVP, 1990) writes:

> *The reference is to the snake spirit of classical mythology which guarded the temple of Apollo and the Delphic oracle at Mount Parnassus. Apollo was thought to be embodied in the snake and to inspire "pythonesses", his female devotees with clairvoyance, although other people thought of them as ventriloquists. Luke does not commit himself to these superstitions, but he does regard the slave girl as possessed by an evil spirit.*

4. Matthew Parris, *The Times*, 27 December 2008, "Africa needs God".

Chapter 2

1. Michael Green, *I Believe in Satan's Downfall*, Hodder and Stoughton, 1981, p. 15.

The Times obituary (31 May 2016) of the redoubtable Professor Dennis Nineham included the comment:

> *In a strong, slightly sharp voice, he would argue that the Bible was shaped by the historical context of its time and by the cultural trappings of its authors. He took the case of a man collapsing to the ground, frothing at the mouth. In the New Testament, Nineham said, such a man would be taken to be possessed and in need of an exorcist. Come to the Middle Ages, the interpretation of his frothing mouth would be that his "humours" were out of kilter. In the modern age, "We would say that he needed a psychiatrist" Nineham concluded.*

This anecdote is presumably referring to the boy (Mark 9:14–29) whom nine of the disciples conspicuously failed to help. This is a typical comment from the theologians of the 1960s. When I was first at theological college, I would probably have accepted this scepticism – perhaps tempering my own interpretation with the thought that the boy was suffering from epilepsy and not in need of a psychiatrist.

2. *The Oxford Dictionary of the Christian Church* on Dualism, Oxford University Press, p. 424.

3. "Wherever the body is, there the eagles will be gathered together" (Luke 17:37, NKJV). In a somewhat fantastic exposition, the body is taken to represent our normal dead spiritual state. The eagles, or for this exposition, vultures, represent evil spirits who attack and invade the body. Hence it is normal for unbelievers to be troubled by evil spirits. This extraordinary exposition would not merit a mention except that it seems to have

influenced a number of disastrous approaches to ministry. To this author, it would seem that anyone who regards the presence of evil spirits as normal has stepped way outside the teaching of the New Testament.

4. Green, *I Believe in Satan's Downfall*, p. 17.

5. Matthew Parris, *The Times*, 27 December 2008, "Africa needs God".

6. Green, *I Believe in Satan's Downfall*, p. 20.

7. Oscar Cullmann, *Prayer in the New Testament*, SPCK Publishing, 1995, p. 141.

8. Simon Magus appears in second- and third-century literature. He seems to have had a Gnostic sect named after him. Possibly he remained a thorn in the side of the early church, despite his unconvincing profession of faith in Acts 8. See, for instance, *The Oxford Dictionary of the Christian Church*, p. 1258.

9. See Chapter 12, pp. 229f and the story from Fortaleza.

Chapter 3

1. William Lane, *The Gospel of Mark*, Marshall, Morgan and Scott, 1974, pp. 84ff. (especially note 141).

2. Michael Green, *I Believe in Satan's Downfall*, Hodder and Stoughton, 1981, pp. 33f.

3. J. V. Taylor, *Enough is Enough*, SCM Press, 1975, pp. 50ff. This prophetic book written by a future Bishop of Winchester was way ahead of its time in raising environmental issues and misdirected foreign aid.

4. Tertullian (160–220), *Ad Scapula* IV:4.

5. Green, *I Believe in Satan's Downfall*, pp. 64ff.

6. We should remember that Jesus sent His disciples out in pairs (Mark 6:7–13; Luke 10:1–20).

Chapter 4

1. Tacitus (*The Annals of Imperial Rome*, Penguin Classics, p. 365) writes with some sympathy for the fate of many Christians who were blamed by Nero for the fire of Rome in AD 64.

2. It is widely accepted that Mark wrote his Gospel, based on Peter's preaching in Rome, shortly after the apostle's execution by Emperor Nero in AD 64 (or possibly a year or two later). Some scholars, while accepting Peter's strong influence, date Mark's Gospel up to ten years earlier.

The death of the leading apostles, Peter and Paul, caused considerable problems for the early church: 1 Clement, section 5, which was written in AD 96, says that "sinful jealousy" caused both their deaths. There is strong archaeological evidence to support Peter's martyrdom in Rome. Dr Guarducci, in *St Pierre Retrouvé*, gives fascinating evidence. During the Second World War, she found a box containing bones on a ledge under which there was a Greek inscription: "Peter is here". The ledge is deep underground directly under the High Altar of the Vatican. The bones are of a man, with his feet missing, aged sixty-five to seventy. All this is in keeping with the tradition that Peter was crucified upside down and that his body was buried in a place carefully marked by the Christians. About a hundred years after his death, the place was marked by something called "the Trophy of Gaius". This is next to *le mur rouge* (the red wall) which Dr Guarducci writes about, and where the inscription above the ledge can be found. Constantine, with great difficulty because of the steep hillside, built the Vatican Church immediately above the site.

This is evidence of considerable importance when considering the historicity of the Gospel of Mark, and the very early tradition that he based his Gospel upon the preaching of Peter in Rome.

3. The manuscripts variously read as the country of the Gerasenes, Gadarenes, and Gergesenes. The nearby city of Gerasa, which is the best attested reading, was some thirty miles from the lake. However, Mark may have been referring to a village situated where the modern town of Kersa is. Gadara, situated about six miles from the shore of the lake, was the capital of the local district. Origen suggested that a more appropriate reading was Gergesa, which was near the lake.

Whichever reading is correct, we can be confident that Mark's account, based on the eyewitness of Peter, is both theologically significant and historically accurate.

4. Bishop Chiu Ban It of Singapore – a well-known charismatic leader in the 1970s.

5. Luke appears in Acts 16:10 (the narrative changes from "they" to "we") and stays in Philippi (Acts 16:40 – "they left"). Then he reappears in Acts 20:6 ("we sailed from Philippi"). Luke is named by Paul in Colossians 4:14 (the doctor), 2 Timothy 4:11 ("only Luke is with me") and Philemon 24 ("my fellow-worker").

6. There is some evidence that evil spirits can remain in families. See Dr Kenneth McAll, *The Healing of the Family Tree*, SPCK Publishing, 1982,

Chapter 2. See also Chapter 6 of this book, p. 125 for an example from Fred Smith's ministry.

7. Fred Smith, *God's Gift of Healing*, New Wine Press, 1986, pp. 128, 130: my wife's bad back (Chapter 5, page 93) was healed one Sunday afternoon through Fred's prayers. He used St Matthew's, Oxford, where I was the Anglican minister, for his evening services. On one memorable occasion, he was tending his bonfire in his garden at Abingdon, when he heard the Lord say, "You are to pray for Billy Graham today." He didn't know that Billy Graham was in Oxford leading a student mission. Billy was also seriously ill with a cracked rib and his team wanted him to pull out of the mission. A few minutes later, Michael Green rang up: "Will you meet John Woolmer and go to the Randolph Hotel to pray for Billy Graham?" It would be nice to record that the great man was dramatically healed. He wasn't. But he was sufficiently well to continue with a very effective mission to the university.

8. Michael Green, *I Believe in Satan's downfall*, Hodder and Stoughton, 1981.

9. William Lane, *The Gospel of Mark*, Marshall, Morgan and Scott, 1974, p. 182, note 9.

10. Ramsay MacMullen, *Christianizing the Roman Empire* AD 100–400, Yale University Press, 1984, p. 60, gives an account of Gregory the Wonderworker using this story. We shall return to this in Chapter 12, p. 241.

Chapter 5

1. See Chapter 4, p. 73.

2. John Bunyan, *Pilgrim's Progress*, J. M. Dent and Sons, 1962, pp. 112f. This incident should be compulsory reading for all who wander into forbidden territory. The key to Christian's escape from Doubting Castle was a key called Promise, which reminds all of us, counsellors and those in need of help, that Scripture is the most powerful and effective way of deliverance.

3. Article written by George Smith, 2004, which can be found by googling "Reiki".

Chapter 6

1. Ken McAll practised psychiatry for many years after the war. He is best known for his book, *Healing the Family Tree*. His friend Eric Liddell was a dedicated fellow missionary (and winner of the 400 metres in the Paris Olympics of 1924) who died in prison – sacrificing his possible freedom for that of a pregnant fellow prisoner. Eric, to this day, is much honoured in

China, not least for protecting his flock in 1937 when the Japanese invaded. He also helped to build an athletics stadium and generally assisted with Chinese athletics. He has recently been honoured with a bronze statue – something usually reserved for Chairman Mao.

2. This was well illustrated for me by a local business family, in which members had been Freemasons for many generations. One young man, while doing exceptionally well in the family business, refused to become a Freemason. All the other members of the family were kindly, helpful churchgoers, who seemed to have a real faith; but he grew much faster spiritually. He eventually left the family business to become a full-time clergyman.

The problems with Freemasonry have been the subject of many books and articles. From the standpoint of this book, the main issue is the rituals and threats that members are subjected to at each stage of their initiation. Most Masons (see note 3 below) literally turn a blind eye to the extraordinary rituals but, as the testimonies in this chapter would suggest, they are anything but spiritually harmless. The use of the name Jahbulon (usually described as a combination of Jehovah, Baal and Osiris) for the supreme deity used in the higher orders clearly breaks the first commandment.

Stephen Knight, *The Brotherhood*, HarperCollins, 1994, pp. 236f. has a very full discussion of this issue.

3. A former Mason explained to me: "During the initiation ceremony of the first degree, the candidate is prepared by removing his jacket and tie and undoing the buttons of his shirt. Any valuable metal items are also removed, including his wedding ring (if appropriate). He is blindfolded and a noose is placed around his neck. As he enters the lodge room, a poniard (dagger) is presented to his naked left breast. The significance is later explained to him in the ritual – he enters Masonry poor and penniless; the dagger implies that if he rushed forward he would be an accessory to his own death by stabbing, the noose implying that an attempt to retreat would be death be strangulation."

4. Paul uses the word "seal" (Greek σφραγίς) on a number of occasions (2 Corinthians 1:22; Ephesians 1:13 and 4:30) to denote assurance that the believer belongs to Jesus. Interestingly, the same word is used in entomology to denote the process whereby a male Apollo butterfly leaves a visible sphragis on a female butterfly with which it has mated. This, like a medieval chastity belt, is to protect the purity of its seed. I always wonder if it was a clerical entomologist who coined the term. See my book, *The Grand Surprise – Butterflies and the Kingdom of God* (Word for Life Trust, 2004, p. 27), which includes a photograph of a female Clouded Apollo adorned with a sphragis.

5. Sozo Ministries is an independent healing organization based in Romsey, Hampshire.

6. I met Carole Lavender at a memorial service for Martin Cavender in Wells Cathedral, 31 October 2015.

7. Fred Smith, *God's Gift of Healing*, New Wine Press, 1986, p. 128.

8. John Woolmer, *Angels of Glory and Darkness*, Monarch, 2006, pp. 36f.

9. Astral travel is an alleged psychic experience where the person travels outside their actual body.

10. Elizabeth Bryan, *Singing the Life*, Vermillion, 2007.

11. Harnhill Healing Centre, near Cirencester, can supply a form of service. The Diocese of Bath and Wells also has a form which includes a powerful responsive version of the Lord's Prayer:

> *Our Father in heaven:* **We thank you that you are Lord over our whole family, and its true father.**
> *Hallowed be your name:* **May glory come to you through this ministry.**
> *Your kingdom come:* **May your reign be established in our family, and your righteousness, peace and joy abound.**
> *Your will be done:* **May your gracious purposes for all in our family find fulfilment.**
> *Give us today our daily bread:* **Remove from us all anxiety, and provide for every need, material and spiritual.**
> *Forgive us our sins as we forgive those who sin against us:* **Help us truly to forgive those who have wronged us especially those who have brought unhappiness to our family.**
> *Lead us not into temptation:* **Help us not to doubt the power of your ministry to us here and now, nor to seek any will but yours in the future.**
> *Deliver us from the evil one:* **Keep us far from our adversary and do not allow him access to our family now or in the days to come. Keep us under the Cross of Jesus.**
> *For the kingdom, the power, and the glory are yours, now and for ever:* **Amen.**

12. From the hymn, "Thou Lord has given thyself for our healing", MP698 by Raymond Browne, a Baptist minister who was converted in the Lowestoft revival in 1924. This beautiful hymn uniquely links evangelism, healing, deliverance, and revival.

Chapter 7

1. To our surprise, on several occasions, Michael Green and I found consecrated water efficacious. Once, the troubled woman (Chapter 4, pp. 71f) said, "You can't help me, you haven't got any holy water." Michael took a jug to a nearby tap and blessed the water. We sprinkled it over her and there was a period of calm as several demons departed. (See also Chapter 9, p. 175)

2. E. W. Heaton, *Every Day Life in Old Testament Times*, Batsford, p. 61.

3. Prebendary Chris Tookey.

4. John Woolmer, *Angels of Glory and Darkness*, Monarch, 2006.

5. This account is very interesting. Things got worse after the first visit – but this was conducted by an advisor who publicly said that, "he didn't believe in this sort of thing". No wonder the visitation was ineffective!

6. Lieutenant Jim Roberts. Simon Daniels, *Enemies at Peace*, wrote a biography of his short life.

7. Augustine, *De Cura Pro Mortuis*, translated in *Nicene and Post-Nicene Fathers*, Volume 3, Hendrickson, pp. 535ff.

8. Kenneth McAll, *Healing the Family Tree*, SPCK Publishing, 2013, Chapter 6.

Chapter 8

1. *The Times*, 1 November 2011, gives a long and detailed, positive account of the work of Revd Ken Gardiner and his book, *The Reluctant Exorcist*. There is also the positive article published on 8 February 2014 in response to my letter. Otherwise, the coverage seems to be entirely negative.

2. I have tried to include some of my mistakes in this chapter. Doubtless I have made many others, for which I am truly sorry. The great chess player Bobby Fischer was the only grandmaster who included some of his losses in his book entitled, *My 60 Memorable Games*. I think we would all do well to emulate this surprising aspect of his character.

3. William Shakespeare, *Cymbeline*, Act 4, Scene 2, line 276f.

In 1604, English canon law forbade exorcism without the express permission of a bishop. There had been a number of notorious cases where people had been induced to pretend to be possessed, or had been forced to drink vile potions which produced extraordinary "demonic" effects. Richard Mainy was subjected, at a notorious place called Denham, to a brutal "exorcism". He commented: "When they had made me in effect mad, no marvel though I spake and fared like a mad man." Shakespeare used the theme of feigned demonization in *King Lear*. Much of his language is based on an official report by Samuel Harsnett, who seems to have been skilled at uncovering cases of supposed possession. One of the most notable cases was that of Anne Gunter who intrigued and, at first, deceived the king. Harsnett also investigated the case of a serving girl, Friswood Williams, who was persuaded by Catholic exorcists that her painful hip was caused, not by a fall in the kitchen, but by a direct assault of the devil. She was also led into a room where she saw "a new halter and two knives" (means for taking her own life), which the priests claimed not to be able to see. Shakespeare used the idea of the imagined knife when Macbeth contemplates using a knife to kill Duncan.

While there may have been some genuine cases, it is virtually certain that most were false. With cases like these, no wonder that, in *Cymbeline*, Cloten's corpse is told, "fear no more ... No exorciser harm thee!" (see James Shapiro, *1606 Shakespeare and the Year of Lear*, Faber and Faber, 2015, Chapters 4 and 10).

4. Pope Gregory the Great c. AD 591 seems to have been largely responsible for this erroneous idea.

5. Marlon James, author of *A Brief History of Seven Killings*, which won the 2015 Man Booker prize, told *The Times*, 30 May 2016, that about twenty years ago he had undergone an exorcism by the ex-gay movement in Jamaica. After initially feeling great, he realized that nothing had changed. He rejected the church, but kept his belief in God "and that worked wonderfully". Presumably there are people who have been helped in this way but they seem strangely silent. The ex-gay movement seems to have gone through a number of crises.

6. See Captain F. M. Woolmer, "Some memoirs of a field cashier", *The Lion and Rose*, February 1941. In it he recounts walking along the beach at La Panne (just north of Dunkirk) with one other officer. It was early on a morning in late May 1940. My father wrote:

> *I have never believed in miracles and did not believe one was going to occur – it seemed just too fantastic to imagine that some boats of the British Navy would appear as on a magic carpet on the calm sea in front of us. Without food or water the only possibility seemed capture by the Germans. My companion and I discussed whether we would eventually surrender or go while the going was good with the last two bullets in our revolvers.*
>
> *We joined up with a party of 250 Royal Engineers. No one knew which way up the coast we should walk. One officer went off in one direction,*

but, naturally disliking walking into the unknown returned a few minutes later. It all seemed so hopeless in this tremendous stretch of sand.

Then I saw a light flashing faintly out at sea. I was carrying my signalling torch – what if I could remember Morse now? I thought of three months of misery at Catterick just eleven years earlier. The T.E. officer was all against signalling, and said it might well be a German submarine. I retorted that one might as well go to Germany in a submarine as in any other way, and asked how he proposed to get in touch with the Navy otherwise... I signalled out a VE that would certainly not have passed the entrance test at Catterick, and to the answering flash, I sent the reply, "Where are the boats?" Then came the reply sent very slowly so that even I could read it. "Two miles this way; hurry up!"

Twenty minutes later the miracle occurred, the sound of oars, the shape of boats...

Personally, I think Dunkirk was a miracle. First, Hitler, overruling his generals, refused to give the order for Germany to attack and, surely, annihilate the BEF. Secondly, the king ordered a National Day of Prayer on Sunday 26 May. Thirdly, on 28 May there was an extraordinary storm over Flanders which grounded the Luftwaffe while many troops reached the beaches. Fourthly, the sea was unbelievably calm, which enabled the small boats to cross the Channel.

7. See, for example, Chapter 4 and the account of the deliverance of the pastor's wife in Zambia

8. Liz Smith writes about her conversion in Toronto in my book, *Encounters* (Monarch, 2007, pp. 222f.).

9. See for instance Arnold Dallimore, *George Whitefield*, Banner of Truth, 1970, at numerous points.

10. In *Angels of Darkness and Glory*, Monarch, 2006, pp. 173f., I recorded an account of a false, but highly plausible, prophetic ministry in Finland, which did immense harm.

11. Christopher Cook, Andrew Powell and Andrew Sims, *Spirituality and Narrative in Psychiatric Practice*, RCPsych Publications, 2016.

Chapter 9

1. Revd Peter Hancock was for some years Bath and Wells Diocesan Healing Advisor. We shared many times of ministry together – notably my first SOMA trip to Zambia in 1990.

2. *Common Worship*, Church House Publishing, 2000; *Alternative Service Book*, Oxford University Press, 1980 – this has the advantage of a much simpler form of service.

3. The responsive Lord's Prayer is particularly helpful – see Chapter 6, note 11.

4. For Church of England guidelines see also *A Time to Heal*, Church House Publishing, p. 181.

Chapter 10

1. Justin Martyr, *Apology II*, Chapter 6, quoted by A. J. Gordon, *The Three Great Classics on Divine Healing*, Christian Publications, 1992, p. 156.

2. Ramsay MacMullen, *Christianizing the Roman Empire AD 100–400*, Yale University Press, 1984, p. 27.

3. Michael Green, *Evangelism in the Early Church*, Hodder and Stoughton, 1970, p. 190, Irenaeus *Adv Haer 2:32*.

4. Origen (translated by H. Chadwick), *Contra Celsum*, Cambridge University Press, 1965, pp. 450, 478.

5. R. A. N. Kydd, *Healing Through the Centuries*, Hendrickson, 1998, p. 23, quoting Minucius Felix Octavius, 27:5 LCL399.

6. Kydd, *Healing Through the Centuries*, p. 24, Tertullian, *Ad Scapula 4*.

7. MacMullen, *Christianizing the Roman Empire AD 100–400*, p. 134.

8. Kydd, *Healing Through the Centuries*, p. 26, Cyprian, *Idols 7*.

9. M. Kelsey, *Healing and Christianity: In Ancient Thought and Modern Times*, SCM Press, 1973, and Augustine (translated by H. Bettenson), *City of God Book 22*, Penguin, 1984, Chapters 8–10.

10. *Nicene and Post Nicene Fathers* – Augustine, *On Care of the Dead*, First series, Volume 3, Hendrickson, 1995, pp. 535ff. See also John Woolmer, *Thinking Clearly About Angels*, Monarch, 2003, p. 170f.

11. Sulpicius Severus, *Life of St Martin of Tours*.

12. MacMullen, *Christianizing the Roman Empire AD 100–400*, p. 119.

13. William Dalrymple, *From the Holy Mountain*, HarperCollins, 2011, pp. 388f.

14. Dalrymple, *From the Holy Mountain*, pp. 133ff.

15. Dalrymple, *From the Holy Mountain*, p. 163.

16. Dalrymple, *From the Holy Mountain*, p. 188f.

17. Dalrymple, *From the Holy Mountain*, p. 407. It is outside the scope of this book, and this writer's competence, to consider in any depth exorcism in

other faiths (see also FAQ 22). Suffice it to say, the Leicester Deliverance Team is quite often called upon by people of other faiths – especially Hindus, but sometimes Muslims. We have seen examples of Muslims seeking help from Christians in Syria and Egypt.

There are also regular reports (for instance in *Time Magazine*, 3 March 2014) of the Coptic priest Father Samaan Ibrahim performing exorcisms in Cairo, mainly for local Muslims. His story is a modern miracle – a miraculous call based on Acts 20:9–10; a miraculous building of a huge church built for the poorest with very little money. His preaching is evangelical; his ministry, which is entirely Jesus-centred, draws many troubled people from different faiths who are seeking God's help.

18. Bede, *Life of Cuthbert*, Chapter 15. Michael Mitton mentions this incident in *Restoring the Woven Cord*, Darton, Longman and Todd, 1995, p. 107, and then in more detail in a talk to Ichthus leaders given in January 2011.

19. AMR, 182, v. 3.

20. Seckendorf, *History of Lutheranism*, BIII, p. 133.

21. *The Journal of John Wesley*, 23 October 1739.

22. John Pollock, *George Whitefield and the Great Awakening*, Lion, 1972, p. 147f.

23. Kydd, *Healing Through the Centuries*, p. 41 and Gordon, *The Three Great Classics on Divine Healing*, p. 220.

24. Ann Meakin, *Anna Hinderer: Pioneer Missionary*, Connaught Books, 2015.

25. See the story in Chapter 9, p. 183 of the man who came to the healing service in Wells Cathedral.

26. Elizabeth Gaskell (edited by Jenny Uglow), *Curious, If True*, Virago, 1995 – see *Lois the Witch*.

27. Dalrymple, *From the Holy Mountain*, makes this clear.

28. In the first edition of *Evangelism and the Early Church*, Michael Green makes this cautious comment (subsequently revised in the light of some of the experiences recorded in this book):

> *Where medical knowledge is so advanced as it is in the West, where 2,000 years of Christian evidences, not to mention the sacred Scriptures, abound to authenticate Jesus' Messiahship, the conditions would appear to be lacking in which we might have a right to expect miracles in the New Testament sense, though we cannot exclude the possibility. However, in missionary areas, where there is only a tiny church in a vast pagan stronghold, where there is a shortage of medical means, where there may*

be no translations of the Scriptures available, or where the people are as yet illiterate, where, furthermore, there are definite spiritual lessons to be reinforced by it – there, on the fringes of the gospel outreach, we have a situation in which we may expect to see God at work in miraculous ways today. That He does so is attested by all missionary societies working in primitive areas.

It is good to know that my great friend, like St Augustine 1,600 years earlier, revised his views in the light of experience!

29. Bede, *The Ecclesiastical History of the English People*, World's Classics, 1994, p. 58, records Pope Gregory's warnings based particularly on Jesus' response to the mission of the seventy: "However, do not rejoice that the spirits submit to you, but rejoice that your names are written in heaven" (Luke 10:20).

30. Meakin, *Anna Hinderer: Pioneer Missionary*, p. 123.

Chapter 11

1. Matthew Parris, *The Times*, 27 December 2008, "Africa needs God".

2. Lynette Oates, *Not in the Common Mould: The Life of David Lithgow* (see end of Chapter 12).

3. Athanasius, *Life of St Antony*; Sulpicius Severus, *Life of St Martin of Tours*; Gregory of Nyssa, *Life of Gregory the Wonderworker*.

4. Neema Crafts is a project in Iringa which employs about 100 disabled people (mainly deaf or polio victims) in making high-quality goods for tourists and markets in Dar es Salaam, and running a restaurant, conference centre, and small guest house. For details see Neema Crafts' website.

5. *ReSource*, "Healing and Deliverance", November 2006. Thirty-three back issues are available via their website.

6. Andrew Fanstone, *God Plus One*, New Wine Press, 2016, pp. 34f.

7. Michael Green, *I Believe in Satan's Downfall*, Hodder and Stoughton, 1981, Chapter 4, pp. 78ff.

8. Bayes' theorem: $P(A/B) = \dfrac{P(A) \times P(B/A)}{P(A) \times P(B/A) + P(A^*) \times P(B/A^*)}$

A/B means A given that B has occurred. A* means that A doesn't occur.

To give a simple example: I throw two dice, one red the other blue. I tell you that I scored 11 or more. What is the probability that the red dice was six? A is the probability that the red dice was a 6 (1/6); B is the probability that the total score was 11 or 12. $P(B/A) = 1/3$ (if A scored 6, B has to score 5 or 6). $P(A^*) = 5/6$; $P(B/A^*) = 1/30$ (the only possibility is that the red dice threw a 5 ($1/5$ not $1/6$ because there are only 5 possibilities for the red dice given that a 6 has not been thrown), and the blue dice threw a 6). Hence $P(A/B) = 1/6.1/3 \ / \ (1/6.1/3 + 5/6.1/30) = 2/3$

This can be seen more simply as follows: if I score 11 or 12 there are only three possible throws, (6,6) (6,5) (5,6) and two of these have the first dice scoring 6. In other words, the expectation that the red dice scored 6 is now four times as likely as if we had no information about the final score. Equally, the probability that the red dice scored 1, 2, 3, or 4 is zero!

Now consider Mark's Gospel and in particular the accounts of evil spirits talking to Jesus (Mark 1:24, 5:7ff.).

$P(A)$ is the probability that Mark's account of evil spirits is essentially true. We give this the value k.

$P(B/A)$, the probability that I meet an English-speaking evil spirit in rural Zambia, given that Mark's account is essentially true, is still unlikely say 10^{-4}. I must have prayed with about several thousand people on my five trips to Zambia. But $P(B/A^*)$, the probability that I meet an English-speaking evil spirit in rural Zambia, given that Mark's account is unreliable, is unbelievable say 10^{-10}. What this is saying, in simple terms, is that examples of this curious phenomenon can only really be explained on the basis of the deliverance stories in Mark. It is still unusual but I do know at least four other people who have witnessed this type of event.

The result is that assigning any reasonable value to $P(A)$ leads to a value for $P(A/B)$ of almost 1. It is really stating the obvious! The unlikely event of English- (or French-) speaking evil spirits in rural Zambia (or inner city Brazil) is just credible if, and only if, Mark's account of Jesus' ministry in Galilee is essentially true.

Interestingly, Revd Thomas Bayes (1701–1761) first used this theorem to allow new evidence to update old beliefs.

9. Fanstone, *God Plus One*, pp. 62f.

10. For a detailed discussion, see John Woolmer, *Angels of Glory and Darkness*, Monarch, 2006. Angels are an important part of the biblical revelation. If angels exist, evil spirits will exist and vice versa. Among many testimonies of God's protection and provision of guardian angels, when Jane and I visited PNG in 2005, we received this from Anita Synnott, who works with her husband with the Wycliffe Bible Translators at their headquarters in Ukarumpa in PNG:

My name is Anita, my husband is Sean and we have two children of our own, Lachlan (five years old) and Courtney (four years old). We live in Ukarumpa in the Eastern Highlands of Papua New Guinea. Our job here is to provide a home for the children of missionaries who are working in this country. We currently have six children boarding with us. We have been up here for four years and we pray every day for our safety and for angels to surround us. God has been so faithful! One day, Courtney and I needed to go to Lae (a town on the coast) to join Sean and Lachlan who were there already. We were travelling down with friends in a twelve-seater van. Again, before we left, we prayed for angels to surround us and we put our lives in God's hands.

About twenty-five minutes into the trip, we were about to cross a single lane bridge and our left-hand tyre hit the left-hand side of the bridge. For a few seconds, we were on the side of the bridge balancing on our axle. I remember thinking, "How are we going to lift the bus off the edge of this bridge?" The next thing I remember, there was a lot of noise and everything was dark. We had tumbled off the bridge, seven metres into the river below landing on the side of the bus.

When we stopped moving, I realized that I wasn't dead, then realized that I was under the water. I was able to push a few people off of me and then get some air. I wasn't sure how deep the water was, but knew that we had to get out of the bus quickly. There were five children, and five adults on board. At the time of the crash, Courtney wasn't sitting with me and there are no seat belts fitted in the back of these buses. When I was sure that I wasn't dead (it sounds silly now, but it seemed to make sense at the time!) I realized that I had to find little Courtney. She was wearing a brightly coloured dress and I could see it in the water about a metre from where I was. I was able to reach into the water and pick her up. By this time, there were some people outside the bus to help us. So I passed Courtney out and then we all followed. We all walked away from the accident! Another miracle!

Later that day, I was talking to Courtney about the "big bump" and was reassuring her and trying to make her understand that it was God who protected us. I told her that God is everywhere and will always look after us. After thinking this over for a few seconds, she piped up with the comment that she didn't see God there. I was wondering how I was to explain this to a child, when she said, "I didn't see God, I just saw the angels."

As tears filled my eyes (and still do every time I think of it!) I asked her what she meant. "The angels were there and when the bump came, they hugged me." She said that they were warm and fluffy and all of the colours of the rainbow. I was full of questions and was overwhelmed with the image of my God protecting my child with His angels. Meanwhile Courtney told me of the angels singing to her, and she asked what my angels sang to me!

There are so many details that God worked out for us! The way that we were all sitting, the seat belt that was repaired for the driver just the day before and that no luggage was on top of Courtney! The river was only about a metre deep – any deeper and we would have been in trouble and any less, and the impact of landing could have been devastating. Instead, we all walked away with only a few minor injuries.

To me, that story is utterly convincing. I can see no rational explanation and I'm very happy to think that Courtney's guardian angels were out on patrol!

Chapter 12

1. Origen (translated by H. Chadwick), *Contra Celsum*, Cambridge University Press, 1965, p. 476.

2. Ramsay MacMullen, *Christianizing the Roman Empire AD 100–400*, Yale University Press, 1984, pp. 59ff.

3. Athanasius, *Church Fathers: Life of St Antony*, sections 13, 41, 48 and 80. It is worth remembering that Athanasius knew Antony very well. This must add considerable weight when we consider the historicity of his writing.

4. MacMullen, *Christianizing the Roman Empire AD 100–400*, p. 112.

5. Bede, *The Ecclesiastical History of the English People*, World's Classics, 1994, p. 58.

6. Eddius Stephanus, *Life of Cuthbert in the Age of Bede*, Penguin, 1965, p. 59.

7. In the 1990s there was a very violent rebellion in Bougainville, a large island to the north east of Papua New Guinea. Times were very dangerous, many people were killed, and Christians had a very difficult time. As so often in these situations, there were also many remarkable stories of God's protection and of his angels. Here are a few examples supplied by my friends Conrad and Phyllis Hurd, who have spent much of their life translating the Scriptures into local languages in Bougainville:

When the people, who were faced with hardship, sought the Lord in prayer and took cover in his name, many extraordinary things happened. Two local pastors, Micah and Penias testified:

"Armed men would spray innocent men with automatic fire, but the bullets simply fell from their bodies like rain, while the jungle on either side would be scythed to the ground. Those who had taken part in violence, did not receive as much protection. Occasionally, God would give them warnings by allowing them to escape death with minor injuries. After two warnings, however, those who didn't repent usually received further injuries that proved fatal."

Samuel Meekera is a minister of the gospel, a member of the United Church. He had some parishioners who were members of the revolutionary forces. They believed that they had the right to rob and pillage the property of those who had fled from the island because of the crisis. He preached, fearlessly, about the need for honesty. Eventually, the revolutionaries had heard enough. One of them pointed his M-16 at him and fired from a range of ten yards. The tracer bullet popped out of the muzzle and landed spluttering in the dirt between them. The gunman fired again. This time the gun roared but the bullet missed. Impressed by what seemed to be Divine protection, the soldier made no further attempts to kill Samuel and the revolutionaries in that area began to have a special respect for the Christian leaders.

John Wesley Kitare lived in the village of Sinare. His wife was at home when helicopters attacked their village in a pre-dawn raid. When his wife saw the hail of fire, she rebuked it in the name of the Lord! As the helicopter swept by, the villagers testified that they saw the tracers visibly diverted away from them.

At the same time, there was a raid on nearby Roreinang. Roreinang is a former Methodist mission station which is now run by the indigenous church. It has a superintendent minister, a large elementary school and a conference centre for the church in southern Bougainville. In 1997, the Defence force started an operation to overrun the Siang and Aropa valleys. The plan was to rout the enemy, even if every village in the area was destroyed in the process. Roreinang was one of the villages designated for a destructive attack.

Ministers from the whole area were just finishing a prayer conference, when helicopters carrying automatic weapons and grenade launchers made a pre-dawn raid. The acting bishop, Meshac Tarurava, jumped out of bed with a strange feeling of militant joy. He said "No hiding place is safe, but God is our refuge. Call out to him!" He then went out and stood in the middle of a nearby sweet potato patch, lifted his hands towards heaven and forbade the bullets and the grenades to do any damage to the Mission Station.

The helicopter circled the station three or four times spraying bullets and launching grenades, but not a single person or dwelling was hit! Later when Meshac sent people out to assess the damage, no one could find a trace of bullet holes or any sort of damage.

When it was all over, one of the locals said rather wistfully, "These sorts of things don't happen any more." I think Cuthbert would have approved!

8. John Woolmer, *Thinking Clearly About Angels*, Monarch, 2003, pp. 232ff.

9. Watchman Nee, *Sit, Walk, Stand*, Kingsway, 1962, pp. 57ff.

10. John G. Paton, *Pioneer Missionary to the New Hebrides*, Hodder and Stoughton, 1893, Part 1, p. 347.

11. Andrew Fanstone, *God Plus One*, New Wine Press, 2016, pp. 59ff.

12. Jacques Teeuwen, *The Secret of Nabelan Kabelan* (contact via jacques. teeuwen@outlook.com).

13. Teeuwen, *The Secret of Nabelan Kabelan*, pp. 34ff. Jacques makes it clear that he'd had no previous experience of deliverance, which makes his quick and decisive ministry all the more impressive. It is interesting that the missionaries at that time were apparently not taught about the reality of evil spirits. I formed the same impression when I visited PNG in 2005. Since then, I am very glad to have been asked to do a day's teaching for future Wycliffe Bible Translators as part of their preparation course.

14. Lynette Oates, *Not in the Common Mould: The Life of Dr David Lithgow*, Wycliffe Media, 1997 (mainly Part 3).

15. Oates, *Not in the Common Mould: The Life of Dr David Lithgow*, p. 171.

16. Professor Antony Flew's book, *There is a God*, is a notable exception.

Postscript: FAQs

1. Canon Dr Michael Green says: "ἀκάθαρτος (akathartos) describes the nature of the spirit, and δαιμονίζομαι (daimonizomai) the grip of the evil spirit. But I think they are interchangeable."

2. In Chapter 4, I mentioned a case of someone who had prayed for "an infilling of the Holy Spirit" and received what turned out to be the "gift" of demonic tongues. Evil spirits will often remain dormant and only come into the open when their host tries to go forward spiritually.

3. Richard Hare, sometime Bishop of Pontefract.

4. See Alison Morgan and John Woolmer, *In His Name*, ReSource, 2008, Session 4, where Alison has a brilliant exposition of 1 Thessalonians 5:23.

Session 5, with references elsewhere, covers the subject matter of this book.

5. I appeared a couple of times on *The Big Question* (BBC TV). On the second occasion, in April 2010, the main argument was about the existence of the devil. An exorcist had claimed that the Vatican was full of demons. The audience was decidedly hostile. It was clear that a number of people had come largely to disrupt the programme. However, it was good to get a Christian viewpoint over. A Christian psychiatrist sitting next to me was particularly eloquent. His views were listened to and carried weight.

6. Books such as *Breaking Strongholds*, Regal Books, 1993, edited by Peter Wagner and Cindy Jacobs, and *Possessing the Gates of the Enemy*, Zondervan, 1994, make strong claims in this area.

7. Read again Oscar Cullmann's perceptive statement (Chapter 1, p. 37).

8. Richard Wurmbrandt, *In God's Underground*, W. H. Allen, 1968. I remember him telling how, after one "Struggle Meeting" where atheism was being vigorously taught by the Romanian authorities, he responded with an eloquent testimony. The commandant said, "Tell that nonsense to Yuri Gagarin. He's been up in space, but he saw no sign of God!" Wurmbrandt replied, "If an ant walked around the soul of my shoe, it could say that it saw no sign of Wurmbrandt" (p. 243).

On another occasion, during a discussion in prison, he held out his hand as if offering an Easter egg and said, "Christ is risen!" A chorus of voices responded, "He is risen indeed" and a powerful, and effective, discussion ensued.

That is the message the devil cannot stand. That is the message that shows that Satan is defeated. That is the message which would seem unnecessary if the devil really had gone missing!

9. John Woolmer, *Encounters*, Monarch, 2007, pp. 168ff. and pp. 186ff. give a number of illustrations of Howard Barnes' powerful ministry.

10. William Shakespeare, *Macbeth*, Act 1 Scene 3, line 107.

11. Fred Smith, *God's Gift of Healing*, New Wine Press, 1986, pp. 124ff.

12. John Knight, *Rain in a Dry Land*, Hodder and Stoughton, 1987, pp. 140ff.

13. Michael Green, *I Believe in Satan's Downfall*, Hodder and Stoughton, 1981, pp. 143ff.

14. William Lane, *The Gospel of Mark*, Marshall, Morgan and Scott, 1974, pp. 140ff. This discussion is another example of this commentator's informative insights into difficult passages.

SCRIPTURE INDEX

INDEX

Selected people, places and spiritual practices (where names have been changed in some of the stories these are not found in the index). Friends of the author are marked with *.